ORDINARY JEWS

ORDINARY JEWS

Choice and Survival during the Holocaust

EVGENY FINKEL

PRINCETON UNIVERSITY PRESS

PRINCETON AND OXFORD

Copyright © 2017 by Princeton University Press

Published by Princeton University Press, 41 William Street, Princeton, New Jersey 08540
In the United Kingdom: Princeton University Press, 6 Oxford Street, Woodstock, Oxfordshire OX20 1TR

press.princeton.edu

Jacket image: Inhabitants of the Kutno Ghetto. Photograph by Hugo Jaeger/Getty.

Library of Congress Cataloging-in-Publication Data

Names: Finkel, Evgeny, 1978– author.
Title: Ordinary Jews : choice and survival during the Holocaust / Evgeny Finkel.
Description: Princeton ; Oxford : Princeton University Press, [2017] | Includes bibliographical references and index.
Identifiers: LCCN 2016043204 | ISBN 9780691172576 (hardcover : alk. paper)
Subjects: LCSH: Holocaust, Jewish (1939-1945) | Jews--Persecutions. | Survival. | Cooperativeness. | Adjustment (Psychology) | Resistance (Philosophy) | Escape (Psychology)
Classification: LCC D804.3 .F5664 2017 | DDC 940.53/18—dc23
LC record available at https://lccn.loc.gov/2016043204

British Library Cataloging-in-Publication Data is available

This book has been composed in Sabon Next LT Pro

Printed on acid-free paper. ∞

Printed in the United States of America

10 9 8 7 6 5 4 3 2 1

CONTENTS

TABLES, MAPS, AND FIGURES

TABLES

MAPS

FIGURES

NOTE ON TRANSLITERATION

For Polish names and places in Poland I use the original Polish spelling. The only exceptions are places that have a standard internationally recognized spelling. Therefore, I use "Warsaw" instead of the original Polish "Warszawa." For places in Eastern Poland I use the pre–World War II Polish form, instead of the later Russian, Ukrainian, Belorussian, or Lithuanian forms. Thus, Białystok rather than Belostok and Wilno rather than Vilnius. In the transliteration of Hebrew words I do not include special characters, such as dots and accents (thus t instead of ṭ, s instead of ś etc.). Hebrew speakers will recognize the correct word without special characters and others will not be affected by this decision.

ORDINARY JEWS

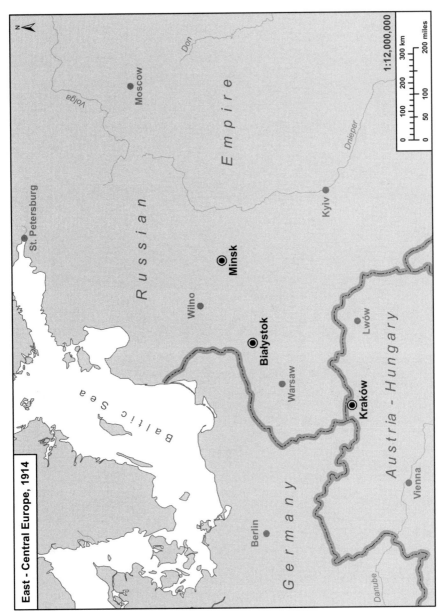

East - Central Europe, 1914

1:12,000,000

Map 1.

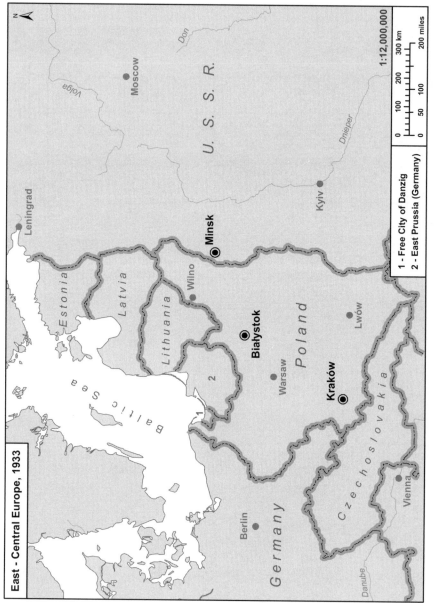

Map 2.

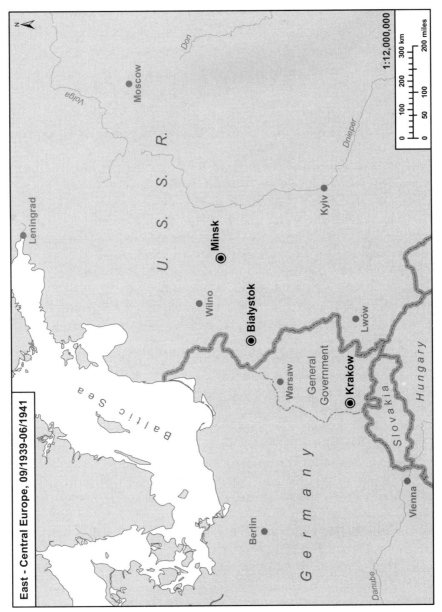

Map 3.

INTRODUCTION

June 12, 1942, Khmel'nik Ghetto, Reichskommissariat Ukraine

June 12, 1942 divided twelve-year-old Israel G.'s[1] life into two unequal parts—before and after the day when the young Jews of Khmel'nik were shot during the Children's Aktion. Israel's travails began a year earlier, when Germany invaded the Soviet Union in June 1941. His father was drafted into the Red Army, while Israel, his mother Alexandra, and a younger brother Venyamin, tried to escape to the Soviet hinterland. They reached Kyiv, but needed a special permit to cross the Dnieper River and continue further east. After considerable effort, Alexandra was able to obtain the necessary paperwork—only to have it stolen by another Jewish family fleeing Khmel'nik. She and her children were forced to return to their town, which had since been occupied by the Germans.

Israel's family was better off than most local Jews. His grandfather, David G., was a coppersmith and the Germans needed his labor. The family also had money. Israel G. was named after his great-uncle, Israel Pinchefsky, who had immigrated to the United States before World War I, was drafted when the United States entered the war, and was killed in France. Until the German invasion, Israel Pinchefsky's mother, who remained in Khmel'nik, received a pension from the United States government.

On January 2, 1942 the Nazi authorities forced the Jews of Khmel'nik, about 4,500 people, into a ghetto. Two weeks later, only 1,000 to 1,500 skilled workers and their families were still alive; the rest had been shot by German mobile killing squad Einsatzkommando 5 and its local collaborators. Then, following several uneventful months, the June 12 Aktion came. The Nazis ordered the ghetto inhabitants to the town's main square, in front of the police building, where all of the children and several old people—360 people in total—were rounded up. By that time Israel G. had already seen enough to understand what would follow. "I somehow made a decision to escape no matter what. . . . Not go to the pit, not to undress, not to wait submissively (*pokorno*) to be shot," he recalled. The police building had large pieces of plywood covering the windows. Israel G. hid behind them and then ran away while seven-year-old Venyamin stayed with the other children. Israel thus became the only survivor of the Children's Aktion, but he never forgave himself for not going with his brother toward certain death. "It is naturally my biggest pain," he admitted in 1995. "Back then, as a child, I didn't understand that, but the older I become the more painful, sharper [the memory] is."

Having lost her younger son and fearing the imminent liquidation of the ghetto, Alexandra G. decided to make another desperate run for her life. With her remaining money she arranged fake IDs in the names of Alexandra and Vasilii Donets, both ethnic Ukrainians, and fled the ghetto with a non-Jewish guide. They crossed the border into Romanian-occupied Ukraine and snuck into the Zhmerinka ghetto, which was considered relatively safe; at this point the Romanians were confining Jews to ghettos but were not killing them *en masse*. Alas, this sanctuary was short-lived. Alexandra and Israel were expelled by the local Jewish authorities for trying to obtain food outside the ghetto. The Jewish police of the Zhmerinka ghetto knew perfectly well that, if caught, Israel G. and his mother would be shot, but they also feared that the refugees' smuggling of food might endanger the entire community. Israel and Alexandra then moved to Murafa, where after bribing Romanian officials they were allowed to remain until liberation in March 1944.[2]

The Puzzle

The story of Israel G. and his family is not unusual. Many, if not most, survivors have similar stories to tell. Dates, places, and details vary, but the basic narratives are tragically similar: survivors recount losing family members, underscore their grief and pain, and emphasize luck and outright miracles. The underlying, but rarely explicitly stated theme of these stories is that of *choice*. Even if under impossible constraints, each and every Jewish person had to decide how to react to Nazi persecution. Lawrence Langer famously calls these "choiceless choices," because no matter what the Jews did, death was the most likely outcome—yet choices they were nonetheless.[3] Each Jew had to select a survival strategy, or sometimes several. Israel G. and his mother first decided to escape, then they coped for a time with the evolving situation inside Khmel'nik ghetto, and then finally escaped a second time. The Zhmerinka ghetto Jewish police *chose* to collaborate with the Holocaust perpetrators—even though their actions put the lives of Israel and

Alexandra, fellow Jewish victims, in grave danger. There were also those who fought back, weapons in hand. The Khmel'nik ghetto had an underground resistance group that obtained weapons and planned to flee to the forests to join Soviet guerilla units.

Another important, but often overlooked feature of the Holocaust is the community-level variation in victims' behavior. Quite a few people escaped, or tried to escape, the Khmel'nik ghetto, but there were other ghettos from which almost no one fled. The Khmel'nik ghetto had an underground resistance, while most other ghettos did not. The Jewish police in the Zhmerinka ghetto collaborated with the Holocaust perpetrators, whereas the Jewish authorities in the Khmel'nik ghetto are usually not accused of collaboration.

The Jewish experience during the Holocaust is not unique when it comes to variation in victims' behavior. In Rwanda, many Tutsis (and moderate Hutus) tried to escape the genocide, while some did nothing. Some Tutsis even joined the Hutu *Interahamwe* killing squads.[4] There was organized Tutsi armed resistance in the Bisesero Hills, but not in other areas. In the Ottoman Empire, Armenian reactions to the 1915 genocidal campaign likewise ranged from armed resistance to passivity to collaboration. During the war in Bosnia, numerous Muslims reaped handsome benefits from active collaboration with Serbs.[5] What explains this variation in behavioral choices and survival strategies?

Genocide and mass killings involve numerous people, usually divisible into three main groups: perpetrators, bystanders, and victims.[6] In recent decades substantial attention has been devoted to studying the behavior of the perpetrators of violence in genocides and mass killings,[7] civil wars, and uprisings.[8] At the same time, the literature on collective violence has almost completely overlooked another crucial group of actors: *the victims*. Because collective violence is a dynamic and relational process, its trajectories and outcomes cannot be fully understood if focus is placed solely on perpetrators.[9] Civilians, when targeted by mass violence, also have choices to make and strategies to adopt. Being targeted by mass violence does not deprive one of agency. Victims of all ages, genders, and walks of life—whether they are Jews, Tutsis, or Armenians—are ordinary people who are forced to act in the face of extraordinary dangers. The analysis of victims' behavior cannot explain why genocides happen, but it can help us to better understand how they happen and what their outcomes are. This book asks the question: *What explains the different patterns of behavior adopted by civilians targeted by mass violence?* To answer this question, I analyze Jewish behavior during the Holocaust at the individual and community levels.

The Strategies

An analysis of Jewish behavior should begin by outlining the strategies that the Jewish victims of the Holocaust had to choose from. I propose a new typology of the strategies in which the Jews could and did engage during the Holocaust: (1) cooperation and collaboration; (2) coping and compliance; (3) evasion; and (4) resistance.

Cooperation and *collaboration* mean working with the enemy by either participating in or facilitating the persecution. The key distinction between the two is the intended goal of the actions taken. Those who merely cooperated with the Nazis wanted to preserve the community and its members; those who collaborated knowingly acted to the detriment of the community's or individual Jews' survival. Cooperation is open and visible, while collaboration can be either public, as in the case of corrupt and self-serving Judenrat chairs, or private, as in the actions of paid Nazi informants.

Coping means confronting the danger and trying to survive while staying put, without (1) leaving one's community or country; (2) engaging in cooperation or collaboration with or; (3) resistance to the perpetrators. An extreme version of coping is *compliance*, which means faithfully obeying the rules that the authorities prescribe and taking no active steps to change one's situation.

Evasion is an attempt to escape persecution by fleeing: leaving the community, emigrating, or assuming a false identity.

Finally, *resistance* is involvement in organized activity that is aimed at physically or materially harming the perpetrators.

It is important to emphasize that this typology makes no normative claims regarding the choices that victims make. There is no moral scale on which I evaluate each type of behavior. Instead, I argue that individual Jews acted as they did for a reason, and that an analytical approach to these reasons is of vital importance for understanding the Holocaust.

My typology builds on but differs from existing work. Raul Hilberg, one of the founders of Holocaust research, suggested the following list of Jews' reactions to Nazi genocide: resistance, alleviation, evasion, paralysis, and compliance.[10] However, Hilberg does not explain *why* people adopted particular behaviors. Furthermore, whereas Hilberg claimed that paralysis and compliance were the most common responses, recent scholarship has shown that other strategies were much more widespread than was previously assumed,[11] and that apparent compliance and paralysis in fact involved numerous additional actions.[12] Hilberg's typology also does not account for the available, though politically and morally controversial, option of collaboration with the Nazis.

Another perspective on victims' behavior was suggested by the historian Yehuda Bauer, who argued that victims' reactions were determined by a combination of the attitude of the local population to the genocide, the nature of the occupying regime, and the traditions of victims' communal leadership.[13] This framework cannot explain the variation in individual victims' behavior. Finally, several psychologists, sociologists, and scholars of literature discuss victims' behavior and stress the importance of norms and social bonds.[14] These studies, however, focus overwhelmingly on concentration camp inmates and are strongly influenced by this very specific setting. Only a minority of Jewish victims actually experienced *life* in the camps—the vast majority were either killed near their hometowns, or sent to the gas chambers immediately upon arrival at a camp. Furthermore, these scholars do not try to classify the different types of behavior encountered, nor do they address the motivations behind each behavioral strategy. Their focus is almost exclusively on coping. The same is also true for the vast literature in the field of psychology on behavior under conditions of stress and violence.[15]

In political science, the most famous typology of individual behavior is Albert Hirschman's "Exit, Voice, and Loyalty" framework.[16] Analytically, "exit" is similar to evasion, while resistance is a clear instance of "voice." But there is no distinct place for collaboration, coping, and compliance in Hirschman's analysis.[17] My framework is more expansive and better fits the empirical realities of the Holocaust. In recent years, social scientists have also started paying increased attention to how civilians survive under conditions of violence. This research on "civilian self-protection" (CSP) is promising, but it is still in its infancy; the typologies of behavior suggested by CSP scholars are still too crude to capture the differences between various strategies, nor do they try to explain why people choose specific courses of action.[18]

The Argument: Who Did What, Where, and Why

This book focuses on two distinct but closely related questions: what made individual Jews choose particular behavioral strategies, and why does the distribution of these strategies vary across localities? My analysis is based on the underlying assumption that genocide is not a one-time event but a complicated social and political process that unfolds over time. During its course, individuals can form and change opinions, gather and evaluate information, and choose and modify their behavior. Which people, then, were more likely to prefer one strategy or another? First, I will demonstrate that Jews who were politically active before World War II were substantially more likely to choose cooperation, public collaboration, or resistance than those who were not. An observable implication of this argument is that pre-Holocaust political activists would dominate both resistance groups and bodies that engaged in cooperation and public collaboration with the Nazis.

Why would people with previous political experience be more likely to engage in cooperation, public collaboration, or resistance? Or, to put it differently, why would they be willing to make sacrifices for the community and the greater good? First, those who engaged in prewar political activism were more likely to choose resistance to, or cooperation with the Germans because they had a history of prior activity aimed at helping, defending, and promoting the community. They also had stronger ties to others engaged in similar activities and had the skills and experience required for successful organization and mobilization.[19] Finally, they were more visible than other members of the community, which made them more likely to assume (or to be assigned) leadership roles, especially when it came to cooperation and public collaboration. It should also be remembered that whereas contemporary political activism is correlated with education and socioeconomic status, this was not the case during the first half of the twentieth century. Back then, people from all walks of life and levels of education could become and indeed did become actively involved in politics. Previous political activism, I will show, is *the* explanation. It is not simply a proxy for education and wealth.

On the other end of the distribution there were those who were consciously willing to increase their odds of survival by harming the community and decreasing the survival chances of other Jews. These people engaged in collaboration, usually private and clandestine but at times also public. They were the corrupt Judenrat chairs, paid informers for the Nazi security services, and Jewish policemen who helped the Germans round up Jews for deportation to death camps in exchange for a promise of personal safety.

The vast majority fell between the two ends of this spectrum. They focused primarily on securing their personal survival and that of their families without either making sacrifices for the community (or ideology) or consciously harming others. These Jews chose compliance, coping, and evasion. Compliance was the strategy of a tiny minority; the majority's choices fell between coping and evasion. This book will show that people who were more integrated into non-Jewish society were more likely to choose evasion. Those who occupied a predominantly Jewish social milieu and had Jewish support networks were more likely to opt for coping.

Finally, building on Kalyvas's argument that violence is jointly produced by macro-level factors and micro-level dynamics, I will demonstrate that the behavior of the Jewish victims of the Holocaust was determined by the interaction between individual, micro-level characteristics (e.g., education, gender, integration into non-Jewish society or political experience) and community-level factors (e.g., local history, relations between ethnic groups in the community, and the community's socioeconomic profile).

The overall menu of available strategies was identical in all locations. When faced with the Nazi onslaught, cooperation, collaboration, coping, evasion, and resistance were the only options, but the distribution of these strategies across communities varied. Some ghettos experienced high rates of evasion while in others almost no one escaped; some rebelled, others did not; and in some communities people died of hunger and epidemics in large numbers while other ghettos had quite efficient food distribution and public health services.

My main argument is that the variation in Jewish behavior was a direct outcome of one key variable: pre-Holocaust political regimes. Pre–World War II states and political regimes collapsed, retreated, and disappeared throughout the first half of the twentieth century, but their past policies continued to influence how their Jewish citizens thought and behaved. More specifically, my analysis will focus on two key sub-areas: states' policies that promoted or discouraged the Jews' integration into non-Jewish society and patterns of state repression of independent political activism.

States and governments have tools to promote or discourage minority integration into the broader society. Arguably, the most effective of such tools are education and schooling. Education and especially mass schooling have a substantial and durable impact on political behavior and attitudes, as Keith Darden and Anna Grzymała-Busse demonstrate; Maristella Botticini and Zvi Eckstein argue that education shaped the course of Jewish history in premodern times.[20] Whether states promoted or discouraged the schooling of Jews in ethnically mixed educational institutions affected the Jews' political attitudes and their familiarity with the majority's culture. In the same vein, a state's willingness or reluctance to allow Jews social and economic mobility outside the Jewish community affected the integration of its Jews into the broader society, as did the government's encouragement or lack thereof of interethnic political and social bodies in the shaping of communal relations—a finding that is supported by empirical evidence from studies of ethnic groups in various parts of the world.[21] Governments can promote interethnic integration for a variety of reasons, not all of them benevolent and aimed at improving the well-being of a minority group as such. Yet, for our analysis, the outcomes of such policies are much more important than the reasons for their enactment.

The level of Jewish integration into broader society had several important consequences. Education, employment, and political activism affected peoples' social networks. Where states encouraged integration, social networks were ethnically mixed; where integration was discouraged, those networks were predominantly Jewish. Integration levels also affected the strength and cohesiveness of the Jewish community. Here, I view community not simply as the total sum of Jews in a certain locality, but as an *organized* Jewish society and its bodies. When the level of integration into the broader society was high, the organized Jewish community and its communal institutions were weaker than in places with little or no integration. A Jew who was well integrated into non-Jewish society could live her entire life without taking part in exclusively Jewish organizations and groups, such as book clubs, charities, schools, and political parties. In places where the level of integration was low and ethnically mixed bodies might not even exist, exclusively Jewish communal organizations enjoyed higher rates of membership and support and could more easily mobilize, coordinate, and control the majority of the local Jewish population.

The result was that during the Holocaust, places with high levels of pre–World War II interethnic integration witnessed high rates of evasion because Jews could, even if not always successfully, use their ethnically mixed social networks to escape the ghetto. More integrated Jews also had an easier time passing as non-Jews than their less integrated coethnics. At the same time, places with high levels of pre–World War II integration suffered from more chaotic coping and quite rampant private collaboration, as strong communal bodies were needed to successfully organize the former and suppress the latter. In localities that had low levels of integration the situation was the exact opposite—they successfully coped as long as the Nazi authorities allowed ghettos to exist and levels of private collaboration were low. Evasion, however, was very rarely practiced in such communities, because Jews had almost no friends and acquaintances to rely upon outside the ghetto, did not speak the local language, and were largely ignorant of the majority's culture.

Finally, the degree of pre–World War II state repression to which the local community and its members were subject determined the sustainability of anti-Nazi resistance. Places and groups that were subject to *selective* pre–World War II repression were more likely to foster sustained Jewish resistance to the Nazi onslaught than those that were not. When pre–World War II governments targeted Jewish political organizations or parties in which individual Jews were active, this selective repression forced some individuals and groups to operate in the underground and thus to acquire the skills necessary for resistance. During the Holocaust, Jews who already knew how to operate underground were better positioned to organize sustained resistance than those who wanted to fight back but had neither the skills to effectively resist nor the time to acquire them.

"If people only appear over the edge of the epistemic horizon just as they are killing Jews, then all we really know about them is that they are killing Jews," notes Timothy Snyder.[22] The same is true for the Jewish victims of the Holocaust; if they appear in an analysis only after their confinement to ghettos and murder by the Nazis, our ability to understand their behavior is limited. The past—both of people and their communities—must be taken seriously if we want to know how and why they chose particular behaviors. That is precisely what this book sets out to do.

Why the Holocaust?

My choice of the Holocaust as the main case study was determined by a combination of theoretical and practical considerations. The Holocaust is an "index case" of large-scale state violence and arguably the best-documented such case.[23] But, despite the availability of research materials, the Holocaust—with some notable exceptions[24]—has been almost completely overlooked by social scientists. This is an omission that demands correction. Furthermore, the Holocaust provides numerous opportunities for comparative research that seeks to identify the impact of political and social factors on patterns of violence. It took place in many countries and involved a wide range of killing methods, but several key variables—among them the ethnic and religious identity of both the key perpetrators and the key victims—remain identical. From Paris to Smolensk to Athens, the main (though not the only) perpetrators were Germans and the main (though not the only) victims were Jews.

Also constant is state strength, another crucial variable. Some regional variation undoubtedly existed, but there is little evidence that the strength of the Nazi state in, say, Warsaw, differed substantially from its strength in, say, Kyiv. Similarly, Nazi territorial control was rather consistent—especially in urban areas of Eastern Europe where the majority of Jewish victims resided. By the time Germany started to lose power and territory in 1943, most Jewish victims were already dead. Finally, the Holocaust is a critical case study for any analysis of civilians' behavior under conditions of mass violence; a theory of victims' strategies that fails to explain the Jews' actions during the Holocaust inevitably loses a substantial portion of its validity. On the other hand, an analysis that can bridge historical studies of the Holocaust and the social science literature on mass violence would contribute to both disciplines.

Case Studies

How can we evaluate the individual and community-level impact of political regimes? To achieve this goal, the book compares three Jewish ghettos[25] during the Holocaust—those of Minsk, Kraków, and Białystok. These communities were selected because of their similarity in a number of important respects. They are comparable in the size of their prewar Jewish communities and in the percentage of Jews in each city. Before World War II, both Kraków and Minsk had a Jewish community of about 70,000, or roughly 30 percent of the population. Białystok had a somewhat smaller Jewish community of about 50,000, slightly less than half of the city's population.

All three cities had ghettos enclosed by a physical barrier and located in what Helen Fein calls the "zone of extermination"—no Jews were supposed to be spared in these cities.[26] Kraków, Białystok, and Minsk were also important Nazi administrative and government centers, which meant that not only macro-level policies, but also the level of the Nazi security services' control on the ground were comparable. Finally, during the Holocaust the Jewish residents of these three cities engaged in all of the available strategies and modes of behavior. In each ghetto there were Judenrats, created to carry out Nazi orders, Jewish police, and individuals who collaborated with and were paid informants of the Nazi security apparatus. Each ghetto also had a Jewish underground resistance. In each there were Jews who tried to escape persecution by hiding and attempting to secure non-Jewish identity papers, while the majority of the ghetto's inhabitants coped with the situation without trying to escape, rebel, or collaborate with the perpetrators.

Despite those similarities, the *distribution* of strategies varied substantially from one city to another.[27] In Białystok only very few Jews chose

Table 1.1. State control of Minsk, Kraków, and Białystok

	Pre–WWI	Interwar	09/1939–06/1941	06/1941–1944/5
Minsk	Russian Empire	USSR	USSR	Germany
Białystok	Russian Empire	Poland	USSR	Germany
Kraków	Austro-Hungary	Poland	Germany	Germany

evasion, whereas thousands escaped from the Minsk ghetto; in Kraków the Jewish underground decided to act outside the ghetto, while in Białystok there was an uprising inside the ghetto walls. In Minsk and Kraków coping was disorganized and chaotic, whereas the Białystok ghetto was known for its order and efficiency. I argue that the reason for this variation is that the three communities varied (but also overlapped) in one key variable: the nature of their pre-Holocaust political regimes. Before the Nazi occupation, Kraków was a part of the Austro-Hungarian Empire and then of the interwar Polish Second Republic. Białystok was a part of the Russian Empire before World War I, belonged to Poland until 1939, and from September 1939 to June 1941 was occupied by the USSR. Minsk was part of the Russian Empire and after its collapse became the capital of Soviet Belorussia (see Table 1.1 and Maps 1–3). Thus, the comparison of Minsk and Białystok, which were both parts of the Russian Empire, will allow evaluation of the impact of Soviet and Polish interwar policies; the comparison of Kraków and Białystok, both parts of interwar Poland, will highlight the legacy of the Habsburg Empire and the impact of Soviet occupation of Eastern Poland in 1939–41. It is the comparison of the distribution of strategies across the three ghettos that will allow us to evaluate the effects of pre-Holocaust political regimes at the community level.

Data

The book employs both qualitative and quantitative data. The main, qualitative part of the study is based on more than five hundred Holocaust survivors' testimonies—mostly videotaped interviews and written accounts that archives and oral history projects throughout the world have collected. The bulk of the testimonies come from the Yale University Fortunoff Video Archive for Holocaust Testimonies (HVT), the Oral History Division of the

Avraham Harman Institute of Contemporary Jewry at the Hebrew University of Jerusalem (OHD; predominantly Projects 58, 110, 188, and 223), and the Yad Vashem Archive in Jerusalem (YVA; Record Group O.3). A smaller number of testimonies come from the U.S. Holocaust Memorial Museum Archive (USHMM) in Washington DC, the University of Southern California Shoah Foundation Visual History Archive (VHA), the Jewish Historical Institute Archive (ŻIH) in Warsaw, Poland, the Jabotinsky Institute Archive and the Massuah Institute for Holocaust Studies Archive in Israel, and the University of South Florida Libraries Oral History Program.[28]

In addition to testimonies, I also use published memoirs and a wide range of Holocaust-era sources, such as official documents, diaries, and letters that Jewish victims of Nazi persecution produced as the Holocaust unfolded. Overall, I rely on primary and secondary data in four languages: English, Hebrew, Russian, and Polish. I do not speak Yiddish, but I am confident that the number and diversity of materials I collected compensate for the lack of Yiddish-language sources and that the inclusion of Yiddish-language materials would not have altered my findings.

My goal is to understand internal Jewish perspectives and decisions. For that reason I intentionally do not rely on materials produced by the perpetrators. This is in contrast to the currently prevalent "integrated history"[29] approach, in which Holocaust scholars draw on sources originating from all three main groups of actors. For the most part, the Nazi authorities knew little and cared less about what was *really* going on inside the ghettos. Moreover, their perspective was inherently biased due to the Germans' position as an omnipotent outsider, even when local German officials did not view the world through racial or ideological lenses.

The use of survivors' testimonies as the key data source has both advantages and limitations. I outline and discuss these in Appendix 1: Data and Archival Methods.

The quantitative data, which I use in chapter 2 and in the analysis of ghetto uprisings (Appendix 3), consists of three large-N datasets, two of which (the Jewish Ghettos Dataset and the Zionist Elections Dataset) offer an opportunity to analyze data that scholars have not previously analyzed.

JEWISH GHETTOS DATASET

For this book I have collected data on 1,126 ghettos that the Nazis established in Poland, the Baltic states, and the USSR. The dataset includes information on each ghetto's dates of establishment and liquidation, its population, whether or not there was a mass killing of Jews prior to the ghetto's establishment, and whether it was "open" or "closed," as well as pre-war census data on the Jewish community, and data on various forms of Jewish organized resistance.

1928 POLISH NATIONAL ELECTIONS DATASET

Out of a total of 1,126 ghettos included in the previous dataset, 677 were established in the territory of pre–World War II Poland. For each "Polish" ghetto, I have collected local-level electoral data from the communities in which the ghettos were established. I chose the 1928 election because it was the last free and fair election held in interwar Poland.[30]

1937 AND 1939 ZIONIST ORGANIZATION (ZO) CONGRESS ELECTIONS

This dataset contains local-level returns from elections to the ZO[31] World Congress in pre–World War II Poland. The data thus allows me to extract the number and the distribution of political preferences among politically active Zionists in Poland.

Structure

The book is structured as follows. Chapter 2 sets the stage by outlining the concept of the ghetto, its defining features, and how ghettos looked across Nazi-occupied Eastern Europe. It provides a historical overview of the Jewish communities of Minsk, Kraków, and Białystok before and during the Holocaust. Chapter 3 discusses what the Jews in the three cities knew or were likely to have known about Nazi policies and to what extent this knowledge affected or failed to affect their behavior. Chapters 4 through 7 are devoted to the strategies: cooperation and collaboration (chapter 4), coping and compliance (5), evasion (6), and resistance (7). These chapters show how pre-Holocaust political regimes impacted the level and content of Jewish political activism, Jewish integration into non-Jewish society, Jewish social networks, and the patterns of state repression in each city. They also demonstrate how the policies of pre–World War II states affected the adoption and viability of different survival strategies during the Holocaust. Chapter 8 presents conclusions and suggestions for further research on victims' behavior. Appendix 1 discusses methodological aspects of working with testimonies and oral histories. In appendix 2, based on the coding of randomly selected testimonies, I show the distribution of strategies within and across the three ghettos. Finally, appendix 3 provides an econometric analysis of ghetto uprisings and identifies factors that made Jewish armed resistance inside the ghettos more likely.

Goals, Contributions, Limitations

The aim of this book is to contribute both to general theoretical explanations of human behavior under conditions of mass violence and to specific empirical knowledge of the Holocaust. The book is also an attempt to bridge the social sciences and Holocaust studies. Social science concepts and methods can substantially improve our understanding of one of the defining events of modern history, and yet the amount of mutually beneficial dialogue between the two fields remains minimal. It is my conviction that a "political science of the Holocaust"[32] is both feasible and desirable. The Holocaust is simply too important to be ignored by social scientists.

The book contributes to several disciplines and research agendas. Its key contribution to social science is in demonstrating the impact of preexisting political regimes on individual and collective behavior, even under conditions of extreme violence and even when the regimes themselves no longer exist. Its main contribution to political violence research is in shifting the focus from the behavior and choices of perpetrators to those of victims. To Holocaust scholarship and genocide studies, the book contributes a new typology of victims' behavior and a controlled comparison of several communities—a staple method in the social sciences research but one rarely encountered in the humanities.[33] Additionally, the book introduces new information on and analysis of three important but understudied ghettos. Finally, I hope that the personal stories and experiences of the numerous Jewish victims presented and discussed throughout the book will help readers, academics and general audiences alike, to deepen their knowledge of the period. It is crucial that the Holocaust be viewed as not simply an act of killing, but as a social and political process. Jews not only died in the Holocaust, they also lived in it.

In numerous studies of the Holocaust "implicit assumptions regarding the victims' generalized hopelessness and passivity . . . have turned them into a static and abstract element of the historical background."[34] The key goal of this book is to bring Holocaust victims from the background to front and center in the discussion, to take their agency seriously, to analyze the choices these people made and to present the entire gamut of their behavior. In the West, Holocaust victims and survivors have acquired an iconic, quasi-religious status. This reflects a noble desire to restore the dignity of the victims—which the Nazis worked so hard to take away—but it also has the unintentional effect of somewhat dehumanizing them once again. We seem to view these people primarily through the prism of their death and suffering and all too often disregard anything that might distract our attention from the tragedies they experienced. In our effort at commemoration we overlook the entire spectrum of their actions and decisions. Would it not be better to view the Holocaust's Jewish victims for who they were—ordinary human beings? Their ordeal was not of their choosing. While enduring it, they behaved like any normal human beings would. They hoped and despaired, fell in love and broke up, promised and cheated, gave and stole, believed and lost their faith. This book tries to restore their agency, choices, and behavior—in all their positive and negative aspects and inherent complexity.

The book also has important limitations. No study can explain all cases and each person's behavior. My goal is simply to demonstrate general behavioral patterns. My argument also does a better job of explaining why a particular survival strategy was adopted than of explaining why one strategy was sometimes abandoned in favor of another. Because of this, some readers will find the analysis wanting and will view my findings as crude generalizations. Generalizations they inevitably are, though I did my best to make them as fine-grained as possible. It is also important to remember that this book is not a history of the Holocaust. It is not even a history of the Minsk, Kraków, and Białystok ghettos. It is first and foremost an attempt to understand the Jews' behavior in these ghettos and therefore, by design, it almost entirely excludes important actors such as the Germans and, to a lesser extent, the local Slavic population. The Germans, of course, were crucial in creating the context and the background of the drama that unfolded in the ghettos; they set the rules, and they decided who would be killed, when, and how. But whether to escape or stay put, enlist in the Jewish police or join the resistance, that was the choice of the Jews. Limited and hopeless as it usually was, it was still *their* choice, not that of the Germans.

Writing this book was a frightening experience, especially when it came to accounts of collaborators, paid informants, and those who stole from fellow victims. It is my duty as a scholar to distinguish right from wrong and label them as such, but in this case doing so would be an act of boundless arrogance on my part. For me, a Jew born in Eastern Europe, the question is not entirely a theoretical or normative one. The main thing that differentiates me from Israel G. and numerous others discussed in the following pages is that I happened to be born in the 1970s rather than the 1920s or 1930s. Had I been born fifty years earlier, how would have I behaved? I like to think that I would have made morally right decisions, but I will never know for sure. If I were Israel G. on that day in June 1942, would I have hidden and survived as he did, or would I have gone to my death? And what would have happened had Israel G. decided not to escape? I do not have an answer and I do not pass judgment. I do my best to understand, but fear that I never will.

* * *

August 12, 1990, Khmel'nik, USSR

Every year, in August, the Khmel'nik ghetto survivors gather to remember the dead. On August 12, 1990, Israel G. came to Khmel'nik with his wife and with a grandson who was the same age as Israel G. had been at the time of the June 1942 Aktion. The family visited a small hill on the outskirts of the town, where the victims of the 1942 Children's Aktion had been buried. Israel G. was quiet. The grandson was impatient and inattentive. His mind was elsewhere; by the end of the month he would leave Europe forever and go to live in a different land. As they walked around the hill, Israel G. began sobbing. The grandson looked at him in amazement and disbelief. Never before had he seen his grandfather, a strong, stocky man in the dark-blue uniform of the Soviet *Aeroflot* airline, crying. "This could have been my grave. This *is* my grave," Israel G. said.

May 4, 2016, New York, USA

May 4 is Israel G.'s birthday. Twenty-six years have passed since my first personal encounter with the Holocaust, back there in Khmel'nik with Israel G., my maternal grandfather. His videotaped testimony was the first I watched when I started this project and the last one I watched when I had finished it. He passed away a year before I began working on my doctoral dissertation, from which this book emerged. He would have likely disapproved of my focus on the Holocaust, but a part of me is still on that hill in Khmel'nik with him. At least I know something about his experiences.

My other grandfather, Lev Finkel was, strictly speaking, not a Holocaust survivor, but he was no less of a victim. Born in Borszczów when the Austro-Hungarian Empire was in its death throes, he grew up in Eastern Poland. In 1939, the Soviets came. In 1941 he was drafted into the Red Army. His family, parents, and sisters, stayed behind. A decorated artillery officer, he returned home from the war in 1945. None of his relatives were alive; they had either been shot locally or gassed at Bełżec. He never mentioned them, and I can barely recall him laughing. We lived in L'viv, less than 150 miles from his hometown but he never went there, not even once—and neither did we. Ninety-six years old, he passed away several days before I finished the first draft of this book. I never interviewed him, knowing how painful it would be for him. Now I wish so much that I had. I dedicate this book to my grandfathers and to their siblings. *Yehi zichram baruch.*

CHAPTER 2

SETTING THE STAGE: JEWISH GHETTOS DURING THE HOLOCAUST

Before we explore the Jews' behavior in the ghettos of Minsk, Kraków, and Białystok, we need to understand what the ghettos were. This chapter will present a general overview of the Jewish ghettos during the Holocaust and then will describe in depth the three ghettos on which this book focuses. I will show that despite numerous similar features—being surrounded by a physical barrier, having similar ghetto institutions, and being subject to the Nazis' total extermination policies—there were substantial differences in Jewish behavior across these three communities. In each there were Jews who engaged in cooperation and collaboration, coping and compliance, evasion and resistance, but the distribution of strategies varied from one place to another. These Holocaust-era differences, I will argue throughout the book, stem from the pre-Holocaust political regimes under which each city lived.

JEWISH GHETTOS: AN OVERVIEW

"[T]he ghetto phenomenon was central to Jewish life under the National Socialist regime and is a keystone of Holocaust consciousness and memory," writes Holocaust historian Dan Michman.[1] Before the twentieth century, ghettos—that is, specific residential areas for Jews—existed in many European towns. The word itself derives from the name of the island where Venetian Jews were forced to live beginning in the Middle Ages. Yet the Nazi ghettos were very different from medieval Jewish quarters. On September 21, 1939, three weeks after the Nazi invasion of Poland, Chief of the Reich Main Security Office Reinhard Heydrich held a meeting to discuss occupation policies in the newly conquered Polish territories; in attendance were his adviser for Jewish affairs, Adolf Eichmann, and several other officials. Heydrich was explicit about his plans: "The Jews are to be concentrated in ghettos in cities, in order to facilitate a better possibility of control and later expulsion."[2] Heydrich's order notwithstanding, the main ghettoization drive did not begin until 1941. Eventually, the majority of Jews in Nazi-occupied Eastern Europe was concentrated in more than 1,100 ghettos, scattered from western Poland to the northern Caucasus. Not every locality in which Jews lived had a ghetto, but most towns and cities with a sizable Jewish population did—even if only for a short time.

The Nazi authorities "never elaborated a clear and unequivocal definition of what the ghetto was or should be,"[3] but the ghettos did share several defining features—namely the resettlement and concentration of the Jewish population into an area only for Jews and severe restrictions on entering and leaving said area.[4] The term "ghetto" itself, however, is rarely mentioned in the Nazis' official discourse and documentation; instead, the neutral and inconspicuous "Jewish Residential District/Area" is generally used. Martin Dean subdivides ghettos into the following types: open, closed, destruction, and remnant. Open ghettos were the officially declared Jewish Residential Areas, which were not enclosed by any physical barrier, although any Jew caught outside the ghetto would likely be shot. Many ghettos were initially open but later enclosed; a substantial number, however, remained open throughout their entire existence. Closed ghettos were physically surrounded by fences of wood, stone, or barbed wire. The Warsaw ghetto with its high brick walls is an iconic example of a closed ghetto. Destruction ghettos existed for a short time only; there the Jews were gathered prior to mass shootings or deportation to death camps. Finally, remnant ghettos were established to house those not selected for deportations or mass shootings, usually Jews with needed skills and their families. Most often those spared were doctors, pharmacists, tailors, cobblers, and providers of other essential services. In the ghetto of Trembowla in Galicia, the Germans temporarily "spared only two engineers, two doctors, and three schnapps brewers as needed specialists."[5] Although conditions varied from one ghetto to another, life in the ghettos was uniformly harsh, with confined Jews suffering from overcrowding, lack of food, and epidemics.

As important as the ghettos' physical attributes were their social structures. Raul Hilberg saw the ghetto as a form of government externally imposed on Jewish populations by an external force in order to improve its control over them.[6] Hilberg's view, however, oversimplifies the political and social features of the ghettos. Most scholars recognize that the ghetto was an externally imposed structure, but they note that important elements of local prewar Jewish society continued to exist there—that in many respects the ghetto was a continuation of the prewar community.[7] Given the salience of community-level political and social factors, the ghettos are a natural unit of analysis in a quest to better understand the impact of pre-Holocaust social and political factors on individual and collective behavior.

For this book I collected data on 1,126 ghettos established by the Nazis over a large territory, ranging from the western parts of Poland, about 250 miles east of Berlin, to the Northern Caucasus, not far from Chechnya. The smallest ghetto (Obol' in the USSR) had about ten inmates; the largest (Warsaw) contained almost half a million Jews. In Belopol'e, Jews made up only 0.72 percent of the prewar population, whereas Kamenka and Voik-hovshtadt were purely Jewish settlements. The majority of ghettos, as Figure 2.1 shows, were established in the territory of interwar Poland. Quite surprising is the relatively high number of ghettos established in the USSR, for the Holocaust in the Soviet Union has generally been described in the literature as a wave of mass shootings that did not involve large-scale ghettoization of the local Jewish population.

Many ghettos were destroyed very soon after their establishment, but a substantial number were allowed to exist for more than a year, and some even for several years (Figure 2.2). There was significant regional variation in the pattern of ghettos' existence, as Figure 2.3 clearly demonstrates. In the

Figure 2.1

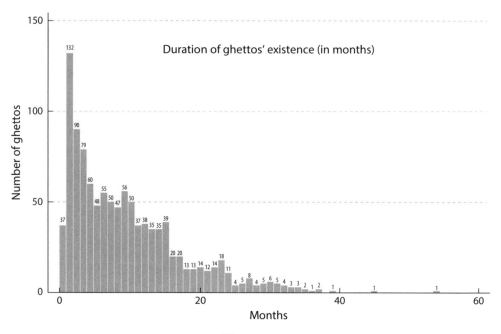

Figure 2.2

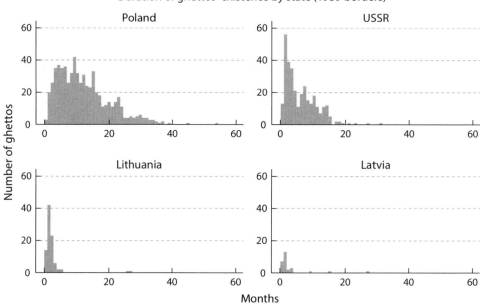

Figure 2.3

territories invaded by Germany in 1941, ghettos generally existed for a short period of time, being liquidated in a matter of months if not weeks after their creation. The most striking examples of these dynamics of persecution and destruction are Lithuania and Latvia, where Germans and their local collaborators killed the vast majority of the Jewish population immediately after the German army occupied these territories.

The data also show that many ghettos were established during the advanced stages of the Holocaust (Figures 2.4, 2.5). The last ghetto to be established by the Nazis was set up in April 1943, two months after Stalingrad.

Another surprising finding is the large number of open ghettos (Figure 2.6). The iconic image of a Jewish ghetto during the Holocaust is that of a closely guarded area surrounded by a wall or a fence. The reality, however, was much more complicated. It should also be noted that my data presents only a static representation of a ghetto's status: if the ghetto was created as open, but enclosed shortly before the final liquidation, the ghetto will still be coded as closed. Furthermore, it is possible that many of the ghettos for which I do not have data on enclosure were in fact open ghettos.

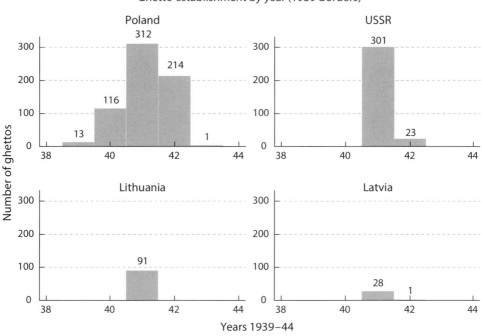

Figure 2.4

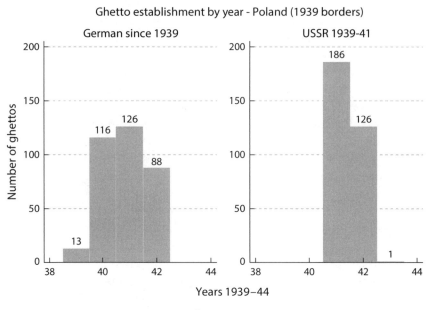

Figure 2.5

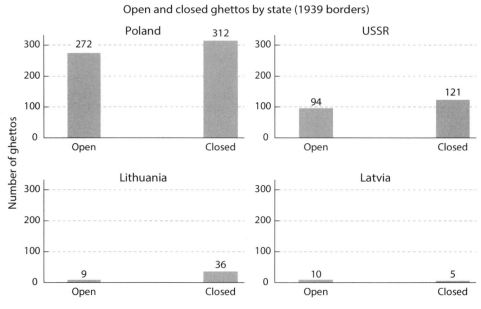

Figure 2.6

Research on Jewish ghettos during the Holocaust tends to focus on the largest ghettos, such as those in Warsaw and Łódź, but these—undoubtedly important politically, historically, and symbolically—were outliers when the wider spectrum of ghettos is considered. Those of medium size were more common, but they are less studied. The next section looks at three such ghettos—in Minsk, Kraków, and Białystok.

Minsk

Germany invaded the USSR on June 22, 1941. It was a Sunday, and many children were in summer camps or out of town with their grandparents. In Minsk, the grand opening of a huge manmade water reservoir, the Komsomol Lake (*Komsomol'skoe ozero*) was scheduled. Although the German offensive started at 4 a.m., Soviet citizens did not officially learn of the attack until noon. Many recall hearing on their way to or from the lake opening ceremony. Soviet authorities urged them to stay put and not panic. Most testimonies stress the relative normalcy of the first two days of the war; citizens were kept ignorant of the rapid German advance, and many still believed the promises of Soviet prewar propaganda that the enemy would be swiftly defeated. Almost no one outside the Communist leadership knew the truth about the catastrophic situation at the frontlines.

All that changed with the first massive German air raid on June 24. The exact number of casualties is unknown, but entire neighborhoods of Minsk burned to the ground. The authorities abandoned the city without organizing the evacuation of the rest of the population, and Soviet rule effectively ceased to exist.[8] At this point many city residents, Jews and non-Jews alike, decided to escape to the east. They did not get far. Most had chosen to flee via the main highway to Moscow, and after several miles were stopped and turned back by German paratroopers who had blocked the road. Some people were simply not allowed even to attempt to escape. Margarita F.'s father worked in the city's flour mill and was forbidden to leave until the day before the Germans entered the town. He was one of the few who anticipated their brutality, and as a Communist Party member probably knew that he would be among the first to be targeted. Yet by the time he was authorized to escape, it was already too late.[9]

In the city, chaos reigned as people who had lost their dwellings and belongings frantically searched for shelter and food. Arkadii P.'s story is similar to many survivors' experiences. He had come to Minsk before the war broke out to visit relatives. The family's house burned down during the

German air raid and Arkadii had to go out to search for food, but the stores were closed. For him, as well as for many others in the city, the only way to obtain food was to loot. Arkadii P. describes finding an open store where people were taking supplies off the shelves. He had moral qualms—after all, it was stealing—but eventually decided to go inside. All he could find by that time was caviar and champagne. Everything else was already taken, so Arkadii P. helped himself to a bag of delicacies and engaged in surrealistic barters. "We traded champagne for potatoes. Potatoes and caviar—[now] we had food!"[10] Both eleven years old at the time, Leonid Okun'[11] and Tsilya Bryson[12] each grabbed a box of candies. Many other testimonies describe the chocolate factory, where looters emptied huge vats of molasses. Some fell into the vats and drowned, but this did not stop others from taking as much as they could.

German troops entered Minsk on June 28, 1941. One of the first actions that the Germans undertook was to summon Minsk's entire adult male population to a camp at Drozdy, where they were kept for a number of days without food or water. Several hundred Jews were shot, while the rest, both Jews and non-Jews, were eventually released. On July 19, German authorities ordered the establishment of the ghetto. The initial order allowed the Jews only five days to move into the designated area; the timeframe for resettlement was later extended to two weeks. Jews could take into the ghetto only what they could carry. Non-Jews residing in the area had to move out. German authorities also began requiring Jews to wear round yellow patches, ten centimeters in diameter, affixed front and back to their clothing. Leaving the ghetto without permission and failure to wear the patches were both punishable by death. Although German authorities initially planned to erect a brick wall around the ghetto, this idea was eventually abandoned and the area was enclosed by barbed wire instead.[13]

The ghetto, which initially housed 75,000 to 80,000 Jews, was extremely overcrowded. Living quarters were allocated on the formula of "1.5 square meters per person," and several families had to squeeze into one room. For example, Girsh K. and four other people lived in a room of approximately seven square meters.[14] In Asja T.'s home, eleven people lived in two rooms;[15] twenty-seven resided in Tatyana G.'s three-room apartment.[16] During the initial period of the ghetto's existence, the only "legal" way to obtain food was to join a forced labor squad. But even then the official daily food allotment—100 grams (0.22 lb) of bread per day and a watery soup—was insufficient to sustain an adult working person, and hunger was prevalent. "In the ghetto, we had two main worries: how to get out of this situation, and what to eat tomorrow," recalled Nina Shalit-Galperin.[17] Most Jews initially tried to deal with their predicament by finding work and obeying German orders, but they soon discovered that coping and strictly following the rules was unlikely to ensure survival, even in the short run. Some began to engage in black market activities and to barter with the non-Jewish population, exchanging whatever they still had left for food, while others escaped the ghetto altogether by assuming fake identities, hiding with non-Jews or fleeing to the forests.

Shortly after the creation of the ghetto, a Jewish anti-Nazi resistance began to emerge. Initially chaotic and disorganized, it eventually coalesced around a group of communist activists led by Hersh Smolar, a Jewish refugee from Poland. Viewing itself as part of the broader Soviet anti-Nazi struggle, the Jewish resistance closely cooperated with the non-Jewish underground outside the ghetto and with Soviet detachments in the countryside. The underground turned the ghetto into a supply base for Soviet guerilla units and led numerous Jews out of the ghetto to the forests. The ghetto also had a Judenrat, though it was later disbanded. The Jewish police and a number of Nazi collaborators spied on other Jews and helped the Germans to fight the underground. Some of these collaborators were organized into a unit that closely cooperated with Nazi security services, while others acted independently.

Killings and seizures for forced labor began in mid-August 1941. Initially the Germans, assisted by Ukrainian and Lithuanian auxiliary troops and by the Belorussian police, seized males, who were then taken to the central square of the ghetto, beaten, and driven away to an unknown destination. None of them returned home. According to some sources, starting in late August women also were captured. About 5,000 people were caught and later executed during the August roundups.[18] The first large-scale massacre took place on November 7, 1941, the anniversary of the October Revolution. Ghetto inhabitants knew that something was brewing because skilled craftsmen, professionals, and members of the Judenrat were moved to the "Russian" part of the city on the evening of November 6th. Yet the scale of the killing shocked everyone. Local Jews, building on their historical experience, called it a "pogrom." The general assumption was that people would simply be thrown out of their apartments and probably beaten—no one imagined large-scale shootings in which thousands (10,000–12,000 is the estimated number) would perish.

At 5:30 a.m. German troops and their Ukrainian and Lithuanian auxiliaries entered the ghetto and cordoned off several streets. Many victims were shot on the spot, but the majority were pushed onto trucks and taken to the brick factory in Tuchinka on the outskirts of the city, where they were shot and buried in huge pits. Almost all were killed, but by a miracle a few survived. Some crawled out of the pits during the night and made their way back to the ghetto. The next Aktion was on November 20, and again thousands were shot.

The Germans' motivation for these killings was to create room in the ghetto for Jews who were being deported to Minsk from Germany, Austria, and Czechoslovakia. When the first transports with Central European Jews arrived in Minsk they were housed in buildings where dozens of dead bodies still lay on the floors. There were no beds, no electricity, no running water or heat; the German Jews had to build open fires inside the buildings to keep warm. Eight to ten people lived in Curt Parker's room. Arthur Menke slept in a bunk bed, built on the spot with raw wood.[19] From November 1941 to October 1942, nearly 24,000 Central European Jews were transferred to the city. Those who were not killed immediately upon arrival were put into the so-called *Sonderghetto* (special ghetto), which was separated from the "Soviet" ghetto by barbed wire. The first transport of German Jews arrived from Hamburg, so the place became known as the "Hamburg Ghetto."

Yet another Aktion took place on March 2, 1942. More than 5,000 Jews, including 300 children from the ghetto orphanage lost their lives. Then, in April, the Germans carried out a number of smaller-scale night raids. On each of these nights, several hundred Jews perished—shot, beaten to death, stabbed, or burnt alive. From July 28th to the 31st, another wave of killings erupted. This time, in addition to shootings, the Nazi authorities also used gas vans (*Gaswagen*), which the locals called the "soul destroyers" (*dushegubki*) and "black ravens." The ghetto hospital, including all of its patients and personnel, the leadership of the Judenrat, and a large part of the Jewish police force were slaughtered. After this Aktion, the ghetto was spared for just over a year. During that time, realizing that their days were numbered, up to 15,000 Jews tried to escape into the forests, where Soviet partisans had established their bases. Many were caught and killed by the Nazis, by local collaborators, or sometimes by the Soviet partisans themselves, but thousands, possibly as many as 10,000, managed to reach safety and survive. In August 1943, when the German army rolled back after its defeat at Stalingrad, German units once again surrounded the ghetto. People tried to find refuge in bunkers and hideouts, but they were often discovered by police dogs, or by Jews who worked as informers for the German security services. Most were shot on the streets or taken to the Trostenets camp near the city and killed there. By October 1, 1943, there were only about two thousand Jews left in the ghetto. On October 20th and 21st the ghetto was liquidated and its last inhabitants were killed or deported.[20] On July 3, 1944, the Red Army liberated Minsk.

Kraków

German troops invaded Poland on September 1, 1939. Some Cracovians sensed the coming tragedy and made frantic preparations, but for the majority the beginning of hostilities came as a shock. Eleven-year-old Avraham Blum was ecstatic—war meant there would be no school—but almost everyone else was terrified.[21] Unlike many Polish towns, Kraków was spared heavy bombing and was practically undamaged by the German advance. On September 6, 1939, German troops entered the city. When the war started, a large number of Jews, mostly males, fled to the eastern part of the country. Wawel, the city's castle and the historical seat of Polish kings became the residence of Hans Frank, the head of the General Government—a newly created administrative unit that encompassed those parts of prewar Poland that had not been annexed by either Germany or the USSR. The city's name was changed to Krakau.

The persecution of Jews began almost immediately after the city's occupation. During the first days of Nazi rule anti-Jewish actions consisted mainly of the looting of Jewish-owned stores and apartments, random beatings, occasional murders, and haphazard roundups for forced labor. With the consolidation of German control over Kraków, the persecution took a more organized and bureaucratized form. On September 8, 1939, all Jewish enterprises were required to be marked with a Star of David, and Jews were prevented from receiving rations in breadlines. In late October, Frank issued the order that all Jews would be subject to forced labor. In November and December, virtually all Jewish educational institutions were shut down.

In November 1939, a census conducted by the city's Judenrat counted 68,482 Jews in Kraków and several suburban communities. Starting December 1, 1939, all Jews over the age of twelve were required to wear a Star of David on their right arm. In January and February 1940, Jewish businesses were seized and transferred to Aryan "trustees" (*Treuhandler*). By April of that year, 700 Jewish enterprises in the city had been taken over by these German-appointed "trustees."[22]

The next blow to the Jewish community came in April 1940, when Frank ordered the expulsion of the city's Jews in order to make his seat the "most Jew-free city" in occupied Poland. Wehrmacht generals were complaining bitterly that they "had to live in apartment buildings where the only other tenants were Jews,"[23] and Frank found this intolerable indeed. Thus the vast majority of Kraków's Jews were to be removed from the city, leaving only about 10,000 who were to remain as indispensable skilled workers. Initially the Jews were urged to leave voluntarily, but in July 1940 their forcible removal commenced. By the beginning of October, the Jewish population of the city had declined by about 50 percent, but many eventually managed to return to the city.

On March 3, 1941, German authorities announced the establishment of a ghetto in the poor suburb of Podgórze. It was enclosed by a wooden fence and a 9.8-foot-high brick wall. In the ghetto area, all Polish signs and public inscriptions were to be replaced with ones using Hebrew script.[24] This confinement of a large number of people to a small area caused a housing crisis. The allocation of space was by windows—four people per window. Because many rooms had more than one window, it was not uncommon for eight or more people to squeeze into one room. Dora R. lived with nine other people in one room.[25] Erna R. and her family of five lived in a kitchen.[26]

The majority of ghetto residents chose coping as their preferred survival strategy. They found work outside the ghetto walls—in various factories, at the airfield, or cleaning offices for German officials. In the ghetto, however, coping was a chaotic and disorganized business, for there was little community-level guidance or intervention, and each family was largely on its own. In October and November 1941, small suburban communities were incorporated into the city and the additional 5,000 Jews who lived in these places—many of them previously expelled from the city—were forced into the ghetto.

The ghetto was crowded, food was in short supply, and living conditions were harsh and humiliating, but the Jews of Kraków nonetheless enjoyed relative safety until the summer of 1942. The first mass deportation to the Bełżec death camp took place in June of that year, following the registration of the ghetto Jews and the distribution of ID cards (*Kennkarten*) to those who were considered useful workers. The lucky ID bearers were allowed to remain in the ghetto; others (approximately 7,000) were deported. According to the Nazi authorities, the deportees had been sent to a labor camp in Ukraine, and it was some time before the Jews of Kraków discovered what "deportation to the East" really meant. A week after the first deportation, a new roundup took place in the ghetto. The next major Aktion was on October 28, 1942, when at least 6,000 Jews were sent to their deaths, and another 600 were killed in the ghetto. Following this Aktion, the ghetto was reduced in size and subsequently divided into two sections: Ghetto A for those who were able to work, and Ghetto B for those who were not. The final liquidation of the Kraków ghetto began on March 13, 1943. The able-bodied from Ghetto A, at least 8,000 people, were marched to the Płaszów labor camp. The remaining Jews were either murdered in the ghetto or sent to Auschwitz.[27] Numerous city Jews escaped the ghetto and moved to the so-called Aryan side, where they assumed false identities as non-Jews, or were hidden by non-Jews.

During its existence, the ghetto had a Judenrat, a Jewish police force, and a number of Nazi collaborators. Some of those collaborators were organized into a special unit that worked closely with the Nazi security services, while others assisted the Germans on an individual basis. The ghetto also had two Jewish resistance groups. One, *Iskra*, was led by communists and saw its main goal as helping the Soviet Union to win the war. The other, *Hehalutz Halochem*, was Zionist and strove to preserve and protect Jewish honor. The groups joined forces in bombing the Cyganeria coffee house, packed with German servicemen, in December 1942. After the bombing, both resistance organizations were eliminated by the Nazis.

The Płaszów camp replaced the liquidated ghetto. It was established in 1942 under the authority of the SS, and was originally a forced-labor camp. It was the site of the city's old Jewish cemetery, and gravestones were used as construction materials. Subsequently it was converted into a concentration camp where thousands of inmates, mainly Kraków Jews, were worked to death. Amon Göth, the camp commander, took special pleasure in personally killing prisoners on a daily basis, and was considered a sadistic monster even by the Nazi standards. Some Płaszów prisoners were lucky to find employment in the Emalia factory, located outside the camp and owned by a German named Oscar Schindler. In 1944, following the rapid Soviet advance, Płaszów was dismantled. The prisoners were transferred to other concentration camps or murdered in Auschwitz. More than one thousand were rescued by Schindler, who transferred his employees and some additional camp inmates to Brünnlitz (currently Brněnec in the Czech Republic), where they remained until liberation in May 1945. Kraków itself was liberated by the Red Army on January 19, 1945. By August 15, 1945, there were 4,262 Jews in the city. By the end of the year their number had doubled, and in 1946 4,300 more Jews returned from the USSR,[28] but the community has never recovered from the Holocaust.

Białystok

The German army occupied Białystok for the first time on September 15, 1939, and it controlled the city for just one week. At that time the Germans were refraining from large-scale anti-Jewish actions. Because Białystok was located in territory that, according to the Molotov-Ribbentrop Pact (1939), was assigned to the Soviet Union, Soviet planes flew over the city several days after the German occupation and dropped leaflets that notified the local population of the forthcoming "liberation of Western Belarus from the Polish yoke." Several survivors recall that as the German troops marched out of the city, some Jews threw stones at them. "We will return!" the Germans shouted back.[29] And return they did.

German troops reoccupied the city on June 27, 1941, five days after attacking the USSR. Immediately upon their arrival in the city, police battalions 309 and 316 and Einsatzkommando 8 started massacring the local Jewish population. Many were shot in a public garden, and around eight hundred were herded into the city's Great Synagogue, which was then set ablaze. Only a few managed to escape the building with the help of the Polish janitor. On July 3rd and July 12th, additional shootings took place. Over the course of two weeks about seven thousand Jews perished. However the city did not experience anti-Jewish pogroms, unlike the surrounding countryside, where in dozens of places Jews were killed by their ethnically Polish neighbors.[30]

On July 26, 1941, the creation of the ghetto was announced. A 2.5-meter (8.2-foot) high wooden fence, topped with barbed wire, surrounded it and enclosed forty-three thousand Jews. In September 1941, about five thousand Jews were expelled from the ghetto to the small town of Prużany. In July 1941, the city became the capital of Bezirk (District) Bialystok, a separate German administrative unit. Bezirk Bialystok was placed under the authority of Erich Koch, the Nazi leader of East Prussia, who governed the territory from his seat in Königsberg. It was initially intended to incorporate the district into the German state, but even though the German Reichsmark was introduced as the regional currency and border check-points were put in place between Bezirk Bialystok and the rest of Poland, the plan was never implemented. Throughout the war, the district remained a separate administrative unit, never fully annexed to the Reich.

The ghetto was overcrowded, with the allocation of living quarters based on the "three square meters per person" principle. Hana Birk shared a room with five other people.[31] Thirty people lived in Lipa A.'s apartment.[32] Life was harsh and many survivors recall being constantly hungry. However, in Białystok, unlike in many other places, the Jews did not die of hunger and there were no major epidemics. As long as it lasted, coping was a reasonably successful and attractive strategy in the Białystok ghetto, much more so than in Minsk or Kraków. The work of coping was directed and coordinated by the Judenrat, which played a very important role in the life of the ghetto and controlled it with the help of the Jewish police. The Nazis did have some collaborators inside the ghetto, but the Judenrat eventually neutralized them.

On February 4, 1943, the Gestapo notified the Judenrat of a plan to deport 17,600 Jews from the ghetto, but eventually the number of deportees was reduced to 6,300. The Aktion, which began on February 5, 1943, lasted an entire week. About 8,000 Jews were rounded up and sent to the death camps; another 2,000 were killed on the spot. "In the cemetery I saw rows upon rows of dead small children, [all in] red socks. I was perplexed: how come all have red socks. It took me a moment to realize that this was blood," recalled Hadasah Levkowitcz.[33] After the deportation, about 30,000 Jews remained in Białystok.[34] In late July 1943, the Nazi leadership decided to liquidate the ghetto. On August 16, 1943, the ghetto Jews were ordered to assemble at the deportation point. The underground, which consisted of both communist and Zionist groups, raised a rebellion, which was brutally put down by the German troops. The majority of the ghetto population complied and quietly went to the deportation point. Very few tried to escape or hide.

Over the next week 25,000 Jews were sent from the ghetto to death camps; those chosen for work were sent to labor camps in the Lublin area. On August 21, about 1,260 ghetto children, many of them orphans, were sent to the Theresienstadt ghetto. According to a rumor, they were to be sent to Switzerland and exchanged for German POWs. The exchange plan fell through, however, and from Theresienstadt the children were shipped to Auschwitz and gassed.[35] The remaining one thousand Jews, including the Judenrat's leaders, were kept in the city in what was called the "Small Ghetto" until early September 1943, and then they were deported and killed as well. When the Red Army liberated Białystok on July 22, 1944, the only Jews in the city were a small group of female Jewish resistance members living on faked papers. More than a year after the liberation, in August 1945, there were only189 Jews in the city. By the end of that year, 167 remained.[36] The Białystok Jewish community had effectively ceased to exist.

THE SHADOW OF THE PAST

The three ghettos, as can be seen from the description above, were subject to Nazi control, confinement, and, eventually, total extermination policies that were in the main similar. Yet the behavior of the Jewish inmates differed

Table 2.1. Main differences between the Minsk, Kraków, and Białystok ghettos

	Collaboration	Coping	Evasion	Underground	Uprising
Minsk	Organizations and individuals	Disorganized	High	Communist	No
Kraków	Organizations and individuals	Disorganized	Medium	Communist and Zionist	No
Białystok	Individuals[1]	Organized	Low	Communist and Zionist	Yes

[1] Until the final deportation from the ghetto.

from one ghetto to another. The most notable of those differences, which will be described in much greater detail in subsequent chapters, are summarized in tables (see also appendix 2).

What explains these differences in behavior between ghettos, populated by members of the same ethnic and religious group? I argue that to understand how the Jews behaved during the Holocaust, we need to begin by looking at the sociopolitical realities of their earlier lives. The Nazi occupation of Central and Eastern Europe changed a lot. It erased and imposed borders, created and broke up countries, drove millions from their homes, reshaped societies, and obliterated communities. But the war and the Nazi occupation did not change *everything*. The monumental shifts and changes brought by the Nazis unfolded against an easily overlooked, but important backdrop of processes that began long before World War II, and these shaped the violence in every place that had the misfortune of being taken over by the Nazi Empire. Given the scale of the tragedy that befell Europe's Jews, it is natural to focus on the immediately visible changes wrought by the Nazis—the yellow stars, the ghetto walls, the mass graves, and the smoke billowing from the chimneys of the crematoria. But if we want to understand more deeply, we should take a serious look at the pre-Holocaust period, not only as a setting, but also as an element of the *explanation*. As the following pages will demonstrate, this analysis of the pre-Holocaust period should focus on the interaction of macro-level state policies and local, community-centered factors.

The next sections will briefly introduce the pre-Holocaust political histories of the three communities, their important similarities and their no less important differences. More specifically, I will demonstrate how the three cities varied in the degree to which their Jews were integrated into the broader society and in the strength of their organized Jewish community. It was these differences that shaped the Jewish community in each place and, down the road, led to variation in Jewish survival strategies across the ghettos.

Minsk

Minsk's Jewish community is one of the oldest in Eastern Europe. The first reference to a Jewish presence there dates to the late fifteenth century, when the city belonged to the Grand Duchy of Lithuania, which later merged with Poland. After Poland's second partition (in 1793), Minsk joined the Russian Empire and was included in the Pale of Settlement—the western part of the state, where Jews were allowed to reside. In the late nineteenth century, the Minsk Jewish community was about fifty thousand strong, comprising a majority of the city's population.

Minsk was a vibrant, if economically troubled town. Most local Jews hardly made ends meet, struggling to eke out a living as tradesmen, craftsmen, and manual laborers. Virtually everyone spoke Yiddish—in the 1897 census 98 percent of the community declared it as their mother tongue.[37] There was also, however, a small, but influential group of educated, Russian-speaking professionals and wealthy businesspeople who dominated local Jewish politics. The Jewish community did experience pogroms, but it knew how to protect itself and how to strike back. Mink's self-defense was in fact a joint endeavor of two very different groups—physically vigorous carriage drivers and butchers,[38] and educated, politically active, middle-class males.

In 1918, following the Communist Revolution in Russia and the signing of the Brest-Litovsk Treaty, German troops occupied the city and expelled the nascent Communist authorities. The experience of what proved to be a largely benevolent German rule played an important role in defining what many Jews expected from the Germans in 1941. In 1918, German authorities restored order, revived economic life, and allowed political parties to resume their activities—all in the wake of an extremely disorganized and repressive period of revolutionary turmoil. Even later, when the Germans began limiting political freedoms, things were still much better than under the Communists. After Germany's military collapse, a second short-lived period of Soviet rule followed, only to be replaced by a brutal Polish occupation. The Jews of Minsk recalled the eleven months of Polish rule in 1919 and 1920 with horror. It was a period of humiliation, lootings, beatings, and the occasional murder of Jews by Polish troops. Against this background of

Polish and Soviet violence, German rule was remembered as a time of peace and stability.

In May 1918 elections for the Minsk Jewish Community Council took place. The socialist, anti-Zionist Bund received 20 percent of the votes, while the Zionists won the majority. In the 1920 elections, the Zionists came out on top once again.[39] Yet the consolidation of Soviet rule after the Polish army's withdrawal led to the swift demise of Jewish ethnic politics. The Bund was forced to merge with the Communist Party, and by 1928 Zionist political groups were outlawed. Persecution of Jewish political parties went hand in hand with the Soviet authorities' attacks on Jewish communal and religious institutions. The Soviet government closed synagogues and religious learning institutions, and a series of public trials of Jewish ritual slaughterers, rabbis, and circumcisers took place.[40] Unable to continue their activities legally, some Jewish organizations disappeared, while others tried, largely unsuccessfully, to continue operating illegally. Until the mid-1930s, there were small underground cells of Zionist youth movements in Minsk, and Rabbi Zvi Neria provides a detailed account of an underground yeshiva that operated in the city.[41] These efforts notwithstanding, old religious and political institutions and practices gradually vanished as the city's Jews became increasingly Soviet not only in citizenship, but also in political outlook and behavior.

The 1920s and early 1930s were not only a period of political repression. During that period, Minsk became a major center of blooming Yiddish (but communist in content) culture and education.[42] At the same time, the Soviet government also made upward social mobility and integration into the broader society possible for the Jews. Czarist-era prohibitions and ethnic quotas restricting the number of Jews in the universities were abolished; anti-Semitism, while it still held considerable sway among the Slavs, became a criminal offense and diminished compared to pre-Soviet times. Young Jews responded enthusiastically to these changes and began integrating into non-Jewish society in large numbers. Thus, less than 50 percent of the city's Jews listed Yiddish as their mother tongue in the 1939 census. Jews, only 6.7 percent of Belorussia's population, made up more than half of the republic's physicians and dentists and a quarter of the managers of its industrial and agricultural enterprises.[43] Among young Jews, intermarriage and friendship with non-Jews, virtually unthinkable only two decades prior, became widespread. By World War II, the demographic and socioeconomic transformation of the city's Jewish population, while still incomplete and affecting the younger generations more than the old people, was already irreversible.

In the late 1930s Soviet official policy toward the Jews underwent dramatic changes. Yiddish schools were shut down; and many prominent Jews, as well as former political activists of the Zionist parties and the Bund perished during Stalin's Great Terror. Most Jewish communal bodies and organizations ceased to exist. At this stage, integration became not simply an individual choice, but a mandatory state policy. Despite the overrepresentation of Jews in the Communist Party and in the government's lower- and mid-level tiers, only a very few Jewish officials held high rank, and their numbers decreased even further after the Molotov-Ribbentrop Pact and the subsequent Soviet-Nazi rapprochement. Another consequence of the pact was a full stop to the previously extensive negative coverage of Nazi Germany and its policies, including its anti-Jewish ones, in the Soviet media. As a result, most Minsk Jews knew very little about what was happening to their coethnics in areas under Nazi control and often grounded their thinking on their largely positive encounters with the Germans during World War I.

In 1939, the Jewish population of Minsk was 70,998, almost 30 percent of the city.[44] Following the German invasion of Poland in September 1939, numerous Jewish refugees arrived in town. These Polish Jews, newcomers to a city whose Soviet Jews had for twenty years been cut off from Jewish communities in neighboring states, were treated with curiosity, suspicion, and sometimes outright hostility.[45] The stories they brought of the Nazis' anti-Jewish actions were more often than not met with disbelief, in part because the Soviet official media silenced reports of Nazi persecution.

Kraków

The Jewish community of Kraków dates back to 1176 and is among the oldest in Poland.[46] After a fire in 1494 destroyed parts of the city, including the Jewish quarter, King Jan Olbracht ordered the Jews expelled from Kraków and resettled in Kazimierz, a separate community on the opposite bank of the Vistula River. After that, and until the nineteenth century, there was no Jewish community in Kraków proper, although several families continued to reside in the city. The Jews, however, did not feel that they had left the town. Though now settled in Kazimierz, they continued to call themselves the Kraków community.[47] During the sixteenth century, this community became a center of Talmudic learning and scholarship. Following the eighteenth-century partitions of Poland, the Jews of Kraków/Kazimierz came under the rule of the Austro-Hungarian Habsburg Empire, which was much more benign in its treatment of its Jewish subjects than was neighboring Russia.

The period of the late nineteenth and early twentieth centuries was an era of major transformation for the Kraków Jews. Even though the city officially preserved its ghetto until 1867,[48] the Austro-Hungarian Empire eventually granted Jews full citizenship rights and eliminated institutionalized discrimination in fields such as education, employment, and residence. As a result, many Jews embraced the Polish and German languages and cultures and assimilated into the larger society. In sharp contrast to Jews in other parts of Poland, Kraków's Jews, even those who belonged to ultra-orthodox religious groups, used Polish or German as their first language, and many did not even understand, let alone speak Yiddish.

In 1900, Jews numbered 25,000, 28 percent of the city's total population. The majority were engaged in commerce and crafts, but by the beginning of the twentieth century they were also well represented in the professions. Thus in 1910, Jews constituted 17 percent of Krakow's engineers, 24 percent of its physicians, and 52 percent of its lawyers.[49] This relatively high degree of assimilation drove many toward the politics of liberal Polish nationalism and "in the last decades before World War I, a group of Jews . . . participated in various organizations working for the resurrection of Poland."[50] Many of them, while still considering themselves Jewish, eventually cut their ties with Jewish communal institutions such as synagogues, Jewish political parties, social clubs, and youth movements.

Another major political force was Zionism. Under the leadership of a charismatic rabbi, Ozjasz Thon, Zionism became the most popular political ideology among Kraków's Jews, not least because the Polish population proved less than enthusiastic about the Jews' assimilation. Yet, even if they failed to fully assimilate into Polish society, in Kraków they were substantially more integrated than the Jews in the rest of Poland. The city's Zionist periodicals were published in Polish, rather than in Yiddish or Hebrew. Even the socialist, anti-Zionist Bund, widely known for its passionate attachment to the Yiddish language, published its Kraków journal in Polish. The city was indeed a center of Polonized Jewish culture; Jewish students were for the most part enrolled in state-run interethnic schools, and even in private Jewish schools Polish was the dominant language.[51]

The Habsburg Empire's collapse paved the way for the establishment of an independent Polish state. Because of the Austro-Hungarian policy of ethno-religious tolerance, the political culture of Kraków was generally more moderate than that of the ex-Russian parts of Poland. But even this relative moderation could not prevent bloodshed. For the Kraków Jews, integration and violence went hand in hand. First, there were anti-Jewish pogroms in 1918 and 1919, which were met by Jewish self-defense units,[52] organized by Austro-Hungarian army veterans. The most important Jewish institution in the city, the *Nowy Dziennik* newspaper, was bombed by right-wing Polish terrorists in 1923.[53] In 1931, the city's Jagiellonian University witnessed three weeks of anti-Jewish violence.[54] Numerous testimonies recall beatings, brawls, and anti-Semitic attacks during the late 1930s.[55] Still, even if not an island of ethnic peace, the city was safer for Jews than most of the rest of Poland.

During the interwar years, Kraków was dominated politically by the Polish Socialist Party (PPS) and other pro-government political organizations.[56] The right-wing, anti-Semitic National Democrats had only a meager following in the city. Between 1933 and 1939 the mayor was Mieczysław Kaplicki, a Jew who had converted to Christianity, while Bernard Mond, the only ethnically Jewish general in the Polish army, commanded the city's garrison. Among the Kraków Jews, Zionists were the dominant political force, followed by the ultra-orthodox Agudas Yisroel party. In the Zionist camp, the moderate General Zionists claimed the largest following.

In 1939 there were about 65,000 Jews in Kraków, comprising 26 percent of the population.[57] Throughout the 1930s, 45 percent of Jews were employed in trade (they were approximately 60 percent of the city's traders), and about a third were employed in industry and crafts. Jews also played an important role in medicine and other professions. Sixty percent of the Jewish work force was self-employed.[58] The community's internal social life was vibrant, and more than 300 Jewish political, educational, and cultural institutions existed in the city during the interwar period.[59] At the same time, Kraków also had a sizable number of Jews who were culturally, socially, and politically assimilated into Polish society and did not belong to any Jewish bodies and organizations.

Before the outbreak of the war, the Kraków Jews were not only informed about Hitler's anti-Semitic policies, but also directly affected by them. In October 1938 the German authorities decided to expel Jews who did not possess German citizenship. The German decision was a reaction to the Polish Ministry of Internal Affairs' decree that the passports of Polish citizens residing abroad had to be revalidated by October 29, 1938, and that those who failed to do so would lose the right to return to Poland. In late October, the German police rounded up seventeen thousand Jews throughout the country, many of whom had resided in Germany for decades or had even been born there, and drove them across the Polish border into the vicinity of Zbąszyń. Because of the city's history of Austrian rule and its Jews' close ties with Germany, almost every Jewish family in Kraków had relatives or acquaintances among the deportees. The refugees flocked to the city, producing a housing crisis. The vast majority of survivor testimonies mention the refugees, who were housed with families or assisted in other ways. The refugees' stories also had a substantial effect on Jewish behavior during the early stages of the war and most people, while surprised by the outbreak of the hostilities, did anticipate there would be persecutions if the Germans were victorious. No one, however, foresaw how far the anti-Jewish violence would go.

Białystok

Białystok was first settled in 1320, and in 1703 the Polish king Jan III Sobieski awarded the city to Count Branicki, who invited Jews into his domain.[60] After the third partition of Poland in 1795, Białystok became part of the Prussian kingdom and the capital of its New East Prussia province. Under Prussian rule, many Białystok Jews promptly embraced German culture and language,[61] but the Germanization process halted abruptly in 1807 when the city came under the control of the Russian Empire, where it remained until the end of World War I.

The first textile mills in Białystok were set up in the early nineteenth century by Saxon soldiers who settled there after the Napoleonic wars.[62] Eventually, Jewish manufacturers began to dominate what became a booming textile industry. Due to its industrial output, Białystok quickly became known as the "Manchester of the North." Its population swelled and by 1897 Jews accounted for about 75 percent of Białystok's 63,000 residents.[63] Jewish domination of the city's economic life was uncontested; by 1921 close to 90 percent of Białystok's factories were owned by Jews,[64] making it not only the "Manchester of the North," but also the "Jaffa of Lithuania."[65] An uneasy mixing of people and languages, with "Jews, Russians, Poles, Ukrainians and Lithuanians taunting each other"[66] on the city streets gave rise to the most ambitious attempt ever undertaken to create a world language. Białystok native Ludwig Zamenhof invented Esperanto, a so-called universal language that was quite popular throughout the world in the first half of the twentieth century.

Early in the new century, the socialist anti-Zionist Bund and the Polish Socialist Party dominated the city's political landscape. Białystok was also an important Zionist center, with Shmuel Mohilever, one of the early leaders of Zionism, as the city's rabbi. In 1906, in one of the bloodiest pogroms in modern history, eighty-eight of Białystok's Jews were murdered, and close to seven hundred wounded.[67] The pogrom was carried out mainly by Russians, some of whom were brought to the city with the explicit task of "beating the Jews." Poles by and large refrained from taking part in the violence. The Jewish self-defense force made desperate attempts to fend off the mobs, but failed because the attackers were actively supported by the police and the army.

During World War I, the city was occupied by German troops. Białystok Jews, who had few reasons to support the Russian Empire, welcomed the Germans as their "liberators and emancipators,"[68] a pro-German attitude that was adopted notwithstanding the fact that the invading German forces had bombarded the city, uprooted thousands, and set hundreds of homes on fire. A noticeable outcome of the fighting was a swift and substantial decrease in the city's Jewish population during and after the war years.

Politically, the city was a hotbed of left-wing revolutionary politics. In the first Jewish community (kehila) elections in 1918, socialist parties (the Bund and the Ferajnigte) came out on top, winning twenty-five out of a total of seventy seats. Zionists came in second with nineteen seats, and Orthodox parties third. So strong was the socialists' hold on communal institutions that in 1919 kehila leaders refused to welcome Ambassador Henry Morgenthau Sr., a prominent American-Jewish diplomat visiting the city, because he was a representative of a capitalist state.[69] Indeed, left-wing parties dominated local Jewish politics throughout the entire interwar period.

The Białystok area was contested after World War I, and its status was not clearly defined until the early 1920s. During the Polish-Soviet war (1919-1921), Soviet troops captured the city only to be driven back by the Poles. Eventually, the Polish government decided to annex the region. Many Białystok Jews were hostile to the Polish state, and a proposal was made to conduct a plebiscite that would determine the fate of the city. Numerous Jews wanted Białystok either to be annexed by the Soviet Union, become part of Lithuania, or even be declared a special international zone. The local Yiddish language newspaper argued against the annexation of Białystok by Poland, and this, naturally, enraged the Poles. The city's Polish media promoted the image of a Jewish-communist conspiracy (even though the actual number of Jewish communists in the city was very small) and portrayed the Jews as a "devious, subversive entity, dangerous to the stability of the new Polish nation, and lethal to Polish Catholic society."[70]

In its residential patterns and in the social ties between the Jewish and Polish communities, the city was radically segregated. Jews tended to reside in the city center, while the Poles lived in the outskirts and in the adjacent rural communities that were incorporated into the municipal boundaries in order to decrease the percentage of Jews. In 1921, almost 77,000 people resided in Białystok, of whom 51.6 percent were Jewish. In 1936, out of 100,000 people living in the city, Jewish numbers were down to about 43 percent.[71] The Jews' hostility to both pre–World War I Russia and the interwar Polish state, coupled with toxic interethnic relations in the town also gave rise to an exceptionally strong city-centered, Yiddish-speaking Jewish *Białystoker* identity that was not dependent on an individual's physical location. Historian Rebecca Kobrin argues that for the Białystok Jews, the city was the center of the universe and that it remained so for a distinct, active, and strongly attached diaspora spread throughout the world, from New York to Palestine to Buenos Aires to Melbourne.[72]

The Jewish population was mainly working-class and poor. After the city was cut off from the vast Russian market, its local textile-based economy experienced an acute crisis with unemployment reaching an astronomic 40 percent. In subsequent years the situation improved, but the city and especially its Jewish community were never able to fully recover. Even though the Jews were no longer a majority in the city, they still dominated local economic life and owned close to 80 percent of local businesses.[73]

Professional organizations, chambers of commerce, and trade unions were no less ethnically segregated than residential patterns. Interethnic relations, already tense and hostile at the onset of the Polish rule, only deteriorated with time. "Growing up in Bialystok [*sic*] I saw how Poles hated Jews and how Jews hated and feared Poles," recalled Charles Zabuski.[74] Even though the Jewish and the Polish communities in the city were not totally isolated from one another,[75] the Jews' integration into non-Jewish society was severely limited, even among the educated classes. The vast majority of Jewish children studied in exclusively Jewish, Yiddish or Hebrew-language educational institutions; only a few attended state schools where Polish was the language of instruction. Allen Seder recalls that he was the sole Jewish student in his state-run elementary school. He was constantly insulted and beaten; his schoolmates also demanded to know why he, a Jew, was attending a Polish school.[76] A number of testimonies state that Jews were scared even to enter Polish neighborhoods or walk in public parks.[77] This lack of integration and interethnic contacts also meant that few Białystok Jews spoke Polish well. In 1938 the local Polish authorities cut funding to Jewish schools,[78] but did nothing to make the Polish-language, state-run educational system more hospitable and attractive to Jewish students. In contrast to Minsk, where the authorities simply shut down Jewish schools and forced Jewish students to enroll in interethnic institutions, in Białystok Jewish schools were allowed to exist; the goal of the policy was not to promote integration, but simply to make the Jewish community's life more miserable. Students who could afford the increase in tuition kept attending Jewish schools, while those who could not either dropped out or had to rely on intraethnic charitable bodies.

A testament to the lack of integration was the status of the Yiddish language. So strong was the position of Yiddish in the city that even the local Zionist newspaper was published in that language, notwithstanding Zionism's ideological animosity to the diaspora language.[79] Another consequence of limited integration, coupled with passionate attachment to the *Białystoker* identity, was the strength of the city's organized Jewish community and communal institutions. In Białystok virtually every Jew took part in exclusively Jewish organizations, such as schools, religious societies, political parties, trade unions, charities, and youth movements.[80] This was not the case in Kraków or Minsk.

At times, ethnic tensions and fights between youngsters escalated into full-on street riots. The most notable fracas took place when the annual *Lag Ba-Omer* parade of Zionist youth movements happened to take place on a Sunday. The parade was supposed to pass by a church and the Zionist youths were advised to change the route for fear of violence, but they refused. As expected, when the parade reached the church, the Jews were attacked by a Polish mob, which started beating them. Jewish porters, butchers, and carriage drivers from all over the city rushed to defend their coethnics and dispersed the Poles. One Polish soldier was killed, and an unknown, though substantial number of rioters were wounded.[81] Undoubtedly, at least some of these porters and butchers belonged to the anti-Zionist Bund and did not support the parade's political message. Yet despite all internal conflicts and cleavages, when faced with external threat, the Białystok Jewish population demonstrated a very high degree of internal cohesion.

THE SOVIET INTERLUDE (1939–41)

After the city was occupied by German troops for a week in 1939, the Red Army entered Białystok only to be greeted by jubilant and cheering Jewish crowds. The Soviet tanks were "bombarded with flowers," recalled Abraham Vered.[82] It was *Yom Kippur*, the Day of Atonement, according to Jewish religious tradition a day that should be devoted to prayer and fasting, but as many witnesses noted, the entrance of the Red Army turned the fast into a holiday. Soviet rule was welcomed by almost every Jew, including staunch anti-communists. The father of Lipa A., a businessman, was extremely happy when the Red Army took over. It meant that there would be no German or Polish anti-Semitism to suffer from, and losing his business was a small price to pay for such a happy eventuality.[83]

One of the first things the Soviet troops did after securing control of the city was to go on a wild shopping spree, emptying the stores and buying virtually everything they could lay their hands on. "[T]he Russians liberated us, they liberated us from butter, from sugar, from milk, from meat," said Michel Mielnicki, sarcastically describing the first days of the Soviet rule.[84] Watches were an especially sought-after item.[85] Shortly after the Soviet takeover, the city was declared the capital of Western Belorussia, and elections for the Western Belorussian Supreme Soviet were held. The elections were rigged and tightly monitored by Soviet officials who flocked to the city, but many young Jews, especially those belonging to left-wing groups, enthusiastically participated in the election campaign.[86] Unsurprisingly, the elected Supreme Soviet unanimously expressed the wish of the liberated people of Western Belorussia to join the "Soviet family of nations," and the territory was promptly annexed by the USSR.

The enthusiastic embrace of Soviet rule by many Jews and the opportunities it offered to this previously oppressed minority aroused the hostility of local Poles, who lost their prominence (and their state) overnight.[87] Quite often, Jews who were for the first time in their lives allowed to assume positions of authority used those powers to demonstrate to ethnic Poles their newly inferior status. "We did not behave properly towards the Poles," admitted Mina Dorn. "[Many Jews] said: they were anti-Semites, so let them get what they deserve."[88] This swift reversal of the preexisting ethnic hierarchy poisoned the already poor intergroup relations in the city, with ultimately tragic consequences. In the meantime, however, social and ethnic conflicts were prevented from exploding by the Soviets' rigorous security apparatus.

One of the main problems the Soviets had to confront was the presence of the tens of thousands of Jewish refugees who had flocked to Białystok from Nazi-occupied Poland, causing acute housing and food shortages.[89] Synagogues, schools, and public buildings were converted to sleeping halls, but there was still not enough space to accommodate everyone. The conditions in the city were so appalling, in fact, that some refugees decided to smuggle themselves back to Nazi-occupied territories.

Eventually the Soviet authorities decided to solve the crisis by presenting the refugees with a stark choice: either accept Soviet citizenship or register to move back to the German-occupied zone. The exact data are unavailable, but about half of the refugees refused Soviet passports.[90] Some managed to return to the German zone, but the majority were arrested by the Soviet security services and deported to the Soviet interior, where most survived the war. After the deportation of the refugees, the food and housing situation in the city substantially improved.

Those who stayed, as well as the native Jewish population, became Soviet citizens. To consolidate their rule, Soviet authorities tried to cleanse the city of unreliable and subversive "elements" such as political activists, religious figures, and many professionals. Especially hard hit were the Bund and the Zionists. Ironically, by targeting these people, deporting them to Siberia, or incarcerating them in the Gulag, Soviet authorities unintentionally saved the lives of thousands of Polish Jews.

The Soviet government also completely reshaped the social and economic life of the Białystok Jews. Private enterprises were nationalized; synagogues were converted to clubs and warehouses; Hebrew- and Polish-language schools were forced to switch to Yiddish or Russian virtually overnight. "My entire knowledge of Russian consisted of *tovarishch* (comrade) and *do svidaniia* (goodbye), and with that vocabulary I had to start," recalled Hadasah Levkowitcz, a high school teacher. As the students did not know Russian either, they were willing to tolerate Levkowitcz's "rather disastrous" instruction.[91] Jewish communal and political organizations were disbanded. Saturday became a regular working day, which meant that most religious Jews had either to desecrate the Sabbath or to face unemployment and potential punishment.

The regime, however, did not *only* punish and deport. For many, Soviet rule brought numerous tangible benefits, such as employment, universal health care, access to secondary and university education, and upward social mobility, benefits not available to the vast majority of Jews in Poland. As a result, many young Jews enthusiastically joined in the new social order. Soviet indoctrination in schools had an effect as well. David Gofer joined the Pioneers, the Communist Party's youth organization, where he was taught about Pavlik Morozov, a Soviet youth who denounced his anti-communist parent. Gofer's mother was involved in the banned kosher slaughter business, and following the footsteps of his Pioneer role model he threatened to denounce her to the authorities.[92] Some Jewish youths, on the other hand, clung steadfastly to their pre–World War II political beliefs. In Białystok and elsewhere in Soviet-ruled Eastern Poland, Zionist youth movements went underground. For the Marxist *Hashomer Hatzair* Zionist youth movement, known for its sympathy to the Soviet Union, the decision to go underground was difficult. "Can we, as socialists, be in the underground in the Soviet Union?" a movement activist in Białystok pondered.[93] The members of the movement decided that they could. The Hashomer underground was a local initiative of several members, recalled Aharon Liak.[94] Initially, it met in groups of ten to fifteen, but later reorganized into small groups with less than five members. Their goal was mainly to preserve the organization, its ideology, and structure rather than to harm the Soviets. The socialist *Dror* and the right-wing *Betar* movements also had underground cells in the city.[95]

The impact of Soviet policies was mixed. On the one hand, Soviet rule offered many Jews economic and educational opportunities as well as social mobility. But it was also detrimental to the large number of Jews who saw their businesses nationalized, synagogues closed, and parties disbanded. Two years of communist policies shattered old social structures and ethnic hierarchies and caused interethnic animosity to rise to unprecedented levels. At the same time, the period was too brief to allow for the building of new identities or to forcefully integrate the city's ethnic communities, as took place in Minsk.

Despite all the changes, the key threat to the Jews of Białystok at this time was external, not internal. Even those Jews who did not benefit from the opportunities offered by the new regime still appreciated the basic fact that Soviet rule was preferable to that of the Nazis. By preventing German rule over Białystok, the Soviets "commuted a death sentence to life imprisonment," a popular joke went. On June 22, 1941, Germany invaded the USSR, and the Jews of Białystok soon came to realize how darkly prophetic a joke this was.

Concluding Remarks

As this chapter has shown, there were many similarities between the Jewish communities of Minsk, Kraków, and Białystok, both before and during the Holocaust. All three were old and well established, and they shared a similar "deep history" of Polish rule, imperial (Russian and Austro-Hungarian) control before World War I, and generally positive encounters with Germans and German-speaking culture prior to the Nazi occupation. Historically, all three were centers of religious scholarship, had vibrant civil societies, and enjoyed high levels of political activism. All three had experienced pogroms and had decisively fought back. The cities and their Jewish populations were fairly similar in size, served as important administrative centers, and suffered total destruction during the Holocaust. Yet there were important differences between them in the type and intensity of their interethnic relations, the extent of Jews' integration into broader non-Jewish society, the strength of Jewish communal institutions, the ideological and linguistic commitments of the Jewish population, and the information available to them about Nazi anti-Jewish policies. Most, though not all of these differences were recent, having arisen during the first half of the twentieth century as a direct outcome of the Austro-Hungarian, Russian, Polish, and Soviet regimes' social, economic, and state-building policies.

Before the Nazi occupation, a typical middle-aged or older Minsk Jew would have been a Yiddish-speaking working-class craftsman or manual laborer who had limited social contact with non-Jews. A loyal Soviet citizen, he would have respected Soviet rule and obeyed its laws, but would not have believed wholeheartedly in communist dogma. He would have known little about Hitler's anti-Jewish policies and would remember German rule during World War I as a mostly positive experience. His children, however, would have been different. Better educated and more integrated into the broader society, they would have spoken fluent Russian and/or Belorussian. They would have viewed social ties with, and even marriage to non-Jews as perfectly normal behavior. They would have been atheists and would have believed in communism. Their social networks would have been inter-, not intra-ethnic. They would have known slightly more about Hitler's policies and would have had no personal memories of a benevolent German occupation. By 1941, even if self-identifying as Jews, members of neither the older nor the younger generation would be part of an organized Jewish community or belong to exclusively Jewish institutions, as these were largely destroyed by the Soviet regime.

Minsk's was a *Soviet* Jew; Kraków's was a *Polish* one. She would have spoken Polish as her mother tongue, been familiar with Polish history and culture, and have had quite extensive social contact, though not necessarily friendship, with ethnic Poles. She would likely have had a middle-class or lower-middle-class background, been at least somewhat familiar with the Jewish religion, and have supported either the Zionists or the non-Jewish center and center-left political parties. She would have known a lot about the situation of the Jews in Germany, but at the same time (and this was especially true for older people), she would have felt a connection to German culture and to the late Austro-Hungarian Empire. More likely than not, she would have been a member of at least some Jewish organizations, but in Kraków there was nothing automatic about self-identifying as a Jew and belonging to an organized Jewish community. In fact, she easily could have lived her life without any contact with or membership in Jewish institutions.

In Białystok, the typical local Jew would have been a Yiddish speaker from a working-class background, and a supporter of Jewish socialist parties, Zionist or otherwise. She would have been struggling economically, have had very few, if any contact with ethnic Poles, and would have felt no attachment to the Polish state, its symbols, or institutions. At the same time, she would have taken special pride in her local identity, limiting the outreach of the "imagined community" to other Białystok Jews wherever they were. A citizen of Poland and later the USSR, she nonetheless would have been neither a Soviet nor a Polish Jew, but a *Białystok* Jew; a member of the city's organized Jewish community and its various educational, social, and political bodies. Polish and Soviet influences would have impacted her identity and behavior, but only to a degree.

Obviously, these depictions are simplified sketches of a complex reality and do not do justice to the nuances of Jewish life in these three cities. Nevertheless, they are useful because they capture the most important characteristics, strengths, and behavioral patterns of (and inside) each community. In the following chapters I will show how these characteristics—products of the political regimes under which each Jewish community lived—translated into actual survival strategies when confronted with the reality of mass murder. I will also show how and in what ways these strategies are similar to, and different from one another in these three communities.

CHAPTER 3

WHAT DID THE JEWS KNOW?

Israel G. had never seen Jews like these before. They did not look or speak like Khmel'nik Jews. The older people in town still remembered Jews in traditional Hasidic garb, but to Israel and his secular, Soviet-born friends these Jews with their yarmulkes and sidelocks were a novelty. They were refugees from Poland who arrived in town after the outbreak of World War II, but how and why this small group reached Khmel'nik, hardly a coveted destination or a major urban center, nobody knew. What to do about them was also unclear. In the meantime, they were housed in the synagogue building.

During their stay in town the refugees told local Jews about the place they had escaped, about the Nazis who made them flee, and about what they went through before reaching the Soviet Union. For many Khmel'nik Jews these stories were the first they had heard about what Germans were doing to the Jews. Some locals treated the accounts with suspicion, because the Germans were known as "a civilized nation." Israel's family, it seems, took them more seriously. When in June 1941 Germany invaded the Soviet Union, Alexandra G. packed the family's most essential belongings, took Israel and Venyamin, and fled eastward. But many of their neighbors who had heard the same stories stayed put.

* * *

To analyze the Jews' survival strategies it is incumbent upon us to understand what they knew. This chapter will evaluate what the Jews in the three communities knew, or were likely to have known about Nazi policies, especially during the initial stages of the war, when German actions were yet to be directly observed. The chapter will make three key arguments. First, that the political regimes under which the Jews of Minsk, Kraków, and Białystok lived prior to the Nazi occupation shaped what people in these communities knew and could know about German policies. Second, that this knowledge and information did have an impact on the distribution of behavioral strategies across the three cities, but—and this is the third argument—knowledge and information alone cannot explain the variation in behavioral strategies across and especially within communities.

The argument that the Jews acted on the basis of the knowledge they had is intuitive. But, as I will show, our ability to explain, let alone predict, individual behavior by simply looking at the information people had is limited at best. What this chapter will demonstrate is that the information available to the Jews was cacophonous, contradictory, messy, and could serve as the grounds for a variety of behaviors. The Nazis themselves did not know how their anti-Jewish policies would unfold and what, in practical terms, their end result would be. After all, the Wannsee Conference, at which the Final Solution was announced and adopted as state policy, did not take place until January 1942.

As Amos Tversky and Daniel Kahneman's classic article and subsequent scholarship convincingly demonstrate, decision making under conditions of uncertainty is subject to various "heuristics" (rules of thumb used by humans to reduce complexity), which are generally "quite useful, but sometimes . . . lead to severe and systematic errors."[1] One such heuristic, consistently present in numerous testimonies, is the well-documented tendency to believe that the past is a useful predictor of the future.[2] Other heuristics were undoubtedly also used by the Jews in the three cities, but the format of the testimonies and the available data do not allow for a detailed analysis of psychological mechanisms of decision making. What the testimonies do show, however, is that even if exposed to the same information, the Jews could and did choose different responses. Knowledge, this chapter argues, was indeed a factor that affected behavior, but it was hardly the only factor, nor was it the most important one.

What did the Jews know about and expect from the Germans and their policies? Of the Jews in the three cities, those in Kraków had access to the most comprehensive information on Nazi pre–World War II anti-Jewish measures. The local media reported extensively on the plight of Jews in Germany and Austria, and the city was flooded with Jewish refugees from Germany. Furthermore, many Kraków Jews spoke German and had firsthand access to German sources of information, such as Hitler's anti-Semitic speeches and writings. As a result, the city witnessed a massive exodus of its male Jewish population during the first days of World War II. At the same time, Kraków's history in the Austro-Hungarian Empire and the affinity of its Jews for German culture made quite a few people less likely to fear the Germans. And indeed while many escaped, others stayed put.

In Minsk, the Soviet official media did not report Nazi anti-Jewish policies in 1939–41, and independent sources of information were scarce. In this vacuum two competing tendencies emerged. On the one hand, the Minsk Jews could rely on a sizable number of Jewish refugees from Poland as a source of information; but on the other, the older generation fell back on their memory of the benevolent German occupation during World War I. Soviet citizens, moreover, were constantly exposed to state propaganda that promised a swift victory if the Germans dared to attack.

The Jews of Białystok had access to information on Nazi policies pre-1939, but unlike Kraków the city did not have a substantial number of Jewish refugees from Germany before World War II. Between 1939 and 1941, the city was flooded with refugees from other parts of Poland, but it was also exposed to the same Soviet propaganda and censorship as Minsk. Given the disparate and conflicting nature of the signals they received, it would make little sense to expect the Jews to base their initial responses to the German occupation solely on the knowledge they had.

This chapter will also demonstrate how knowledge of Nazi persecution changed over time and how the realization of the Final Solution emerged and became internalized by the Minsk, Kraków, and Białystok Jews. Yet the reaction to changing knowledge was not uniform, and new information did not always lead to changes in behavior. Some Jews did choose to abandon previously adopted survival strategies in favor of actions better fitted to newly available information, but many others clung to the choices they had made earlier, even when they realized that death would be the most likely outcome. Knowledge and information, therefore, did play a role in determining survival strategies, but other factors, described in greater detail in the following chapters, were more important.

MINSK

In Minsk, knowledge of Nazi anti-Jewish policies was scarce prior to the German invasion. As a result of the Molotov-Ribbentrop Pact, Soviet Jews were cut off from reliable information on Nazi activities in Poland in 1939–41. "The newspapers and the radio were silent. At that time the Soviet Union and Germany became close friends . . . so the truth about the Nazis' actions did not reach us," lamented Aleksandr Gal'burt.[3] After the pact, in the Soviet media "all the information was pro-German," agreed Solomon Zuperman. "And of course we believed the media. There were no other sources of information." There was quite a lot of information on Nazi anti-Jewish policies during the pre-1939 period, many survivors recall, but it did not have much impact on the Minsk Jews' attitudes. Those who whole-heartedly supported the Soviet state believed the official propaganda that the Germans would be swiftly defeated and therefore did not even imagine that they might experience Nazi policies firsthand. Those who treated the Soviet government with suspicion discounted reports published in official media.[4] As a result both groups downplayed the severity of the threat. Pol-ish Jewish refugees were one of the few sources of firsthand information on Nazi policies; they warned Soviet Jews about German atrocities, but many thought that their stories were exaggerated.[5]

On June 28, 1941, German tanks were already on Leonid Okun's street, but eleven-year-old Leonid, influenced by Soviet interwar propaganda, still pictured Germans as weaklings with horns on their helmets.[6] He was astonished to discover that real Germans were "big, impressive, and well-groomed."[7] Even the Germans themselves were genuinely surprised to dis-cover how ill-informed Soviet Jews were about the Nazis' anti-Semitism and their persecution of Jews.[8] By mid-1941 Poland was already covered by a dense network of Jewish ghettos, yet in Minsk people often had no idea what the very word "ghetto" meant—some thought it derived from *get*—a divorce in Jewish religious tradition.[9]

Consequently, in the initial period of Nazi rule many Minsk Jews based their decisions on preexisting knowledge of German behavior, drawing mainly on the period of German occupation during World War I. Joseph Gavi's maternal grandfather, Kiva, had owned a business before the revo-lution but lost his livelihood under the communists, who also briefly imprisoned him. When the war began, he refused to evacuate: "I am not worried about the Germans. They were nice people during the occupation in 1918, certainly better than the Communists," he claimed.[10] That Gavi's grandfather was able to keep his business under German rule during World War I, but lost it under the Soviets, determined his initial choice of be-havioral strategy during World War II. He was killed in the ghetto. Nina Shalit-Galperin escaped from Minsk before the Germans captured the city. However, on their way to the east, some who had initially decided to flee started talking about their experiences under German occupation in 1918, and as those experiences had been "pretty good," they claimed that it made sense to return to the city.[11] Albert (Alik) Lapidus describes how he lost his brother. When the Aktion of November 7, 1941 began, Lapidus's mother, who had recently given birth to a baby boy, could not hide both children fast enough. Albert's grandmother, however, instructed her to hide with Albert and leave the baby outside, saying: "I remember well that . . . [during World War I] Germans did not kill babies—leave him here, they won't touch him—save Alik."[12] German soldiers killed the baby.

Some (though very few) knew what to expect based on their initial encounters with German troops. A German officer, who did not know Tatyana G. was Jewish, assured her that life would be great after the Germans killed all the Jews and the communists. Being both, Tatyana was ready for the coming danger. Later, when she was already in the ghetto, a German soldier explicitly advised her to escape. But even then Tatyana G. still hesitated—she knew that the ghetto was an extremely dangerous place, but her ability to act upon this knowledge was limited, as she had nowhere else to go.[13] A German soldier warned Sara Goland that as long as the military was in charge, the Jews would be fine, but the moment the SS took over, they would be in trouble, and therefore should save themselves. The soldier also warned Goland that her son was suspected of helping Soviet POWs, a behavior that easily could have cost the young man his life.[14] On most, however, the realization of Nazi policies dawned only after they had witnessed and experienced German actions firsthand. "These are not the Germans of 1918. These are real beasts," admitted Leonid Rubinshtein's grandmother after seeing Nazi soldiers rape and kill a Jewish neighbor girl.[15]

Information was also crucial for coping with the situation in the ghetto, particularly when Jews desperately hoped for good news to help them through their daily struggle. Radios were forbidden; listening to news broadcasts, like any other transgression, was punishable by death. Tamara, Anatolii Rubin's sister, did not look Jewish and lived outside the ghetto, passing as Russian. She did so mainly to help the family obtain food, which was much easier done outside the ghetto. No less important, she brought news, publications, and rumors. When no news was brought from the "Russian" side, people in the ghetto just made it up.[16] "Regardless of education and intellect, [in the ghetto] everyone consumed the same spiritual food—rumors," noted Albert Lapidus.[17] Therefore, it is not surprising that there even emerged a "news agency" called YIVO,[18] which stood for *Yidn Viln Azoy* (Yiddish for "the way Jews want it") and produced optimistic, but totally false news. YIVO was a "narcotic that helped people hold out against the incessant German roundups in the ghetto streets. . . . The ghetto even saw the birth of a new profession of news broadcasters" who claimed that their fabricated good news helped entire families.[19] The existence of this "good news agency" is remembered by other survivors as well.[20] Interestingly, a "news agency" with the very same name is also mentioned in the Białystok ghetto, even though we lack any evidence of communication between the two ghettos.

In addition, there was also an official German newspaper, called the *Minsker Zeitung*, and it was possible to glean some reliable information from it by reading "between the lines," just as people had done with the Communist Party mouthpiece *Pravda* during Soviet times. Given the importance of information, one of the key areas of communist underground activities was the distribution of leaflets with summaries of Moscow radio news broadcasts.

Knowledge was often important not only for the adoption of a certain strategy, but also for moving from a presumably failed strategy to another that was seen as more likely to ensure survival. One of the key examples of this phenomenon took place during the first days of the war. When Germany invaded the USSR, many young and middle-aged Jews who wholeheartedly believed the Soviet government and its promises that the enemy would be swiftly defeated, decided to stay rather than leave the city. When, after a massive air raid and the disintegration of Soviet power in Minsk, they grasped the true situation, many tried to escape. Unfortunately, for most of them it was already too late. For people who believed that German rule in 1941 would be as benign as it had been in 1918, the disintegration of Soviet rule was no cause for a change in behavior.

It was also important to know that previously unattainable or restricted survival strategies were becoming available. One of the first actions of the Jewish partisan detachment, led by Shalom Zorin, was to pin leaflets to the electricity poles in the ghetto that said "Jews, save yourself, leave the ghetto—in the forest [we are] waiting for you!"[21] Fourteen-year-old Fima Shapiro worked with his father in a German military mechanical shop. They did not plan to escape from the ghetto, but one day a German soldier came to Fima's father and told him: "What are you waiting for? Hitler said in his book *Mein Kampf* that he has to wipe the Jews off the face of Earth. Go to the partisans." This short conversation made Fima and his father reconsider their behavior; they left for the forest.[22] Esfir Movshenson's employer, a German officer, explicitly instructed her to escape to the partisans or she would be killed.[23] She escaped. Anna Karpilova's friend Riva

Eisenstadt worked with a German who told her to flee and even promised to get her a gun.[24] Similarly, Yekaterina Perchonok-Kesler was told by a German driver at her workplace that she should join the partisans before it was too late.[25]

Arkadii Krasinskii and his father were the only members of their family to survive the July 1942 Aktion. His father's five sisters and their families were all killed in the ghetto. After that, it became clear to them that "their chances of survival in the ghetto [were] equal to zero . . . and only then the father finally decided to leave for the forest."[26] Lev Pasherstnik, too, tried to stay in the ghetto as long as he could, and decided to change his behavioral strategy only after realizing that the ghetto was about to be liquidated. He then escaped to the partisans.[27]

Conflicting information also played a role in determining the behavior of German Jews. Many of them "had a totally false notion of what awaited them. The Nazis assured them they were the vanguard of German colonization in the east."[28] When the first group of German Jews boarded the train to Minsk in Hamburg, they were told that the German secret police had promised the leadership of the Hamburg Jewish community that nothing bad would happen to the deportees. "The local Jews told us: 'You all are going to be killed,'" admitted Henry R. "But we said 'It's humanly impossible to kill everybody.' They told us about the death of at least thirty-five thousand Jews thus far, but we couldn't believe it."[29] Until the very end, many German Jews were confident that they would be spared and that mass killings, resistance, and flight to the forest were the *Ostjuden*'s (Eastern Jews') lot, not theirs.[30] Iaakov N., a Soviet Jew, once met a Jewish woman from Hamburg who was married to an ethnic German. Until her death in the ghetto, this woman refused to believe that German Jews were going to be killed as well, and was confident that eventually she would be allowed to return to Germany.[31] German Jews, unlike their Soviet coethnics, were also cut off from almost any external sources of information and had little knowledge about what was happening outside Minsk. Sometimes, recalled Eric Floss, friendly German soldiers would share bits and pieces of information about the external world, but beyond that they knew nothing.[32]

What the German Jews did know well was that if one of them escaped, collective punishment would be meted out and numerous inmates would be murdered.[33] Knowing that they might be killed if someone else escaped, German Jews strongly disapproved of attempts to leave the ghetto, and sometimes even took actions that prevented others from escaping. Yet while collective responsibility was also applied to Soviet Jews, it did little to prevent them from engaging in prohibited behavior.

KRAKÓW

Unlike the Jews in Minsk, those in Kraków knew that German rule would likely bring persecution, but the exact nature of the upcoming Nazi violence remained unfathomable. As described in chapter 2, the city was swamped with Jewish refugees from Germany who shared stories of Nazi anti-Jewish measures with anyone who cared to listen. In addition, unlike the Jews of Minsk, who knew only what the Soviet government told them, the population of Kraków had access to external sources of information and, no less important, the linguistic skills to understand them. Many people in the city, especially those who spoke German at home or were schooled during the Austro-Hungarian period, carefully monitored German radio; some even listened to Hitler's speeches.[34] Unsurprisingly, when the war started many people, first and foremost the males, decided to leave Kraków and escape to Eastern Poland. One of the causes for this mass exodus must have been the Polish government's desperate call for all able-bodied males to flee eastward to where the Polish army was to be reorganized after initial defeats—but testimonies and memoirs only rarely mention the government's call as the reason for escape. Almost all the Jews who fled to the east did so because they believed that the Germans were going to target males, while women and children had little reason to fear for their safety.

The sources of this expectation are hard to trace. Rosalie S.,[35] David R.,[36] and Solomon S.,[37] among others, testify that there was a rumor going around town that young Jewish males would be targeted, and Solomon S. goes even further, saying that the rumor was that men would in fact be used as human shields by the Germans. People who cited this rumor were of different ages when the war started, lived in different parts of the city, and belonged to different social strata, so it is plausible that the majority of Kraków's Jews (if not all of them) were exposed to it. As a result, many people tried to flee the city, as civilians usually do during armed conflicts. What is more surprising is that despite the available information, some chose to stay put.

Among those who preferred to stay in Kraków, some cite purely material or logistical reasons, but many admit that their decision was shaped by prior experiences with the Germans and by their presumed knowledge of the Germans' real character. The closer their prior relations with Germans, the less likely they were to try to escape. Quite typical in this regard is the story of Luna K., whose father was an officer in the Austrian army during World War I and had strong pro-German feelings.[38] The family's exposure to German culture went beyond her father's military service, for many of Luna K.'s relatives had studied in Germany. Moreover, her father disliked the Jewish expellees from Germany and claimed that it was Germany's sovereign right to expel Polish Jews who lived there. When the German army occupied Kraków, a high-ranking German officer came to visit Luna K.'s family—her father's best friend from World War I. After the visit, Luna K.'s father told her that the horror stories about the Germans were just propaganda. Leon K. tells a similar story. His parents remembered their life under Austrian rule as peaceful and pleasant, and the Germans as nice and cultured, much better than the Poles. Leon K.'s family was aware of the persecution of the Jews in Germany, but dismissed it as the isolated actions of a "bunch of hoodlums." "In a way, [his parents] were happy" when German troops occupied the city, he testified.[39]

In the household of Menachem S., German was the language spoken.[40] When the war started, it would have been possible for the family to escape, but his grandfather decided that they would not leave Kraków. His rationale was that he had known Germans all his life, and considered them "the best people in the world." For him, all the rumors about the anticipated German atrocities were just that—rumors. For William S., Germany was "the door to culture," and he knew that the Germans were "the smartest people, the cleanest people in the world," so he refused to leave Kraków.[41] Reena F. cites her grandparents' experiences during World War I as the main reason for the family's behavior during the first days of World War II. The grandparents, she recalled, always talked about World War I and about Reena F.'s uncle, who was killed fighting for the Habsburg monarchy. Based on these past experiences, the family anticipated that there would be little food, but that people would survive.[42]

An expectation that the current war would not be very different from past wars also guided the behavior of the family of Ada A., who was the granddaughter of an Austrian army captain. By the time of the German invasion, her grandfather was no longer alive, but the grandmother was still with the family, and she convinced her relatives that they had nothing to worry about. In World War I only the men were affected, she argued, so "this all does not concern us, women and children." When German soldiers came to search for valuables in her apartment, she expected them to salute the portrait of her late husband in his Austrian uniform and to kiss her hand. She was genuinely surprised when this did not happen. "And little by little, we saw that Grandma wasn't right, it wasn't like World War I, it was a different kind of a war."[43] The family of Rosalyn O. was also unprepared for the changed nature of warfare. Rosalyn O.'s father, an officer in the Polish army, was a POW. Her mother, believing that as the wife of a POW officer she was protected by the Geneva Convention, did not hide and did not try to get a job. She was deported to Bełżec and gassed.[44] Alexander A.'s father was also a Polish army officer and a POW. During a selection in the ghetto, Alexander A.'s mother showed the relevant parts of the Geneva Convention to the SS officer who conducted the selection. The officer hit her and she was eventually deported to a death camp.[45]

Knowledge of Nazi policies and plans also affected behavior when things settled down after the initial period of turmoil and uncertainty. Reliable information on Nazi plans and the war situation was very hard to come by, and therefore during the first months of the German occupation, the incipient underground focused mainly on transcribing and distributing BBC broadcasts.[46] Whenever Meir B. and his friends got together in the ghetto, they immediately discussed what they had heard on the BBC.[47] Yet underground newspapers, leaflets, and transcripts of BBC broadcasts, while they did circulate, could reach only a limited audience. The majority had to rely on rumors, which were incomplete, contradictory, and generally unreliable.

"Everything was from rumors," recalled Moshe B.[48] "We did soak up the news from secret broadcasts and we searched it out in the underground press," even the "German-inspired [Polish language] gutter press" was used as a source of information, wrote Mordecai Peleg.[49] Later in the war, knowledge of German losses kept many people going and helped Jews to cope with the situation and not lose the will to survive. "Any half-mile of [Russian advance] was like music to our years. It gave us hope that we would be eventually liberated," recalled Henry S.[50] "Every day there were discussions about [General Governor] Frank's latest speeches or the current war communiqués; from these observations chances of survival were evaluated," remembered Tadeusz Pankiewicz, the ethnically Polish owner of the ghetto pharmacy.[51]

Knowledge was often important for changing behavioral strategies. Ludwig B. had a relative in the underground who informed the family that the ghetto was going to be liquidated. Immediately after receiving this information, Ludwig's mother escaped. The family hid until the city was liberated by the Red Army, and they survived.[52] Heszek Bauminger, who managed to smuggle himself to Kraków after spending some time in German-occupied eastern Ukraine and witnessing the mass murder of Jews by German mobile killing units, was able to use this information to mobilize his friends in the still safe Kraków ghetto to organize an underground resistance organization. Nathan Gross's uncle heard a rumor about Jews being killed in large numbers, and this prompted the family to purchase fake ID papers that would allow them to hide outside the ghetto.[53]

The importance of knowledge can also be clearly seen when we analyze the behavior of Kraków ghetto inmates during deportations to death camps. Initially, argue the survivors, no one knew what the term "deportation to the East" meant, and German authorities invested considerable effort in spreading rumors, mainly through their Jewish collaborators, that the deportees were being sent to Ukraine, where they would work in labor camps and agriculture. "No one imagined that those who were deported were being killed," recalled Henry T.[54] "We knew that Auschwitz was a concentration [rather than death] camp, but what was going on there we had no idea," claimed Solomon S.[55] Ida L. believed that Auschwitz was "a special camp for older people."[56] Regina L., like most other Jews in the ghetto, believed that she was being sent to a labor camp in Ukraine, and worried more about her family members who stayed behind, hidden with a Polish peasant, than about her own fate. But prior to boarding the train, she was told by a Ukrainian guard that she did not need new shoes and water because she was going "straight to the oven." Regina L. and her sister jumped off the train and survived.[57] In her case, it was new and unexpected information, received from a person who certainly had not planned to help her, that prompted Regina L. to change her survival strategy.

Only later on did the news about the real nature of "deportation" start trickling into the ghetto. Unlike in Minsk, where most killings were carried out locally, only a few miles from the ghetto, in Kraków knowledge of the Germans' genocidal plans came later, and precise data regarding German policies and intentions was much harder to come by. German authorities were less than forthcoming about their long-term plans and employed a network of Jewish collaborators who spread false rumors and tried to convince Jews that they needn't fear. Many Jews tried to get information from non-Jewish friends and Polish railroad workers. Frederic B. even hired a Polish woman to follow the trains carrying deportees. The woman came back and reported that the trains entered the forest and then all traces of the people who rode them disappeared.[58] Bruno Shatyn heard a similar story from the Polish railroad workers he knew: the trains enter a station, the German crew takes over and drives them to an unknown destination, where Polish railroad men are not allowed. The cars then return empty and thoroughly cleaned.[59]

After the first wave of deportations, the trains' true destination was harder to disguise. Aliza Avnon recalls that in the ghetto they had no idea about the death camps, but after moving to the nearby Płaszów labor camp they became aware of what Auschwitz truly meant.[60] This new information prompted many Jews to try to secure their existence by seeking more promising employment, building hideouts, or escaping. Ida L. recalls that she knew perfectly well that if deported, she would be killed, so she escaped from the ghetto to Płaszów, which seemed to provide its inmates with better long-term survival chances.[61] That the Kraków Jews eventually had learned the true meaning of deportation is best evidenced by the story of the Schindler Jews transferred from Płaszów to Brünnlitz. The men were taken directly to the new camp, but the women were sent first to Auschwitz for registration and delousing. Pushed into the showers, they were confident that they are going to be gassed and were ecstatic when water started pouring in.[62]

Knowledge of the Nazis' plan for the total extermination of the Jews eventually became widespread in the ghetto, yet not everyone acted upon it. While some in Kraków, as I will demonstrate in later chapters, did change their initially adopted survival strategies, many—contrary to the expectation that new information is the driver of behavior—did not.

BIAŁYSTOK

As in Minsk and Kraków, information did play a role in the Białystok Jews' choice of behavioral strategies. Kraków was flooded with Jewish refugees from Germany who gave firsthand accounts of Nazi persecution, but in pre–World War II Białystok knowledge of German policies came mainly from newspapers and other media sources. Białystok Jews read about the refugees but did not meet them in the city, recalled Leon F.[63] The troubling news from Germany was also somewhat mitigated by the history of local Jews' rather positive encounters with the Germans.

Michel Mielnicki's mother's family came from the part of Poland that had belonged to Germany before World War I. His mother taught her children to speak German and, based on her memory of German troops saving Jews from a pogrom, she dismissed any reports of German anti-Jewish policies.[64] The father of Eva Kraczowska, a well-known physician, was taken away by the Germans during the first days of the occupation and shot. Kraczowska's mother spoke German and held Germans in high regard. For months she believed that her husband was still alive simply because she could not imagine that Germans might be capable of killing doctors.[65]

At the same time, several people who before the war had personally witnessed German actions did fear them. Ralph B. happened to have been in Czechoslovakia when German troops marched into the country. The first thing he did after returning to Białystok was to write a letter to his uncle in Chicago, asking him to sponsor his immigration to the US. The uncle was happy to help, but unfortunately the immigration paperwork was likely to take up to three years, and before it was completed Ralph B. was already in the ghetto.[66]

German troops occupied Białystok for one week in 1939. The Jews were harassed, beaten, and sometimes even killed, but German actions were perceived mainly as local wartime aberrations rather than as part of a general strategy. Under Soviet rule, information about German policies in central and western Poland could come from two key sources—Jewish refugees from the Nazi-occupied parts of Poland and the Soviet media. Jewish refugees flocked to the city in the fall of 1939, but testimonies report rather contentious relations between them and the local Jewish community. Moreover, after discovering that life under the Germans was harsh at that time, but tolerable, numerous refugees returned to their hometowns. The local Jews of course noticed that many preferred going back to German-controlled areas to staying in the communist paradise.

The second potential source of information was the official Soviet media. All other independent media outlets had been shut down by the new regime. Following the Molotov-Ribbentrop Pact, however, and the subsequent cooperation between Hitler and Stalin in redrawing the map of Europe, the Soviet media minimized or silenced negative coverage of Germany. The Soviets "started publishing the *Białystoker Stern*, a new Soviet-controlled 'Jewish' newspaper with a communist orientation. . . . [T]he paper deliberately concealed the Nazis' treatment of Jews," recalled Charles Zabuski. Only "through the grapevine" were the city Jews able to learn that "Polish Jews in German-occupied Poland were being humiliated, tortured, and murdered," he added.[67] But the grapevine did not reach everyone, and its credibility was uncertain. Thus, in this regard the situation in Białystok did not differ greatly from that in Minsk.

After the ghetto was established and sealed, knowledge about what was happening in the outside world became an extremely valuable commodity.

Even though no newspapers were allowed in and listening to radio broadcasts was a major offense that could easily cost a person her life, news did reach the ghetto. Some Jews refused to turn their radio sets over to the authorities, and there were even cases of Jews who had radios charging other Jews money for listening.[68] Virtually every political movement in the ghetto had its own radio, notes the historian and ghetto survivor Szymon Datner,[69] and not surprisingly one of the first actions of the underground was the distribution of transcripts of London and Moscow radio broadcasts. Moshe Goldshmidt's mother worked as a janitor in the train station. She supplemented her income by collecting newspapers that the German soldiers left on the trains. The demand for the newspapers was staggering.[70] People knew "how to read between the lines in German newspapers," noted Eva Kraczowska.[71] When Harry Bass went to the Aryan side to engage in black market activities, he made sure to smuggle both food and newspapers back into the ghetto.[72]

Politics became one of the main discussion topics, many survivors testify. Abraham O's job as an engineer in a textile factory protected him from deportation. During the February 1943 deportation to the death camps, he brought several rabbis to the factory to save them. "We were sitting there [just] talking politics," he recalled.[73] "A Jew who was a 'political junkie' told a German officer before being put on a train [to Treblinka]—me, you took, but Stalingrad—forget about it," wrote Mordechai Tenenbaum, the ghetto underground commander shortly after the February 1943 Aktion.[74] The Stalingrad Battle had ended just three days prior to the Aktion, but people in the ghetto already knew its outcome, all the bans on radio and newspapers notwithstanding. Indeed, one of the key reasons why the liquidation of the ghetto in August 1943 took everyone by surprise was precisely that the ghetto Jews were well aware of the political and military situation on the eastern and western fronts. The Soviets were rapidly advancing, German troops were defeated in North Africa, and American and British forces had landed in Sicily. The future looked quite promising for the ghetto inhabitants.

But much of the news that circulated in the ghetto was incorrect. Rumors were prevalent and often affected peoples' behavior. The father of Hana Birk was taken away with many other males after the Germans occupied the city, and he never came back. "There were rumors that here [the men] return, so I came out to the road with a cup of tea for father to greet him, for if he comes back, he will surely be thirsty. . . . [T]here always were rumors. Later we learned that they [were] no longer alive."[75] After the February 1943 Aktion, the ghetto was filled with rumors that were optimistic "up to the point of being idiotic," lamented Tenenbaum. As in Minsk, there emerged a street-level "good news agency" called YIVO.

Knowledge determined the behavior not only of the ordinary ghetto inhabitants, but also of the leadership. Ephraim Barasz, the Judenrat chair, relied heavily on the information he received from his German contacts and was willing to spend considerable amounts of money to bribe people who could provide him with the information he needed. This information included secret German documents concerning the ghetto, and Barasz was convinced that when and if the order to liquidate the ghetto came, he would be warned in advance. After the February Aktion, relying on German documents to which he was privy, Barasz told Tenenbaum that the Łódź and Białystok ghettos would remain intact until the end of the war. Tenenbaum did not believe this, but others did. Among those who believed was Barasz himself. He reassured Tenenbaum that his German contacts had never lied to him on important matters and that he had every reason to trust them. When orders for the ghetto's liquidation arrived from Berlin and no one in the city administration notified Barasz until the very last moment, the Judenrat leader was dumbfounded.[76]

The appearance of new information often (but not always) led people to change their behavior. This can be seen most clearly in the case of the February Aktion and its immediate aftermath. A German informer in the ghetto once asked Yisrael Pransky to sell him some building materials that Pransky supposedly had. Pransky figured out that something was brewing and decided to build a hideout in which he survived the soon-to-be Aktion.[77] Jay M. learned that people who worked in certain industries were exempt from deportation and immediately applied for a job in such an industry.[78] A relative of Luba Olenski owned a kindergarten for children from families of the ghetto's intellectual elite. By February 1943 she had closed down her financially secure business and gone to work in a factory, because employment as an "essential" worker was now perceived to be a wiser strategy.[79] Liza Shtrauch heard people talking about Treblinka and started looking for connections (*protektsiya*) inside the ghetto who could help her get a work permit.[80]

Contemporary sources were not the only ones that were valued; people tried to analyze their current predicament by looking at comparable situations in other places and periods. For Białystok Jews during the Holocaust such a comparative case was the Armenian genocide. From underground archive documents and testimonies, we know that ghetto resistance members closely read *The Forty Days of Musa Dagh*, a fact-based novel that describes an Armenian community's successful self-defense against Ottoman troops.

"The ghetto should be our Musa Dagh," one underground activist insisted during a discussion about the choice of resistance strategy. According to Barasz's secretary, he also gave a copy of the book to a friendly female German official so that she would better understand the Jews' situation.[81] Intriguingly, I could not find references to the book, a mid-1930s bestseller, in either the Minsk or Kraków testimonies.

Information was not only consumed, it was also actively produced in the ghetto. This is probably the main reason why the ghetto underground archive was established and why Barasz and Tenenbaum spent considerable efforts updating it to include as much information and evidence as possible. Immediately after Barasz learned of the killing of Jews in the Treblinka death camp, he sent the information to Tenenbaum to be added to the archive. "Barasz sent me documents and pictures found in the clothes that arrived [in the ghetto] from Treblinka. I am walking with them the whole day; I cannot be separated from them for even a moment. It seems like my pocket is burning. . . . Awful, terrifying," wrote Tenenbaum in his diary.[82] Felicja N. did not look Jewish, spoke good Polish, and had friends in the countryside. After the February Aktion, people in the ghetto urged her "to escape if only to tell later what we lived through."[83]

Did the Jews of Białystok know the fate that awaited them? Survivors' testimonies and memoirs are remarkably consistent in this regard—few people knew about gas chambers before early 1943, but virtually everyone knew after the February 1943 Aktion. In late 1942, according to Avraham K., people still didn't know about Treblinka.[84] When Michel Mielnicki's mother heard that they were going to be deported to a labor camp (in reality they went to Auschwitz), she was optimistic. "They are not going to let us starve in a *labor* camp," she argued.[85] Even Barasz had no idea where the people deported during the February Aktion were taken. According to his secretary, he thought that this Aktion would be similar to the earlier expulsion from Białystok to the Prużany ghetto, and when he learned that they were sent to Treblinka he became depressed. "But what could he do, what could he say?"[86]

The situation changed after the February Aktion. According to Zvi Yovin, people then knew what Treblinka was and that Treblinka meant death.[87] Yekutiel S. knew about Treblinka even though he knew nothing of the Majdanek camp, where he ended up.[88] Rachel Lahower was spared and sent to a labor camp with a stopover in Majdanek. "In Majdanek, until they opened the shower [we] did not know whether it would be water or gas," she recalled.[89] Baruch Piletzki, who was eight years old in 1943 and was attached to a group of women prisoners, recalls an identical moment

of uncertainty experienced by Białystok women who were sent to a different camp. What made the women hopeful that it would be a real shower
and not gas was that two German guards came in to see naked women.[90]
Other children of Piletzki's age "knew perfectly well what Treblinka was,"
and they asked whether they should jump off the train, testified Hadasah
Levkowitcz who was sent with the ghetto orphans to the Theresienstadt
ghetto.[91] After arriving to Theresienstadt, the children refused to enter the
showers, crying, "Don't kill us, we are also Jews!" The local Jewish personnel,
who had no idea about the gas chambers, were genuinely puzzled by this
behavior.[92] People in Dora Kozin's train compartment knew that they were
being taken to the death camp and decided to commit mass suicide. When
the train reached the camp, almost everyone in the compartment was dead.
Kozin's cuts were not deep enough to cause her death and she survived.
Berta Sokol'skaia tells an almost identical story, but it is unclear whether
the two women are describing the same incident or there were several mass
suicides on death-camp-bound trains from Białystok.[93]

Among the Białystok ghetto underground archive documents there is a
letter in Hebrew written by resistance member Cipora Birman on March 4,
1943. In it she asks for assistance in locating her sister. The letter is short and
worth quoting almost in its entirety.

> I would ask to find my sister. Her residence place is Jerusalem, the address I do
> not know. Her name now is Szoszana Fink.
> To send her my regards. From the family I have no news. I was at home last time
> only under the Soviets. For sure [they are] no longer alive. I will also not be [alive],
> in a week, maybe in a month.
> I very much wanted to see her. For minutes at least. Alas. Shalom to her.[94]

Birman survived for longer than a month, but she certainly knew what
the Germans had in store for her. Other Jews in the city knew as well. And
yet, while Birman resisted, most did not try to fight or escape, but instead
clung desperately to the behavior they had originally adopted, even when it
was crystal clear that doing so would most likely lead to death.

CONCLUDING REMARKS

This chapter focused on what the Jews in the three ghettos knew about
Nazi policies and the extent to which such knowledge affected their behavior. The regimes under which the three cities lived before the German

takeover played a crucial role in determining local Jews' knowledge of Nazi policies. In Kraków, the Polish media was free to report on the situation in Germany and many local Jews could access German media sources first-hand. In Minsk and, during the Soviet interlude, in Białystok, information about Nazi persecution of Jews was actively suppressed, which led many to fall back on their previous, benign encounters with Germans. These different levels of knowledge were shaped by the different regimes, and they can explain *some* people's choices and behavior, but they certainly do not explain the whole phenomenon. All Kraków Jews had access to reliable independent reporting and almost none of the Minsk Jews had. Yet in each city people chose different strategies. The information Jews had to rely on was partial, contradictory, and inherently messy, as is almost always the case under conditions of war. The very same information could force different people to choose diametrically opposite responses. And often new knowledge, no matter how consequential, failed to lead to behavior changes. The Jews of Białystok, for instance, knew that deportation almost certainly meant death, and yet during the last day of the ghetto's existence, the vast majority quietly went to the deportation area instead of going into hiding, escaping, or rebelling.

It would be inaccurate to limit an analysis of Jewish behavior simply to the evaluation of the information they possessed. Still, understanding what people knew is important, for knowledge was the necessary background against which the Jews operated and made their choices. Keeping in mind what the Jews knew, the following chapters will proceed to analyze the choices people made, the strategies they adopted, and the ways in which the prewar political regimes under which the Jews lived shaped their behavior under the Nazis.

CHAPTER 4

COOPERATION AND COLLABORATION

Adolf Herschman, the "Ghetto President" of the Zhmerinka ghetto, and Matvei Belikovetskii, the ghetto's police chief, had a problem. The ghetto, which they ran with an iron fist, was a sought-after destination for Jewish refugees. Located in the southern part of central Ukraine, the town was occupied by Romania, an ally of Nazi Germany. It was 1943 and the Romanian authorities were still confining Jews to ghettos, but they were not killing them *en masse*. In the neighboring German-ruled localities, however, the genocide neared completion and those who found the opportunity and the courage did their best to cross the porous German-Romanian control lines and sneak into the relative safety of Zhmerinka.

Herschman and Belikovetskii were generally willing to tolerate the refugees in their midst, but not in all cases and only on their terms. Over the last year and a half the Zhmerinka ghetto leaders had invested considerable effort in cultivating relations with local Romanian authorities and fulfilling their demands. This, they believed, was the community's best survival strategy. The duo's primary allegiance was to *their* ghetto and its residents, not to Jewish people at large. Herschman was willing to take in the wealthy and professionals who escaped from the nearby German-controlled Brailov; the rest of the refugees he tried to move on to other places.[1] Israel G. and his mother, who had escaped from the more distant Khmel'nik, had some money but could hardly contribute to the ghetto economy. What is more, they had tried to obtain food outside the ghetto and smuggle it in. This was a serious breach of rules, as leaving the ghetto was punishable by death. As retribution the Jewish police expelled Israel and Alexandra G. from the ghetto, knowing quite well that if caught outside, the mother and son would almost certainly be executed. The survival of the ghetto demanded sacrifices. Both the leaders and the community were in agreement on that point. We do not know whether the decision to expel Israel G. and his mother was taken by Herschman, Belikovetskii, or by lower level officials. Nor do we know whether Israel and his mother tried to talk the local Jewish authorities out of expelling them. We have no idea whether bribes were offered, declined, or whether they could have made any difference to begin with. What we do know is that Israel G. and his mother had to leave. They survived, but how many Jews lost their lives after being expelled from the Zhmerinka ghetto?

What motivated Herschman, Belikovetskii, and their counterparts in other ghettos? Who were they and why did they take on a job that by definition involved following the perpetrators' orders and taking actions that endangered the survival of fellow Jews like Israel G.? Did they do it for the sake of their personal survival and to advance their well-being, or to help their communities endure under new conditions when prewar war moral codes were no longer valid? This chapter explores the most sensitive and controversial varieties of Jewish behavior: cooperation and collaboration with the Germans.

* * *

"The whole truth was that if the Jewish people had really been unorganized and leaderless, there would have been chaos and plenty of misery but the total number of victims would hardly have been between four and a half and six million people," Hannah Arendt famously claimed in *Eichmann in Jerusalem*.[2] Her accusation is serious—Jewish leaders, she insists, failed not only politically but first and foremost morally, and therefore bear a share of the blame for the Holocaust's death toll. Arendt is not alone in criticizing Jewish leaders in Nazi-occupied Europe, but she does stand apart from others in assigning blame to them.[3] Raul Hilberg argues that Jewish leaders and especially the members of the German-established Judenrats were essential cogs and "indispensable operatives . . . within the German superstructure," but he strongly disagrees with Arendt on the question of intentionality and moral responsibility. In his view, these Jewish leaders were "not the willful accomplices of the Germans." Rather, most Judenrats tried to help the communities they led by employing centuries-old methods that Jewish elites had honed for interactions with threatening and hostile governments. That these time-honored tools were now meaningless the Jewish leaders initially could not know and later on failed to grasp. Theirs was a failure of perception, not intention.[4]

Later scholarship has presented a more nuanced picture of Jewish leaders' behavior and motivations. Strongly rejecting Arendt's accusation, subsequent studies have also disagreed with Hilberg's sweeping, one-size-fits-all approach to Judenrats' behavior and motives. Isaiah Trunk, the author of the first large-N analysis of Judenrat leadership in the ghettos, showed that there was in fact enormous variation in the conditions the Judenrats faced. Most Jewish leaders did experience common problems and chose, to the best of their abilities, similar responses and policies, but any analysis of their behavior cannot be detached from local contexts.[5] The Israeli historian Aharon Weiss also surveyed the behavior of numerous Judenrat leaders in Poland in his Hebrew-language doctoral dissertation. Whereas Trunk emphasized the varying conditions the Judenrats faced, Weiss focused on the temporal aspect of the Judenrats' structure and actions. His assessment is that the first wave of Judenrat leaders were largely well intentioned, if not always competent public servants who tried to improve the lot of their constituencies. However, when these early leaders were removed by the Germans, usually due to their unwillingness to obey blindly, the Nazis deliberately chose as replacements corrupt persons motivated by self-interest and willing to fulfill any and all German orders.[6]

Still other researchers have focused on the motivations and actions of individual Judenrat leaders, most notably Adam Czerniaków in Warsaw, Chaim Rumkowski in Łódź, Jacob Gens in Wilno, and Moshe Merin in Sosnowiec. These biographical studies have demonstrated that some Judenrat heads, like Merin and Rumkowski, were possessed by a "Messianic Complex" and believed themselves chosen by destiny to lead their communities to safety and eventual survival.[7] Others, most notably Czerniaków, understood the reality (and their own role) more clearly and were forced to make pacts with the Nazi devil in the hope of saving whatever could be saved. They were motivated, determined, and resourceful; they had to operate under unimaginable constraints but were hardly passive cogs.

This discussion also revolves around language and a classification of the Judenrat leaders and their behavior. According to Dan Michman, the very term "leadership" does not and should not apply to the Judenrat chairs. Their authority, he contends, emanated from an external source, not from inside the community, and therefore "headship" would be a more appropriate term.[8] A much more loaded disagreement focuses not on their status and the sources of their authority, but on their actions. Negative assessments use the term "collaboration" to describe Jews who were tasked with and consistently carried out German orders to the detriment of their coethnics. The term, however, is controversial. In the context of World War II, "collaboration" is normally associated with Vichy's Pétain, Norway's Quisling, and Hitler's other willing helpers, not the Nazis' Jewish victims. The label serves also as a useful fig leaf for nationalist apologists, especially those from groups whose members were deeply implicated in the Holocaust. Somehow, the existence of Jewish collaborators is supposed to minimize the responsibility and complicity of the non-Jews who cleared the ghettos, participated in mass shootings, or guarded the death camps.

There are also analytical arguments for choosing a different term. Hilberg used the term "collaboration" in the first edition of his monumental *The Destruction of the European Jews* but dropped it in subsequent editions, opting for "compliance" instead.[9] Yet there is a conceptual difference between complying and not resisting deportation to the death camps, and assisting the Nazis in rounding up other Jews. Bauer, building on Trunk's work, stresses that one should distinguish between collaboration, a "collusion based on identical ideological premises or a conviction that Nazis would win the war" and "cooperation," an "unwilling yielding to superior force."[10] Collaboration, Bauer's argument goes, was the domain of the Warsaw ghetto's notorious Office to Combat Profiteering and Speculation (generally known as *The Thirteen*), "undoubtedly a Nazi agency in the ghetto;"[11] the Judenrats and their leaders cooperated, but did not collaborate.

My approach is somewhat different. I fully recognize the moral and the ideological baggage that the term "collaboration" carries. If what Pétain and Quisling did is collaboration, then that term cannot characterize the behavior of Jewish leaders. If collaboration is a collusion based on ideological premises, then by definition no Jew could have collaborated; for even the most ardent Gestapo Jewish informers did not share Hitler's worldview. At the same time, "cooperation" defined as an "unwilling yielding to superior force," is no less problematic a term for the behavior and the motivations of the Jewish leadership. A large body of evidence suggests that quite a few—though certainly not all—Judenrat leaders were utterly corrupt, despotic, and abusive toward ghetto populations. They were often driven by desires for personal enrichment and survival, to the detriment of their communities. This is especially true of the Jewish police force, which tended to be even more corrupt and self-interested than the Judenrats.[12] And those who assisted the Nazis by informing on and betraying other Jews often did so voluntarily, in order to receive monetary rewards, power, and status.

Thus, as we set out to analyze the people who worked with or helped the Germans, the forced dichotomy between "collaboration" and "cooperation" limits our ability to understand their choices and actions. Judenrat leaders engaged in both types of behavior. Some cooperated with the Germans while others collaborated. What is more, the same person could adopt both types of behavior over the course of time and the same actions could have been driven by different motivations. Both "cooperation" and "collaboration" mean working with the enemy by either participating in or facilitating persecution. It is important to emphasize that in this definition persecution is not restricted to the process of killing. The registration of Jews, the confiscation of Jewish property, the organization and supervision of Jewish forced labor, and the guarding of ghetto entries to prevent smuggling and escape were also acts of cooperation and collaboration. The key distinction between the two lies in the intended goals of the actions taken. Those who cooperated acted to preserve the community *and* its individual members; those who collaborated knowingly worked to the detriment of the community's or individual Jews' survival. Cooperation was open and visible, while collaboration could be of two basic types—public, as in the case of corrupt and self-serving chairs of the Judenrats; or private (often, but not always secret), as in the case of paid informants.

Emotionally and morally controversial, collaboration can nonetheless be a rational strategy for survival. Yet precisely due to the incendiary nature of the term, analysis of this behavioral strategy is largely absent from Holocaust literature, confined for the most part to the publication of a small number of biographies, diaries, and memoirs.[13] This limited attention is inevitable and understandable. Like resistance, collaboration was not widespread, and people who engaged in it had few reasons to leave substantial paper trails, to volunteer testimonies, or to agree to oral history interviews. Unlike the other strategies, most of the evidence here comes *not* from people who chose this course of action, but from other, often hostile survivors. Even with this limitation in mind, however, it is still possible to take a deep look at both those who cooperated with the Germans and those who publicly and privately collaborated in the three ghettos, to analyze who they were and what caused them to engage in these behaviors.

This chapter will argue that the prewar political regimes under which the Jews of Minsk, Kraków, and Białystok lived shaped the patterns of cooperation and collaboration in each ghetto and determined what types of people engaged in those strategies. It will also demonstrate that people with previous political experience tended to be overrepresented among those who chose cooperation and public collaboration with the Germans; while at the same time, there was no link between previous political activism and private collaboration. I will show that those who engaged in cooperation and collaboration were driven by the desire to survive, but that survival had a different *meaning* for different types of cooperators and collaborators. Cooperators and public collaborators who were politically active before the

Table 4. 1. Cooperators and collaborators

Type	Goal	Typical role	Willing to sacrifice individual Jews
Cooperator	Community survival	Judenrat Chair	No
Public collaborator (pre–WWII political experience)	Community survival	Judenrat Chair, Jewish Police Commander	Yes
Public collaborator (no pre–WWII political experience)	Personal survival	Judenrat Chair, Jewish Police Commander	Yes
Private collaborator (no pre–WWII political experience)	Personal survival	Informer	Yes

war prioritized the survival of their communities. Private collaborators and public collaborators with no previous political experience were motivated by personal survival. The different types of cooperators and collaborators are described in table 4.1.

MINSK

In the Minsk ghetto, the main public bodies engaged in collaboration and cooperation were the Judenrat and the Order Service (*Ordnungsdienst*), generally known as the Jewish police. The Judenrat was established by the Nazi authorities to carry out German orders and policies, such as the registration of ghetto Jews, confiscation of Jewish property requested by the Nazis, taxation of the Jewish population, and the provision of Jewish forced labor. The Jewish police supervised public order in the ghetto, but at later stages also assisted the Germans in spying on other Jews, preventing escapes to the partisans, and hunting down the underground movement in the ghetto. In addition, there was a Special Operations Unit that worked closely with the Nazi security services, and the Gestapo also had a network of paid Jewish informers in the ghetto. The initial policy of the Judenrat and the Jewish police leadership was one of cooperation with the Germans, with the aim of helping the city's Jewish community. However, after the original Judenrat and Jewish police leaders were killed by the Germans and replaced with compliant and self-serving individuals, cooperation evolved into public collaboration. Individual informers and the Special Operations Unit rank and file were private collaborators.

One of the first things the Germans did in Minsk was to establish the Judenrat. The order was copied almost verbatim from similar orders issued by the Germans in Poland, but the difference between Polish and Soviet pre-Holocaust regimes forced the Nazis to adopt a new, ad hoc strategy of Judenrat appointment. In Poland, prewar community leaders or other prominent Jews usually became chairmen and members of Judenrats.[14] After twenty years of Soviet rule, the situation in Minsk was different. Jewish political and communal institutions did not exist, and ethnically Jewish communists were the first to be killed by the Nazis; their appointment to leadership roles was simply unthinkable. As a result, the Germans had to improvise. The first Judenrat head, Il'ia Mushkin, was chosen simply because he happened to be the only German-speaker in a group of Jews randomly seized on the street.[15]

Data on Mushkin is limited and contradictory. Most sources, including several communist underground members, argue that he was not politically active before the war, but some claim otherwise. Barbara Epstein, basing her contention on the testimony of Zelig Yoffe, the son of Moshe Yoffe, Mushkin's interpreter and successor as Judenrat chair, writes that he was a member of the Communist Party before the war.[16] According to Anatolii Rubin, who claims to have been a classmate of Mushkin's son, the first chairman of the Minsk Judenrat was "a public figure, trade union activist and official" (*obshchestvennyi, profsoiuznyi deiatel'*).[17] Neighbor David Taubkin described Mushkin as "a poor man with loose white hair [who] looked like [Israel's founding father] David Ben Gurion."[18] Mushkin is widely regarded as a decent and honest leader who did everything he could to help the ghetto, its inmates, and the Jewish resistance. His job required him to cooperate and work with the Germans, but he was never a collaborator.

Whether politically active or not, Mushkin was a product of the Soviet political system. This is clearly shown in how he designed the Minsk

Judenrat. Although not much is known about it, we do know that its internal structure was copied from Soviet institutions, and that the names given to its various departments were the same as the terms used in the Soviet administrative apparatus. The registration office was called the *pasportnyi otdel*, the housing department the *zhilotdel*, and the welfare department the *sobes*, all equivalents of Soviet administrative bodies.[19] Even the Jewish Order Service, elsewhere generally known as the Jewish police, was in the Minsk ghetto referred to as the *militsiia*, the name given to Soviet law enforcement bodies. Mushkin's right hand, Moshe Yoffe, was a Polish Jew. He was an engineer who worked for a radio-set enterprise that was moved to Minsk from Wilno shortly after the city became part of the USSR. To the best of my knowledge, Yoffe was not involved in any type of political activism, either in Poland or in the USSR. On the other hand, the first commander of the Jewish police, Ziama Serebrianskii, was active in the Komsomol, the Communist Party's youth branch. Yet he was not a cadre and shortly before the German invasion had served time in prison for embezzlement. Several other key Judenrat officials were card-carrying communists—a fact of which the ghetto communist resistance movement was fully aware.[20]

Shortly after their appointment, Mushkin and Serebrianskii began working with the underground. Serebrianski's cooperation with the resistance is the more intriguing as one of the underground's key members, Anna Machiz, was the public prosecution (*Prokuratura*) investigator who put him in jail.[21] Yet Serebrianskii did not try to exact revenge, though he could have done so easily; had her prewar position became known to the Germans, they would have killed Machiz immediately. While the Judenrat's leaders were willing to work with the underground, the resistance was split on whether it should cooperate with people whom they considered Nazi lackeys. Resistance leadership outside the ghetto was especially disturbed by a partnership that arguably undermined the ideological purity of the struggle. The underground inside the ghetto was more pragmatic and better positioned to understand the predicaments Mushkin and Serebrianskii faced and to distinguish between necessary cooperation and willing collaboration with the Germans. Eventually, the view of the ghetto underground prevailed.

When—we do not know how exactly—the Germans became aware of Serebrianskii's connections with the underground, he was arrested and executed. Mushkin did not survive either. He was arrested in February 1942, tortured, and killed. Most likely, his arrest was not related to his connections with the resistance, as no further arrests of underground activists followed. According to one rumor, he was hiding a German serviceman who had deserted from the Russian front. According to another, Mushkin tried to bribe a German official to secure the release of a certain Jew from prison. At the very same time, Dr. Frank, the leader of Minsk's "Hamburg ghetto," was also accused of bribing a German official, arrested, and beaten to death.[22] It is therefore possible that the bribery rumor is correct, or it might have been simply a German excuse for killing both leaders (if they needed any excuse at all).

After Mushkin's death, Moshe Yoffe became Judenrat chairman. Whereas Mushkin's willingness to go out of his way to help the underground was indeed rare, his sincere attempts to help the ghetto population were not. This aspect of Mushkin's behavior was not different from that of the many other "first-wave" Judenrat chairs who were genuinely committed to the well-being of their communities and viewed cooperation with the Germans as necessary to achieve this goal. After these Judenrat chairs were removed—precisely because they cared so much for their communities—the German authorities took special care to appoint self-interested, compliant, and often utterly corrupt collaborators.[23] And here, the Minsk ghetto's experience *was* different. In a desperate and suicidal move, Yoffe tried to warn the ghetto population about the true meaning of the Germans' July 1942 Aktion and was immediately killed.

The events that followed neatly fit Weiss's argument as to the negative selection of Judenrat heads. After Yoffe's death the Judenrat effectively ceased to exist, and the Jewish police, now headed by Nahum Epstein, became the most powerful Jewish institution in the ghetto. Epstein, who had begun his career in the Judenrat as the head of the labor exchange, was a young and well-mannered refugee from Poland. His closest associates—Weinstein and Rosenblatt—were from Poland as well, and according to some testimonies were connected to the Łódź and Warsaw criminal underworld. Most ghetto survivors considered these leaders of the Jewish police and its Special Operations Unit to be traitors and willing Gestapo agents who hunted down the underground and betrayed Jews trying to escape the ghetto to the Germans. Usually, being accused of underground connections and attempts to escape the ghetto meant death for not only the accused, but also for their families. Survivors' testimonies are replete with horrific accounts of the slaughter of Jews suspected of anti-German activism or of intending to escape to the partisans. Rachil Milechina, a member of the underground, recalls that she feared the Jewish police more than she feared non-Jewish policemen, because the Jewish collaborators were able to recognize underground activists—which echoes Jason Lyall's more general finding that coethnics are more skillful counterinsurgents.[24] Several survivors note that denunciations were common and that people constantly spied on and feared one another.[25] According to some sources, Epstein's antagonism toward the communist underground was politically motivated: before the war he was supposedly a member of the Jewish right-wing Betar movement in Poland.

An important aspect of the Jewish police in the Minsk ghetto was the domination of its ranks by Polish refugees. The reason for this lies in the different social and political orientations of Soviet and Polish Jews, which, once again, were shaped by pre–World War II political regimes. The Soviet Jews who had witnessed firsthand Stalin's Great Terror knew too well that taking the lead, as the Soviet saying went, was dangerous (*initsiativa nakazuema*), and therefore they did not seek to stick out. Polish Jews, on the other hand, had no qualms about being first movers and, given their small numbers in the ghetto, were substantially overrepresented in collaboration. An alternate explanation advanced for the overrepresentation of Polish Jews in the Jewish police is that many of them spoke German.[26] This argument is unconvincing, because quite a few Soviet Jews spoke German as well. Still, it is likely that the German authorities' perception that all Soviet Jews were communists contributed to their underrepresentation in the police force. Overall, however, refugees' domination in the Jewish police was not unique to Minsk. Weiss has concluded that Jewish refugees were overrepresented in this institution because service in the police, and collaboration more generally, provided people who were cut off from their kinship and social support networks with sources of income and influence.

Polish Jews were overrepresented in the Jewish police, but Soviet Jews served as well. Regrettably, very little information exists on the Minsk ghetto Jewish police, but the available evidence allows us to identify several of them, generally the most notorious ones. These Jews joined the police because they perceived police service as offering their best chance of survival, even if it required betraying coethnics.[27] Short-term enrichment also played a role. Smuggling food and merchandise in and out of the ghetto was a lucrative enterprise, which the Jewish police and their non-Jewish counterparts were well-positioned to undertake. Mikhail Treister, who was Rosenblatt's neighbor in the ghetto, recalls that the Jewish police commander was constantly visited by Belorussian policemen with whom he drank and engaged in business.[28]

Jewish police actions against other ghetto inmates were not limited to enrichment, betraying escapees, and fighting the underground. Often it meant going further: decreasing the survival chances of others, even those not engaged in the resistance. Several survivors recall being attacked by Jewish police members, especially the notorious female operatives Mira Markman and a certain Yocha (last name unclear), for trying to sneak food into the ghetto or participating in the black market.[29] The unfortunate smugglers and traders would lose their money, food, and merchandise—a serious blow to their and their families' survival chances.

The hatred toward those viewed as eager collaborators knew no limits. Lazar T. had an aunt who claimed that the biggest desire of her life was to see Rosenblatt go to the gallows because he had once confiscated all the things she had bartered outside the ghetto.[30] Abram Rubenchik was once caught stealing vegetables from a plot of land and beaten up by a "Hamburg ghetto" policeman. He and his brother were so outraged that they decided to "pay this 'Fritz' back" and hit him with a stone.[31] Interesting to note here is Rubenchik's use of "Fritz," a common derogatory term that the Russians used to describe Germans. Even though the policeman was Jewish and a ghetto inmate, for Rubenchik this person was, by virtue of his place of origin and behavior, as much a German as any other. Sara Goland, a resistance activist, described one Berkovskii, a member of the Special Operations Unit that hunted down the underground, as a fascist.[32]

Yet some were willing to acknowledge that survival necessitated such behavior. "[They] were ordinary Jewish people," claimed Vera S.[33] "Some [were] good, some [were] bad . . . they were just doing their job." Joining the police to help one's family was acceptable, but consciously harming other Jews was a serious breach of the ghetto's unwritten moral code. A good indicator of the public's awareness of the distinction (which was obviously based on constant and close observation of the servicemen's behavior) is the fate of police members who escaped the ghetto and reached partisan detachments in the forests. The rank and file who were "just doing their jobs" were generally allowed to join the partisans or faced minimal punishments; eager collaborators were executed upon arrival.[34] Overall, however, very few members of either the Minsk ghetto Judenrat or its Jewish police force survived, and those who did tried their best to hide their involvement with these organizations.

Even less is known about the Judenrat and the Jewish police in the city's "Hamburg ghetto," where Central European Jews were housed. Almost no data exists on Dr. Frank, the first chairman of the Hamburg ghetto Judenrat, or on his five successors.[35] Among "Hamburg ghetto" inmates, being in the Judenrat was considered an extremely dangerous job because "they would be killed first if the Germans didn't like something."[36] More is known about Karl Löwenstein, the first "Hamburg ghetto" police commander. Löwenstein, the offspring of a mixed Jewish and Christian marriage, was a decorated officer in the German Imperial Navy and an aide de camp of the crown prince. However, shortly after his arrival in Minsk, Löwenstein was transferred to Theresienstadt, which was considered the ghetto for privileged people, and there he survived the war.[37] This case of a decorated German officer commanding the ghetto police, while uncommon, is not unique. In the Zamość ghetto (Poland), the Jewish police were led by Alwin Lippmann, a German World War I pilot and a wartime friend of Hermann Göring, the number two man in the Nazi hierarchy. Of the origins, lives, and behavior of rank-and-file "Hamburg ghetto" police, we unfortunately know almost nothing.

Kraków

As in Minsk, in the Kraków ghetto the main cooperation and collaboration bodies were the Judenrat, which was later replaced by the Jewish Commissariat, and the Order Service (*Ordnungsdienst*) or the Jewish police. Kraków's equivalent of Minsk's Special Operations Unit, which worked closely with the German security services, was the Civil Affairs Unit. A network of private collaborators—paid Jewish informers—also existed in the city.

In the previous sections I argued that politically active and visible persons would be overrepresented among those engaged in cooperation and public collaboration with the Nazis. In Minsk, this prediction turned out to be largely incorrect, mainly because the only politically active people among the city's Jews were the communists, and for the German authorities it was unimaginable to appoint communists to leadership positions. In Kraków, the Jewish political scene was vibrant, with multiple parties represented, and the city is thus a better place to test my argument, but as I will show, distinctive local factors also impacted patterns of cooperation and collaboration.

After German troops entered Kraków on September 6, 1939, the remaining Polish city authorities called on prominent Jewish citizens to volunteer for the Judenrat, and on September 17 it was announced that an interim Judenrat had been established, headed by Dr. Mark Bieberstein, an educator, and his deputy, Dr. Wilhelm Goldblat. The list of Judenrat members was drafted by leading figures in the Jewish community and later approved by the German authorities. However, because of the city's importance in Polish political life, many Jewish politicians from Kraków also held prominent positions at the national level and therefore went into exile with the Polish government. Such was the case of the leader of the Kraków Zionists, Ignacy Schwarzbart, who spent the war years as one of the two Jewish members on the Polish National Council in London. Some other politicians, fearing that they would be the first to be targeted by the Germans, fled to Eastern Poland. Yet even though many leaders escaped, the data collected by Yael Peled-Margolin indicates that at least eight out of the initial twenty-four Judenrat members had previously been quite active in Jewish political and social life.[38] We can confidently identify the political affiliations of ten out of the twenty-four, an indication that these people's political past and present were no doubt known to all. Out of these ten, eight were active in various Zionist parties. Because we do not have reliable data on all of the Judenrat's members, it is likely that the actual proportion of the politically active was in fact higher. It is important to note that in Kraków, unlike many other places, the allocation of seats in the council was *not* based on party quotas—a precondition which would have made the claim that politically active people tended to be overrepresented in Judenrats analytically meaningless. As for Dr. Bieberstein, the Judenrat chair, not much information is available, but according to several sources he was, in addition to being a teacher,[39] a member of the (elected) Jewish Community Council before World War II.

Dr. Biebersten's tenure as the Judenrat was short. He worked with the Germans but did whatever he could to improve the situation of the city's Jewish community. During the partial expulsion of Jews from Kraków, Biebersten attempted to bribe German officials to increase the number of Jews permitted to remain in the city. He was arrested and sentenced to eighteen months imprisonment. His replacement was Artur Rosenzweig, a lawyer, and the former secretary of the Kraków city bar association. During the deportation Aktion of June 1942, Rosenzweig refused to provide the Germans with the demanded deportees, and paid for this act of insubordination with his life. The Judenrat's attitude toward its cooperation with the Germans is revealed in the words of an official, Yitzhak Ganani. "People had to cooperate with the Germans. It is hard to say, but this is how it was. Whoever did not cooperate was taken away and someone else was appointed instead.... We didn't like it and could not do anything [about it]. We thought that this or that person can somehow save Jews by negotiating with the Germans," he explained.[40] Ganani's line of argument exemplifies the attitude of many

Judenrat leaders, and in that regard Kraków was not unique. Theirs was a desperate, often misguided and eventually futile, but nevertheless sincere attempt to help the community by cooperating with the Nazis. These were people driven by a desire for the public good, not considerations of individual well-being; Bieberstein's bribes and Rosenzweig's insubordination are the best evidence of such intentions. When Rosenzweig was killed, the Judenrat was dissolved and replaced by the Commissariat, headed by Dawid Gutter. Under Gutter, cooperation turned into collaboration.

The difference between the Judenrat and the Commissariat consisted in more than terminology. The Judenrat was initially selected by the Jews and did its best to represent the Jewish population of Kraków and to protect their interests. The Commissariat was directly appointed by the Nazi security services and saw its main role as strictly obeying German orders. From an initial twenty-four Judenrat members, the Commissariat's membership was reduced to seven, but real authority lay in the hands of Gutter, who before World War II had been a traveling salesman.[41] We do not have any evidence of Gutter's prewar political activism or preferences; most likely he was not politically active. The pharmacist Tadeusz Pankiewicz, owner of the only non-Jewish business that was allowed to operate in the ghetto, recalls a conversation with SS officer Wilhelm Kunde, who explained that Gutter was appointed for purely practical reasons. "[Dr. Rosenzweig] was not a dependable man; he did not care to and could not work like . . . Gutter."[42] The Germans were not disappointed by the new Kommissar, who not only obediently followed their orders, but also tried to copy the Germans in his external appearance. He wore a dark gray uniform with a hat that resembled that worn by Gestapo members, and an armband on which was written in Gothic letters: "*SS- und Polizeiführer im Distrikt Krakau—Distriktjudenrat*" [The Office of SS- and Police Chief in District Krakau—the District Judenrat] implying that the Kommissar saw his position and authority as stemming from that of the District SS and Police Chief and that he considered himself in charge of all Jews in geographically large Distrikt Krakau. Gutter is described by the Kraków Jews as smart, obedient to the Germans, self-interested, and notoriously corrupt. Animosity toward the Kommissar ran so deep that, according to Nurit Guter, her father even removed one "t" from his last name so that it would not be the same as that of the despised official.[43]

However, few of the Kraków ghetto survivors' testimonies or memoirs discuss the Judenrat at any length. This neglect is perfectly understandable, if only because the Judenrat—even when it initially tried to assist the ghetto Jews by organizing medical services, social welfare, and employment opportunities—was the weaker of the two main Jewish bodies in the ghetto. The ghetto, according to Henry T., was run by the Jewish police. "They were the masters of the Jews in the Kraków ghetto," agreed Nachum Meringer-Moskowicz.[44]

The Kraków ghetto Order Service was officially organized under the auspices of the Judenrat in July of 1940, but it soon became the most powerful institution in the ghetto.[45] Initially the Jewish police consisted of forty servicemen, the vast majority unpaid volunteers who lived off business opportunities (mainly bribes and smuggling) made possible by their status and connections. By December 1940, however, the Jewish police had 130 servicemen, and most were members of the intelligentsia who had lost their prewar livelihood after Jews were banned from most professions.[46] The first commander of the Jewish police, who remained in office until March 1941, was Aleksander Choczner, a Polish Army officer about whom little is known.[47] In these early days the Jewish police did indeed attract at least some Jews who were committed to public good and helping the community,[48] but very quickly these were either pushed aside by the force's new commander or chose to leave on their own because they could not reconcile themselves to the new leadership and its actions.

The second commander was Symche Spira, who had been a religiously devout, impoverished glazier before the war. Lacking any formal education, he spoke both Polish and German poorly, but compensated for his lack of linguistic skills with zealous obedience to the Germans. Spira started his career in the ghetto as a low-level clerk in the Judenrat, and when the Jewish police was organized, applied to be transferred to the force. He was immediately popular with his German supervisors and quickly promoted. According to Kunde, "If [the Jewish police chief] position were filled by an intelligent, well-educated man, coming from a different social strata, he would be lost and completely out of place. Instead of working closely with us [the Germans] he would only make our job more difficult."[49]

Numerous sources confirm Spira's image as an uneducated and psychologically unstable, but also very proud and determined person who was obsessed with external signs of power and status. A constant source of mockery was Spira's uniform, which made him look like "a dictator of some South Sea Republic."[50] Walter Karter described his appearance as that of a "a general in South America."[51] Mieczysław Staner recalled: "He dressed himself in a white uniform with gold insignias—an imitation of Hermann Göring—and looking like a circus clown ran around the streets yelling things which nobody could understand."[52] According to some sources,

Spira was promised (whether jokingly or not, we do not know) the position of Tel Aviv police chief, effective after the Germans would have occupied the city, so every morning he rushed to hear the most recent updates from the North African campaign. Indeed, in Kraków relations between the German authorities and the Jewish police were closer than in most ghettos. When Spira married off his daughter, SS and Gestapo officers in charge of the ghetto took part in the celebration alongside Jewish religious authorities. According to a rumor, one of these officers even asked a famous rabbi to bless him.[53]

Spira was mocked and despised, but this did not make his power any less real or fearsome; in fact the jokes and the derisive songs and verses[54] composed about him are typical "weapons of the weak."[55] Buffoonish though he was, Spira was also ill-tempered, resentful, and violent. Survivors' testimonies describe him and his sons beating his fellow Jews for the most trivial offenses. The transformation that the Spira family underwent after their swift rise to power was profound and visible. Iaakov W. escaped from the Prokocim labor camp and made it back to the ghetto, but the Jewish police were not willing to let him in. Finally, Iaakov W. saw one of his best childhood friends in a police uniform, and begged for help. The friend was Spira's son, who refused to even talk to Iaakov W.[56] Halina Buchnik recalls a similar story. Before the war, her grandfather and Spira had prayed in the same synagogue. When her grandfather came to Spira asking for help, Spira refused to even shake his hand.[57] The position of the Jewish police commander made Spira not only powerful, but also wealthy. Avraham Blum smuggled live chickens (later to undergo kosher slaughter) into the ghetto and sold them to affluent Jews. Only a few families could afford his merchandise, and Spira's wife was among them.[58]

The Jewish police were widely resented. They were "very good helpers to the Germans. Not so good to us, Jews, but very good helpers to the Germans," recalled Aneta W.[59] Edward S. went even further, claiming that in some respects the Jewish police were worse than the Germans.[60] Nachum Meringer-Moskowitz considered them worse than either the Germans or the Poles.[61] Yitzhak Ganani, a Judenrat official, argued emphatically that even though the Judenrat and the police were both tasked with implementing German orders, the two institutions should not be viewed as similar because the Judenrat did its best to help the Jews, while the police he hated more than he hated the Germans.[62]

This hatred is hardly surprising because, in addition to keeping public order, the Jewish police were tasked with catching people who tried to escape the ghetto, hunting down those who smuggled food, and fighting the Jewish underground. "If you saw in the movies people jumping from roof to roof—I did that. I jumped from building to building," recalled Joseph B. of his attempt to escape the Jewish police who tried to catch him for smuggling food into the ghetto.[63] He had good reason to escape. Edith Katz was not so lucky and was caught violating the external appearance rules. According to her testimony, she was brought to the Jewish police station and physically abused in a procedure very similar to the strappado torture.[64] Out of the more than 150 Kraków ghetto testimonies that I have read and watched, hers was the only one that explicitly accused the Jewish police of employing such gratuitous violence and, admittedly, Edith Katz's story is quite atypical in other respects as well. Yet, torture or not, the picture that emerges from the testimonies is that the Jewish police did use physical violence against the ghetto's population. More importantly, they did so not only while the Germans were watching, but also when no Germans were present.[65] Whereas the former was generally seen as an understandable, indeed unavoidable behavior, the latter was a blatant violation of existing moral codes. The Jewish police also invested considerable effort in fighting the Jewish underground and managed to arrest several of its leaders—a struggle that will be described in greater detail in chapter 7.

It is therefore unsurprising that service in the Jewish police carried a social stigma. Ida L.'s brother-in-law joined them but resigned two days later when he realized what his duties entailed.[66] Sonia W. also had a brother-in-law who contemplated joining the force, but his fiancée, Sonia's sister, refused to let him, even though by joining he would be helping his parents.[67] William S. was asked to join the police but refused because in the service "you had to be nasty to other people, and I couldn't do that."[68] Mieczysław Gurewicz did not want to join because he considered the police traitors.[69] Rivka Teler recalls how her mother threw her nephew, Rivka's cousin, out of the house when he came to visit with a Jewish police cap on his head.[70] In contrast to opinion in the other two ghettos, almost no Cracovians viewed their ghetto police as "simply doing their jobs" or "being composed of both good and bad people."

In addition to regular policemen, the Jewish police also had a special unit, the so-called Department of Civil Affairs (*Zivilabteilung*), a seven-man group directly linked to the Gestapo. Most, if not all of these people were police informers before the war, and they simply continued to follow their accustomed profession under the new rulers. Finally, the Gestapo also employed a network of informers whose responsibility was to spy on the ghetto Jews, provide the German security services with the information they sought, and uncover Jews who had gone into hiding during and between deportations.[71] One of these people was Danek Redlich. When the war started, Redlich escaped to Eastern Poland, where he made a living as an informer for the Soviet NKVD. When Germany invaded the USSR he returned to Kraków and started working for the Gestapo. After the war, he continued doing what he did best, informing on regime enemies to the Communist political police.[72]

Another well-known informer was a certain Shpitz, whom the Jewish resistance unsuccessfully tried to assassinate.[73] Julek Appel, yet another Gestapo informer, convinced his victims to escape the ghetto and then betrayed them to the Germans.[74] According to Yehuda Friedman, who was employed by the Germans as a truck driver, he could have escaped, but he did not choose this option because he knew "that there are those like Julek Appel" out there.[75] Appel was also responsible for the elimination of the ghetto Zionist underground, which he betrayed (more on this in chapter 7). Ester Zalsberg, who was closely connected to the anti-Nazi resistance, lamented that "even among our friends there were informers (*malshinim*)."[76]

Why did these Jews collaborate with the Germans? Almost none of them did so for ideological reasons—there were no Nazis among the Jewish collaborators. For a tiny minority of professional informers, collaboration was simply a matter of continuing to do what they had done for a living before the Holocaust. But for the vast majority, including Spira and Gutter, their key motivation was the belief that collaboration increased their chances of survival. "Not infrequently one could hear Spira brag: 'Nobody else but Spira will survive the war; everybody else will perish, but Spira will live,'" recalled Pankiewicz.[77] "Some [Jewish police members] were promised survival in exchange for their eager and devoted service," notes Chwalba.[78] These people thought that if they collaborated and faithfully followed orders, they and their families would survive. Service in the Jewish police also provided its members with numerous enrichment opportunities that could be easily translated into tangible benefits such as better food, clothing, the ability to buy fake documents, and the means to pay for shelter outside the ghetto, thus increasing their chances of survival. The majority perished, however. The most notorious informers were eventually hunted down by the underground and fellow Jews, and most Jewish police members were killed once their services were no longer needed. Some fell victim to their German masters because they knew too much about the corruption and enrichment schemes so prevalent among Nazi officials. Their belief that devoted service would save them proved to be utterly self-deluding. Trying to secure personal survival, they took part in the destruction of their own community. In the end, they themselves were destroyed.

BIAŁYSTOK

Like the other two ghettos, Białystok had a Judenrat and a Jewish Order Service (the Jewish police). In addition, the ghetto also had a number of private collaborators who served the German security services as informers. Some of these had long-term relationships with the Gestapo, while others informed on fellow Jews on an ad hoc basis during the February 1943 Aktion.

The Białystok ghetto Judenrat was a stronger and more capable institution than its Minsk and Kraków counterparts. It cooperated with the German authorities in order to help the city's Jews throughout most of its existence, but switched to public collaboration during the final days of the ghetto when Ephraim Barasz, the council's leader, reneged on his promise to inform the underground about the ghetto's impending liquidation and urged the Jews to comply with the deportation order. Before that, for more than two years the Judenrat had worked tirelessly and quite efficiently to shield and if possible save what was left of Białystok's Jewish community. Its leaders, noted historian Nachman Blumental, had a vision, a grand strategy,[79] and they chose to cling to it no matter what. They did as much as they could. And they failed.

The Białystok ghetto Judenrat (or as it called itself—the *Yidenrat*) was established by the Nazis in late June 1941, immediately after the German occupation of the city. There are no documents describing exactly how its members were selected, but evidence from the Judenrat meetings' protocols enables us to reconstruct the process. Following the city's occupation, German authorities summoned the city's chief rabbi, Gedaliah Rosenmann, and appointed him Judenrat chair. The selection of Rosenmann is not surprising given Białystok's political situation prior to the German takeover. Jewish communal institutions had been dismantled by the Soviet regime, so that in June 1941 the rabbi was the most visible Jewish public figure in the city (with the exception of Jewish communist officials, whose appointment was of course out of the question).

Then Rosenmann was tasked with selecting other council members. Initially, there were twelve Judenrat members, but their number was later increased to twenty-four. In selecting the other members, Rosenmann made two crucial decisions. First, he sent his beadle to former Jewish community leaders who were still in town and urged them to join the Judenrat. Those approached could not refuse an explicit request from a highly respected religious authority, and agreed to join the Judenrat even if they had reservations about participating in such a body. Second, realizing that advanced age and limited administrative experience would prevent him from effectively leading the work of the council, Rosenmann appointed Ephraim Barasz, the former general manager of the Białystok pre–World War II Jewish Community Council to be his deputy and the acting chair of the Judenrat. This decision proved to be crucial and shaped the life of the Białystok ghetto during the period of its existence.

Ephraim Barasz was born in 1892 in the small town of Wołkowysk to a middle class, ardently Zionist family. Educated in Germany, Barasz was a mechanical engineer by training. His real passion, however, was Jewish communal and political life. In his native Wołkowysk, he had been president of the Jewish Trade Bank and headed the local Jewish Community Council and the Zionist Organization chapter. In 1934 Barasz's career received a substantial boost when he was invited to join the Białystok Jewish Community Council as its director (general manager). In his political beliefs Barasz was a left-wing Zionist, who had even sent his oldest son to study in Palestine. He was asked to lead the Judenrat mainly due to his administrative abilities, but his fluency in German helped as well. After his appointment, Rosenmann, the de jure Judenrat chair, assumed a largely ceremonial role. Judenrat meetings' protocols show that he usually opened and adjourned the meetings but hardly ever took part in the deliberations or made decisions. That was Barasz's domain. Contact with German authorities was also left to Barasz. One of very few exceptions to this rule took place during the first days of the occupation, when the Great Synagogue burned. The German military governor demanded that Rosenmann sign a declaration stating that the synagogue was set ablaze by retreating Soviet forces. At gunpoint, Rosenmann complied. Immediately after that, the Germans demanded that Rosenmann and the Judenrat pay ransom for the men who had been rounded up (and by that time had already been shot) during the first days of the occupation. Collecting the ransom—five kilograms gold, one hundred kilograms silver, and two million rubles—was among Barasz's first tasks.[80]

As noted above, most if not all Judenrat members were public figures in the city's Jewish community. According to Judenrat member Pejsach

Kaplan (editor of the city's main Jewish newspaper before the war), almost 100 percent of Judenrat members were people previously engaged in public activity. Even if Kaplan's assessment is exaggerated, the available data show that a substantial majority of the council's twenty-four members were publicly and politically active before the war.[81] Judenrat clerks came mainly from the intelligentsia simply because these people could not secure any other source of employment and found it difficult to endure physically demanding manual labor in the various ghetto factories. This also explains the skyrocketing employment figures of the Judenrat's administrative workforce: from six hundred employees in January 1942 (and it was already claimed then that this number was three times of what was needed), it swelled to 2,201 in July of that year.[82] Unlike industrial workers, Judenrat employees did not receive salaries, but they were given increased food rations. Białystok's Jewish police, however, were paid.

Throughout the existence of the Białystok ghetto, Barasz was its undisputed leader. He rarely sought advice from the council and was not accountable to it in any meaningful way. Initially the council met frequently, but toward the end of the ghetto's existence meetings became increasingly infrequent. Barasz also tightly controlled the flow of information and was practically the only ghetto official with access to German authorities. According to his secretary, Hadasah Levkowitcz, there was only one phone in the ghetto, and she was required to be near it at all times, lest someone use it without Barasz's approval.[83] The distribution of office space in the Judenrat building also reflects this institutional hierarchy—Levkowitcz shared a room with the formal Council head, Rabbi Rosenmann, while Barasz enjoyed his own office.

As with many other Judenrat chairs, Barasz's key objective was securing the survival of *his* ghetto, and he had a clear vision of how to achieve that goal. His was a two-pronged strategy. He would cooperate with the local German authorities and strive to make the ghetto so indispensable to the German war effort that its liquidation would become unthinkable. Having graduated from a German university, Barasz knew how to approach German authorities. Some officials, who were known in the ghetto as "good Germans," helped Barasz out of human decency, personal sympathy, or patriotic feelings, because they recognized the importance of ghetto workshops and factories to the war effort. Others were bribed. Leaving the ghetto for conferences with the German authorities, Barasz often took with him jewelry, diamonds, gold watches, or money as "gifts" for the officials he expected to encounter.[84] It should also be noted that even though Barasz had access to substantial resources, donated by or taken from the ghetto population, he, unlike Gutter in Kraków or Epstein in Minsk, was never accused of personal enrichment and corruption. Even those who faulted him with being the Germans' lackey never questioned his personal integrity.

In his dealings with the Germans, Barasz achieved several important successes. First, he was able to prevent the establishment of the ghetto in the most dilapidated part of the city. Later, during the expulsion to Prużany (see chapter 2), he negotiated a substantial reduction in the number of deportees. He was also able to secure a steady supply of food, which made the situation in Białystok better than in virtually any other large ghetto. So high was the level of trust between Barasz and certain local German officials that they even shared with him classified documents concerning the ghetto. Their close cooperation was well known; so well, in fact, that many Jews made a habit of gathering by the ghetto gate, waiting for Barasz's return from his meetings with the Germans. They knew that he would be given reliable information and believed they might predict the future by his facial expression.[85]

The second prong of Barasz's cooperation strategy was to make the ghetto as useful to the German war effort as possible. "The factory is our shield," he claimed during a Judenrat meeting, and urged ghetto Jews to do everything they could to make the ghetto productive. At the peak of its productivity, the ghetto manufactured more than five hundred different items, from shoelaces to saddles to mechanical equipment.[86] The Judenrat even organized a special exhibition that celebrated the ghetto's production and invited visiting German officials to view it. The ghetto laundries washed the soiled uniforms of the entire German eastern front, and according to a popular story, an Ordinance Corps general from East Prussia supposedly notified Berlin that if the ghetto were liquidated, he would close his office because there would be no one to make boots and sew uniforms.[87] The "salvation through work" philosophy was not unique to Barasz; many Judenrat leaders adhered to it. Yet thanks to the city's historical status as a large industrial center, in Białystok its implementation was easier and its productive capacity greater than in most other places.

Barasz's belief in his chosen strategy was unequivocal. When he learned about the ghetto Jews' attempts to employ the "weapons of the weak" against the Germans, he was outraged. "Trucks assembled by the ghetto workers end up without brakes, wheels, or headlamps," he lamented during a Judenrat meeting and demanded that the Jews not shirk their duties. In addition, lest the Germans get the impression that the ghetto was composed of people enjoying comfortable lives and consuming luxury items, the Judenrat urged mothers not to use baby carriages painted in bright colors, closed the front entrances to restaurants, and prohibited the sale of tobacco, cacao, pastries, meat, and fish in ghetto markets and stores.[88] The Judenrat tightly supervised the distribution of staple foods and clamped down on the black market,[89] but at the same time did its best to ensure that all ghetto residents were provided with the minimum resources needed for survival and that hunger and epidemics did not break out in the ghetto.

The relations between Barasz and the ghetto underground should also be viewed against the background of this strategy. A devoted left-wing Zionist, Barasz certainly sympathized with and respected the resistance efforts of left-wing Zionist youth. Zionist underground leaders Chajka Grosman (in her memoirs) and Mordechai Tenenbaum (in his wartime diary) describe close and cordial relations with Barasz, who helped them with documents, permits, living and office space, and money. Some meetings of the underground leadership took place in the Judenrat building; Barasz's adjutant was a member of a Zionist youth movement and active in the underground. However, personal sympathies and a shared Zionist ideology were not the only reasons for Barasz's close relations with the underground. Barasz's secretary recalls that he respected the underground members, but did not believe in the practicality of resistance and its ability to bring about salvation.[90] For him, the underground was a constant threat to cooperation with the Germans and he therefore chose not to fight it, but instead, if he could not control it entirely, at least to be informed about its activities. Because of that the Zionist Barasz urged the Zionist underground leader Tenenbaum to orchestrate a compromise and unite with the communist resistance, which hated the Judenrat leader and viewed him as Nazi stooge. When a member of the communist underground killed a German serviceman in a shootout by the ghetto fence and when there was an explosion in the communists' munitions lab, Barasz had to invest considerable effort in calming down the Germans and making sure no reprisals against ghetto Jews were ordered. A unified underground that kept him in the loop was preferable to a divided one that did not. Barasz also made a promise to keep Tenenbaum informed about all developments affecting the ghetto's fate.

Barasz's strategy *almost* worked. He was able to keep his ghetto intact after most other ghettos had been liquidated. Among the large Polish ghettos, only Łódź outlived Białystok. "Smart people understood that we are facing death," recalled Berta Sokol'skaia, a Judenrat employee. "But we all thought: maybe [the Germans] won't have enough time [to kill us]."[91]

Barasz mistakenly believed that he could rely on his German contacts and that he would be informed if something were going to happen to the ghetto. A rational person, he simply could not imagine that the Germans would destroy a ghetto that contributed so greatly to their war effort. The German authorities in Berlin were also aware of local officials' attempts to shield the ghetto from destruction; as a result they had to bring Odilo Globocnik, the notorious SS commander of the Lublin district, to Białystok to organize the deportation.[92]

Barasz believed that cooperation with the Germans was the best chance to save the ghetto as a whole, but he was also certain that such behavior would lead to his own death. He had no doubt that the Germans were going to lose the war and told his secretary that he expected to be executed when the Soviets returned.[93] He also knew that his conduct was heavily criticized by many Jews, especially the Jewish communists, and resented by the Poles. In public meetings with the ghetto population he addressed this point and claimed they had no reason to fear, because the attitude of any future regime toward the Jews would be guided by high-level political decisions, and not by what the Jews had done during the war. As for himself, he was willing to give his life to save the community.

Barasz's policy of cooperation without collaboration remained intact up until the final days of the ghetto's existence. There was a major deportation of Jews from the ghetto in February 1943, but according to his secretary, he thought that the deportation Aktion would be similar to the previous relocation of Jews from Białystok to the Prużany ghetto. By summer 1943, however, he knew that deportation meant death. The night before the ghetto's liquidation, Barasz's cooperation strategy collapsed in an instant. Devastated, lost, but probably still hoping to save the ghetto in a last ditch attempt, Barasz crossed the threshold from cooperation to public collaboration. His goal—to save the community—remained intact, but now he was willing to take part in the German extermination effort. The Judenrat urged the Jews to faithfully comply with the expulsion order and to present themselves at the deportation point (rather than hiding or trying to escape). In Minsk, Judenrat chair Yoffe warned the ghetto population of the German killing Aktion, while in Kraków Rosenzweig refused to provide the Germans with the demanded number of deportees. Both paid for their insubordination with their lives. Barasz also had little hope of survival and realized that the Soviets would never forgive his cooperation with the Germans and his efforts to make the ghetto indispensable for the Nazi war effort. His actions during those final days of the ghetto were driven not by a lack of courage or the desire for personal survival, but by the delusion that something could still be done to save at least parts of the community. Realizing that the underground would rebel and that an uprising would seal the ghetto's fate, Barasz also reneged on his earlier promise and did not inform the underground of the deportation orders he had received, thus depriving the resistance of several crucial hours of preparation. His desperate attempts failed. The Białystok ghetto was doomed, and not even Barasz's public collaboration could save it.

In addition to the Judenrat, the Białystok ghetto also had a Jewish police force, the Order Service. In many ghettos, including those of Kraków and eventually Minsk, the police were de facto independent from, and often more powerful than, the Judenrat.[94] But in Białystok, which had a strong and competent Judenrat, the Jewish police force was firmly subordinate. With the several exceptions (discussed later in the chapter), they did not try to gain independent power. There were about two hundred Jewish police members in the Białystok ghetto and their mission was to keep public order, patrol the gates, and ensure the Jews' compliance with the German authorities' instructions on such matters as the curfew and the blacking out of windows. We don't know much about the criteria that determined their recruitment. Dora Kozin's husband, brother, and uncle were in the Jewish police. According to her, they were given their jobs because they spoke German.[95] Family connections also likely explain why she had several relatives in the police.

"The first batch of [people who joined the ghetto police] were Jewish crooks. . . . These criminal types didn't last long. . . . [T]he second wave of 'volunteer' police came from the intelligentsia, a lot of mama's boys who believed it was safer than doing other work," recalled Charles Zabuski.[96] Lipa A. disagreed, describing the Jewish police as "the best young people in the ghetto."[97] Although seemingly contradictory, both of these statements are true, but apply to different types of police servicemen. Among the first wave of recruits to the Jewish police were a police superintendent named Pfenigstein and Grisha Zelikowicz, a low-ranking serviceman. Both actively engaged in extortion, blackmailed rich Jews, and informed on ghetto inhabitants to the Gestapo. Pfenigstein acted independently and was quickly killed by his German masters, who did not look favorably on the Jewish policeman's clandestine attempts to amass personal wealth.[98] Zelikowicz and his associates turned out to be a more serious threat, because they had an ambition to gain control over the Judenrat's financial department and probably even to oust Barasz. Had they succeeded, the Białystok ghetto might have become similar to Kraków's, and Zelikowicz would likely have achieved the power and the notoriety of Spira. However, Zelikowicz was outsmarted by the Judenrat leader, and ended up in the Gestapo jail.

After the arrest of Zelikowicz and his group, the Jewish police ranks were purged of 10 percent of their members, who were exposed as corrupt and prone to bribe taking, extortion, and racketeering. The remaining 90 percent continued in service but were constantly urged by their superiors not forget that "[t]he ghetto is not forever. A day will come when we will meet our brothers without the [police] cap."[99] It is not known what the direct effect of such warnings was, but when it came to the February 1943 deportation the behavior of the Jewish police was by and large irreproachable. During that Aktion, they refrained from taking part in the rounding up of fellow Jews, leaving the dirty work to the Germans. Unable to discover the Jewish hideouts themselves, the Germans were forced to recruit private collaborators, who tried to save their own lives by betraying others.

The *mosrim* (literally "givers away" in Hebrew and Yiddish) became the plague of the ghetto during the February Aktion, because they were deadly effective in discovering hideouts. "Three soldiers are walking—an old lady in front of them—an informer. Five Germans—a lad leads them—an informer," lamented Mordechai Tenenbaum.[100] As compensation for their services, they were exempted from deportation.[101] Fear of the mosrim was so high that when Jack R. and his friend left their hideout in the ghetto during the Aktion to search for food and accidentally discovered a bunker full of Jews in hiding, the Jews in the bunker wanted to kill them. Their lives were spared only because one lady in the bunker was from Jack R.'s hometown and she vouched for him.[102]

After the Aktion, a witch hunt began in the ghetto and informers or suspected informers were lynched by outraged mobs. "It was a death penalty" if someone betrayed a hideout, recalled Avraham K.[103] Some informers were identified by members of the Jewish police, who could walk freely around the ghetto during the Aktion and therefore saw the mosrim in action;[104] others were recognized by people who jumped off the trains to Treblinka and managed to return to the city.[105] However, it was "enough to walk on the street and someone would call you an informer from behind to be killed. No one asked, no one interrogated. Just kicked them to death," explained Avraham K.[106] After the Aktion, Baruch Piletzki saw an old man lying on the street, bruised and crying. When pressed, he admitted to betraying—out of a desire to survive—the hiding places of his three sons. "He didn't make it through the night," recalls Piletzki. "We finished him off. All the people. One spitted, another hit."[107] Several testimonies mention the killing of mosrim with hammers.[108] According to Hadasah Levkowitcz even the mosrims' graves were vandalized.[109]

Yet, despite the vividly gratuitous violence employed against them, the actual number of private collaborators in the city was small, hardly more than several dozen.[110] In the grand scheme of things, the cooperation and public collaboration of the Judenrat, intentions aside, proved to be substantially more consequential. By creating an impression of normal life inside the ghetto, lamented Berta Sokol'skaia, the Judenrat "as if put us all to sleep . . . we were not alert, and we were distracted."[111] When the final deportation orders came, this illusion of normalcy collapsed and left Jewish Białystok paralyzed and disoriented. Only a few rebelled or escaped; the vast majority ignored the underground's call to resist, did not go into hiding but just packed their belongings and quietly went to the trains that would take them to Auschwitz and Treblinka.

Concluding Remarks

In this chapter I discussed the most sensitive and controversial of the survival strategies adopted by the Jews—cooperation and collaboration with the Germans. In all three ghettos there were Jews who engaged in cooperation and collaboration, often to the detriment of their communities. Some, like the Judenrat leaders, cooperated and collaborated publicly and openly; others preferred to hide their relations with the Nazi authorities. Those who cooperated—the initial Judenrat leaders—did so out of a desire to save the community; while the private collaborators' goal was to help themselves. Those who cooperated without collaborating are remembered by the survivors with respect; those who crossed the line between cooperation for the sake of public good and self-serving collaboration are despised. Almost none of these people survived. We do not know for certain how many engaged in this behavior, but what is undeniable is that such people did exist. It is impossible to understand Jewish behavior during the Holocaust without considering them and their actions.

People with a history of previous political and social activism were overrepresented in the ranks of the cooperators and public collaborators, especially among the Judenrat leaders. This is certainly true for Białystok and, to a somewhat lesser extent, Kraków. But political activism alone cannot explain the patterns of Judenrat leadership recruitment; the nature of each city's pre–World War II regime played an important role. Thus, were it not for the escape of many Jewish leaders from Kraków in September 1939, the percentage of political activists among the member of its Judenrat would likely have been even higher. In Minsk, the Soviets' complete elimination of non-communist Jewish institutions precluded the emergence of a Judenrat similar in its makeup to that of Białystok or Kraków. However, when the typical Judenrat model of ghetto governance collapsed in Kraków and Minsk, the new institutions that replaced it were led not by community-oriented prewar political activists, but by individuals who prioritized their personal well-being. Nonpolitical ghetto leaders turned out to be more similar to Gestapo informers and corrupt Jewish policemen than to their pre-1939 politically active counterparts who cooperated without collaborating.

The comparison also suggests an inverse relationship between cooperation and private collaboration. In Białystok, a strong Judenrat that successfully cooperated with the Germans was able to substantially limit private collaboration by the ghetto Jews. The only exception was the February 1943 Aktion, when the Judenrat temporarily lost control over the ghetto. The return of control to local Jewish actors went hand in hand with the brutal grassroots purge of those who switched sides and defied the community and its norms by collaborating. In Kraków and Minsk, where the original Judenrats were eliminated by the Germans, private collaboration was rampant.

The chapter also demonstrated that private collaboration did take place and that often it took similar forms in the three ghettos. That in itself is unsurprising. As Stathis Kalyvas argues, under conditions of violence stronger sides will always enjoy a ready supply of people willing to defect and collaborate.[112] Coethnics are much better counterinsurgents than external occupiers,[113] and therefore invaders always have an interest in attracting collaborators and employing them against potential resisters and rule breakers. Collaboration and the power associated with it also reshaped preexisting social relations and hierarchies. This explains why the most notorious private collaborators in the three ghettos were either outsiders, such as the Polish Jews in the Minsk ghetto, or people previously located at the bottom of the social order, such as the poor glazier Spira in Kraków and the low-ranking policeman Zelikowicz in Białystok. For them, collaboration provided an opportunity for social advancement, enrichment, and power.

The most important motivation, however, was survival. People who engaged in cooperation and collaboration perceived this course of action as the most promising means of surviving the war and the genocide. The evidence of such a belief is overwhelming and explicit; the only difference is *whose* survival the collaborators had in mind. While private collaborators and nonpolitical public collaborators were focused on their personal survival, politically active cooperators and public collaborators prioritized the survival of their communities, or at least parts of them. In Minsk and in Kraków, when the physical existence of the community itself came under threat, the cooperation of the Judenrat leadership stopped. In Białystok, Barasz wholeheartedly believed that due to his cooperation with the Germans the ghetto would survive the war, while he himself would be executed when the Soviets returned. Eventually, he became a captive of his strategy, failed to resist the ghetto's final liquidation, and reneged on his promise to notify the underground, thus crossing the line that separated cooperation from public collaboration. In hindsight, the strategy was misguided, but his intentions were noble and sincere.

What this chapter also shows is that cooperators and at least some public collaborators were much closer to those who occupied the opposite end of the behavioral spectrum, the resisters, than they were to private cooperators and collaborators. For this reason it makes sense that Barasz and Mushkin had cordial relationships with the underground and supported many of its actions. Had they been a generation younger, they might well have become resisters themselves. It was situational factors, such as age, tactical differences, and the need to take care of dependents and communities that often distinguished those who worked with the Germans from those who fought against them. On broader goals, they agreed.

Collaborators, on the other hand, focused on their personal well-being and because this was their goal they vastly differed from those who merely cooperated with the Germans. Yet despite their differences, one thing united those engaged in cooperation and collaboration: almost none of them experienced success with their chosen strategy. Morally controversial, cooperation and collaboration also turned out to be ineffective.

CHAPTER 5

COPING AND COMPLIANCE

The Germans, recalled a survivor, "went on a rampage; they smashed windows, fired their guns. . . . Corpses were strewn everywhere, the snow was red with blood, the barbarians were running around and shouting like wild animals: 'Beat the kikes! *Jude kaput!*"[1] This was the January 9, 1942 Aktion that cost most Khmel'nik Jews their lives. Israel G. did not see those pictures.

While the Germans gathered the Jews together in the town square, Israel, along with his mother, brother, and some neighbors—about twenty people in total—hid in a cellar prepared in advance for such an occasion. (As it turned out, they had no need to hide. Israel G.'s grandfather was considered by the Germans an "essential specialist" and would be allowed to survive along with his family.) The grandfather, however, was at this time in the square, where the selection was taking place, as were distant relatives Tzilya Axelrod, her sister Manya, and Manya's newborn baby. Tzilya and Manya took advantage of the absence of Alexandra, Israel, and Venyamin to pose as David G.'s family. They, along with the baby, would otherwise surely have been killed, but the identity swap allowed them to remain in the ghetto and they eventually survived.

Meanwhile, in the cellar where Israel G. and others hid, food was running low and tensions were flaring. Everybody knew that they had to be quiet and motionless; the Germans and their collaborators were going from house to house looking for hideouts. Israel G. had a kitten that had been left outside the cellar, in the house. After some time the pet became hungry. He located the carefully disguised entrance to the hideout and started meowing, asking for food. Realizing that if the Germans were to enter the house they would figure out what is going on, Israel took the kitten in. He gave the kitten some food, but the pet did not stop making noises, this time from inside the cellar. People in the hideout became agitated. Israel G. was given a choice between leaving the hideout with the kitten and killing him. Israel strangled his pet as it scratched and tried to escape.

* * *

Several important studies of the Holocaust would classify the behavior of Israel G., his family, and their neighbors as "passivity" and "paralysis."[2] After all, they did not try to escape or fight back, and the only one they killed in their bid for survival was a kitten. Yet a closer examination demonstrates that even this short episode contains numerous actions, attempts, and split-second decisions that fly in the face of the passivity charge. David G., despite his advanced age, worked hard in a physically demanding job (he was a coppersmith) to ensure his "essential specialist" status. Israel G. and his family had prepared a hideout. Tzilya Axelrod and her sister exploited a split-second opportunity to present themselves as David G.'s family, hardly a sign of paralysis. Finally, there is nothing passive about having to kill a pet.

I view such behavior not as paralysis, but as coping. In my typology "coping" means confronting a danger and trying to survive while staying put, without (1) leaving one's community or country; (2) engaging in collaboration with the perpetrators; or (3) presenting resistance to the perpetrators.[3] Coping, however, does not mean submissiveness and passivity. It often requires breaking rules and laws by engaging in black market transactions, theft, smuggling and bribing, or taking various legal or illegal actions to improve one's chances for survival. The appropriate vocabulary for such a strategy, notes Browning, is not passivity but "ingenuity, resourcefulness, adaptability, perseverance, and endurance."[4] In various anthropological works, first and foremost those by James Scott, many tactics that I classify as coping are viewed as nonviolent, "everyday" or "hidden" forms of resistance.[5] Coping also corresponds in large part to what many Israeli Holocaust historians view as *amidah*, an unarmed (sometimes referred to as "passive") resistance. Bauer, for instance, views *amidah* as consisting of mutual help, underground political life and education, religious life, attempts to obtain food and preserve health.[6] In this book, however, I limit the definition of resistance (described in chapter 7) to organized attempts to actively harm the perpetrators. Doing what you can to stay alive certainly thwarts the Nazi design to see the Jews dead, the sooner the better, but I believe that "coping" is a more appropriate term to describe the phenomenon.

This, obviously, does not mean that none of the Jews were passive or submissive. An extreme version of coping is "compliance," which I define as acting according to the rules and guidelines prescribed by the authorities without taking active steps to change one's situation. With the benefit of hindsight, we can see that in the Holocaust context compliance almost inevitably led to death. People who had to choose their strategies while events were unfolding had no such knowledge and thus could reasonably have opted for compliance. Some did. Almost none of them survived.

Initially, when information about the Nazis' actions and intentions was limited, compliance could seem a sensible course of action. As it became increasingly obvious that compliant behavior was extremely unlikely to ensure survival, coping became the dominant strategy. Yet some people stuck to compliance even as the genocide progressed. An analysis of compliance is inevitably affected by two key limitations. First, this strategy was chosen by a tiny minority of Minsk, Kraków, and Białystok Jews. Second, people who chose compliance as their key strategy almost never survived. Those few who did would naturally be reluctant to admit to their submissiveness, especially against the background of studies, films, and novels that emphasize the Jews' activism, ingenuity, and both passive and active resistance.

The paucity of data on compliance makes it impossible for me to venture comprehensive arguments about who would have been more likely to engage in it. Yet two trends do emerge from such scarce evidence as exists. First, it would seem that people who had more prewar exposure to the German state and its behavior (but not necessarily to German language and culture) were more likely to choose compliance. This is especially true of the German Jews in the Minsk ghetto. And second, compliance was more likely to become the default strategy either when all other survival strategies seemed unfeasible or during periods of great uncertainty, such as the initial stages of an occupation or during the final deportations from the ghettos.

Compliance was a minority strategy. In public perception, however, the image of Jews being led like "lambs to the slaughter" became widespread. This perception, I will show, has little basis in reality because the strategy that the majority of Jews chose was coping, not compliance. Moreover, throughout most of the ghettos' existence coping was arguably the most prudent behavior: other strategies would likely have been judged either prohibitively risky (resistance and evasion) or morally questionable (collaboration). As the mass murder accelerated and the understanding emerged that coping was unlikely to ensure survival, alternative strategies could have become increasingly more attractive, but only for people who had the capacity to engage in them. For the vast majority of Jews who were neither presented with the opportunity nor endowed with the capability to collaborate, escape, or resist, coping remained the dominant strategy until the bitter end.

This chapter will show that coping consisted mainly of a combination of three tactics: securing employment in a needed industry, obtaining food, and preparing a hideout. These three essential components of coping played a role in all three ghettos, but the relative importance of each varied across communities. I will also show that Jews who were less integrated into non-Jewish society and lived and functioned in mainly intraethnic, predominantly Jewish social milieus and networks were more likely to choose coping as their dominant survival strategy. They were also more likely to be successful in obtaining the necessary components of coping and in surviving predations throughout their time in the ghetto. In other words, less assimilated Jews found life *inside* the ghetto easier than their more assimilated coethnics. The pre–World War II strength and cohesion of the local Jewish community, the chapter will show, shaped patterns of coping. In Białystok, neither the Imperial Russian nor the interwar Polish government promoted the integration of Jews into the broader society, and thus allowed strong Jewish institutions and identities to persist until the beginning of World War II. As a result, the city's Jewish community was robust, cohesive, and endowed with powerful communal institutions, leadership, and support networks. Coping took a more organized form and was, throughout the ghetto's existence, more successful than in Minsk or Kraków, where the Soviet and Austro-Hungarian policies of integration and assimilation had given rise to more heterogeneous and weaker Jewish communal institutions and networks.

At the end of the day, compliance and coping were not the best survival strategies; for the vast majority the viability of such behavior decreased as Nazi persecution mounted. But even then, people who had opted for coping often clung to the strategy simply because they had few feasible alternatives. The level of Jews' integration into non-Jewish society and the ethnic makeup of their social networks in Minsk, Kraków, and Białystok were predetermined by the pre-Holocaust political regimes of the cities, and the coping strategy often could not be swiftly amended even as it started to unravel.

Minsk

The most common strategy that the Minsk ghetto inmates adopted was coping. Rakhil Rappoport's motto—"I did everything I could, I did more than I could, and there is nothing else I can do"[7]—is probably the best description of how people in the Minsk ghetto coped with Nazi persecution. At the same time, the business of coping was in Minsk more individual than community-based, and also more chaotic and desperate than in the other ghettos. This was due in part to unrelenting violent assaults by the Germans and to the appalling conditions in the ghetto, but another important factor that shaped the nature of coping in Minsk was the diverse and fragmented nature of the city's Jewish community, a product of twenty years of Soviet social engineering.

Compliance was extremely uncommon in the Minsk ghetto and confined predominantly to the German Jews (described later in the chapter). Among the Soviet Jews, some at first chose to fully obey German orders and instructions due to their positive pre-Holocaust encounters with German authorities. Others were simply too disoriented during the first stages of the German occupation to devise other strategies. Long-term compliance, however, was rendered impossible by the German policy of mass murder and by the abysmal conditions in the ghetto. Even the German Jews, with their penchant for scrupulous obedience to laws and strict discipline, found it almost impossible to survive without breaking at least some rules. Simply put, in the Minsk ghetto, given the meager food rations, compliance could not be a viable survival strategy; those who strictly obeyed stood no chance of survival, even if they were not directly killed by the Nazis and their collaborators.

When compliance failed, coping swiftly emerged as the dominant strategy. In practice, coping meant first and foremost securing three essential things—food, work, and hiding places inside the ghetto. Without all three, the chances of survival were miniscule. The ghetto population was divided into several categories that determined access to these critical resources. First, there were those who worked and those who did not. Those who worked were fed. The rations they received could not sustain an adult person—a bowl of watery soup, a slice of bread, or, if lucky, potato peels—but nonworkers usually did not receive even these. Second, working outside the ghetto provided Jews with opportunities to trade with the non-Jewish population and to barter their belongings for food, which could then be smuggled into the ghetto. And most importantly, people who possessed work certificates and their immediate families were not killed by the Germans during the initial waves of shootings. Most privileged were the skilled workers, the *Facharbeiter*. Having a coveted skilled-worker ID was, at least initially, perceived as one of the best ways to ensure survival.

Workers were also sometimes able to obtain various small things that made a huge difference, such as food leftovers from the Germans. Vera B. and several other young Jewish women worked at the German Air Force unit. Some German pilots tried to help them, but they were too scared to do so openly. Eventually, they came up with ways to help without arousing suspicion—for example, they brought the girls dishes that still had plenty of soup in them and asked to have them washed. Vera B. then brought the soup home and fed her little sisters. At her next workplace, another German helped Vera B. to smuggle salt to the ghetto, where she sold it.[8] A German soldier who was an avid philatelist approached Abram Astanshin-skii at his workplace and asked for Soviet stamps in exchange for bread.[9] Arkadii T. befriended a German supervisor in his workplace; the man always warned Arkadii when there was an Aktion in the ghetto and helped him to get food.[10]

The situation with nicotine was even more desperate than with food, and the demand was staggering. "[My mother] was ready to give bread, everything, for cigarettes," admitted Esfir Movshenson.[11] Working outside the ghetto allowed people to pick up cigarettes butts and either smoke them or sell them in the ghetto.

The imperative to find employment was grasped almost immediately by everyone. "All the supplies of food and soap [are gone]. And you have to live somehow. A job, as a fourteen-year-old without a profession, I won't get. That means that I am sixteen, and I am a cobbler. The documents, obviously, were destroyed in a fire. This is the only thing [in my story] that was true," recalled Mikhail Treister.[12] Working as a cobbler and learning the trade by producing jackboots for the Germans also provided Treister with an opportunity to steal from the factory. According to his account, virtually everyone in his workplace stole leather, insoles, and even entire boots. Treister sold or bartered some stolen boots for food, others he gave to friends, and some were sent to the partisans. Germans, it seems, were well aware of the widespread theft and tried to do something about it. Their solution was simply to give jackboots to every worker and to make sure that they wore only one pair. The idea, recalled Lazar T., failed miserably as Jews simply started coming to work in the morning wearing slippers, and going home in the evening wearing boots.[13] Not everyone was as lucky as Lazar T. and Mikhail Treister. Arkadii T. once stole canned food in his workplace. The German supervisors suspected him, and he was severely beaten. Yet they did not find the food. There were also weapons lying unwatched in the room, but Arkadii didn't touch them—at that time food was much more important.[14]

Because work was one of the key modes of survival, loss of the male head of a household often meant starvation for the entire family. Vera B. remembers how during the 1941 summer and fall roundups, Germans were looking mainly for males. She thus did everything she could to keep her father constantly hidden, because she understood that "he [was] the main-stay (*opora*) of everything in our life."[15] Vera S. was not so lucky; her father and two brothers were taken away and shot.[16] When there were no adult males in the household—either because they had been killed early on, fighting in the Red Army, or had been imprisoned in the Gulag, women and teenage children like Vera S. had to become the main providers for their families.

Many people were willing to go to great lengths to get a decent job. Asia Bressler and her husband bartered their soap for German Jews' clothes, even though personal hygiene products were extremely scarce and badly needed in the ghetto. The reason was simple—the German Jews' clothes were more elegant and gave the Bresslers' appearance a Western European flavor. This was important, because Germans paid attention to how people looked when hiring for good jobs. Wearing the German Jews' clothes, Bressler got a job that substantially improved her survival chances.[17]

Obviously, survival through work depended to a large extent on the Minsk German authorities' willingness to continue exploiting Jews as slave labor instead of killing them. And here, the Germans' self-interest was crucial. As Jürgen Matthäus writes, as late as April 1943, several months after Stalingrad, the regional SS and Police Chief Kurt von Gottberg complained that "even today there are German institutions in the region that think they cannot do without the Jew as a skilled worker."[18] But when Jewish workers became unnecessary or had to be replaced, nothing could protect those Jews who still clung to the coping strategy.

In the long run, coping did not, indeed *could not* be a successful survival strategy for the vast majority of Jews, but in a few cases having highly needed professional expertise did enable them to survive. The Soviet-Jewish writer and a military journalist Ilya Ehrenburg recalled one such story:

> When I got to Minsk it was four hours after the first Soviet tanks had entered the city. The first citizens I met told me there were some Jews still alive where the SD [German security police] was. I made my way there and found them in the SD forge. There were a few people in very poor physical condition. They told me how they had survived. The Gestapo had made use of the more experienced Jewish craftsmen for their own purposes.... There were 200 such specialists in Minsk; most of them, it seems, had been killed by the Germans as they were leaving. This dozen people knew what awaited them and, as soon as they saw the first signs of confusion among the Germans in Minsk five days before our soldiers arrived, they hid in an underground vault they had discovered beneath the SD yard. They stayed there for five days.... One of them was

an Austrian Jew.... [He] survived because a mechanic had been needed on the day he had been sent here.[19]

The second most common way to obtain food was through barter. When it became clear that official rations were insufficient even for basic survival, ghetto inmates began trading their belongings for food. Here, those who lived in the designated ghetto area before the war were luckier than those who had moved into the ghetto from the outside, for they had not lost most of their belongings in moving and thus had more to barter. Those who had previously lived in other parts of the city had fewer things to sell. Barter was dangerous for both Jews and non-Jews, because any contact between the two populations was strictly forbidden. Yet trade still flourished and a black market emerged. "We made our living off bartering our aunt's belongings. This was done at high risk of death, because it was necessary to approach the barbed wire, settle on a price quickly and make the exchange. When the German guard saw what was going on, he shot immediately—obviously, at the person who was behind the barbed wire [inside the ghetto]," recalled Anatolii Rubin.[20] The speed of the transactions provided people with numerous opportunities to cheat. Galina Davydova's neighbor bartered a winter coat for a sack of flour. Too scared to open the sack on the street, she waited until she got home. Instead of flour, the sack was filled with sand. The coat, of course, was gone.[21] Leonid Okun's family sent him to the city to barter boots for food. When he got back home, he discovered that instead of flour he had been given whitewash. "My grandpa yelled at me, and others cried."[22] Albert Lapidus's family received a sack of bleach instead of flour.[23]

The custom of bartering goods for food even spilled over from the "Soviet" to the "Hamburg" ghetto, but when it came to trading, the German Jews' situation was worse than that of their Soviet coethnics. German Jews did not speak Russian—the importance of which is emphasized in virtually every testimony of the Hamburg ghetto survivors—and therefore they were entirely dependent on Soviet intermediaries who often charged high prices. People in the Hamburg ghetto sometimes resented what they perceived as the Soviet Jews' greed, but they could not do much about it. Reuven Liond started a "business" with a German Jew named Max, who was born in Poland and knew some Russian.[24] Max and Liond served as intermediaries, or in network analysis terms "brokers," between the German Jews and the local non-Jewish population. Later on, Liond used his Belorussian trade contacts to obtain a gun and escape to the partisans. Berta Malomed's mother, a baker by trade, opened a primitive bakery that used ingredients that were "arranged" by two German Jews—most likely smuggled into the ghetto or bought from German soldiers or officials.[25] For German Jews, barter was a no less risky behavior than for their Soviet coethnics—Fred Alexander's mother was killed while tried to barter some of her belongings, but it was the only way to get extra food inside the ghetto.[26]

Working and trading could help keep the body and the soul together between German killing sprees, but surviving an Aktion required a very different set of skills. Those who worked outside the ghetto were initially spared, so hideouts within the ghetto were the main need—places to conceal women, children, and the elderly, or entire families during a night raid or a random roundup. According to Iakov N., "pogroms" became the chief topic of conversation in the ghetto.[27] "People start thinking about how to survive. They start building hideouts." The hideouts, called *malinas*, were everywhere. Each house and apartment took steps to build one. Those who had beds just above the entrance to the malina were considered the luckiest.[28] Hiding in the malina required total silence because any sound could lead to discovery and certain death. Women with small children sometimes had to choose—usually under intense pressure from others in the hideout—between leaving the hideout and strangling their crying babies. Older children knew how to remain quiet and motionless for hours. Abram Rubenchik describes how the first thing he did after moving to a new apartment in the ghetto was to organize a hideout.[29] Moisei Gorelik's family did the same.[30] Some hideouts were designed to house large groups of people over substantial periods of time. A group that entered a malina before the ghetto was liquidated in the fall of 1943 set a duration record; they stayed hidden until liberation in July 1944. At night, they occasionally crept out to breathe some fresh air and obtain food from a Belorussian woman who helped them. A number of group members died, but thirteen, literally walking skeletons, survived to see Soviet troops entering the city.[31]

In the desperate struggle to survive, prewar networks played a huge role as people fell back on them when they needed support. "In the ghetto—[Jews] from outside Minsk were on their own," claimed Lazar T. who came to Minsk from the small nearby town of Uzliany.[32] "If people knew one another before the war, they tried to look after one another. And we, we tried to stick together with people from our own town." Those who did not have Jewish friends or relatives in the ghetto suffered even more than others. "I was dreaming about fresh potatoes, bread and soup. Since we did not have any connections, we couldn't buy anything," wrote Maria Epstein, a refugee in Minsk who came from Kraków.[33]

In the Minsk ghetto, coping was desperate, chaotic, violent, and individual/family-focused. Several survivors note last ditch attempts, mainly by the older generation, to revive the city's robust pre-Soviet Jewish community with its intraethnic solidarity and support networks. According to Esfir Movshenson, there was powerful pushback against speaking Russian on the street.[34] Younger, more assimilated Jews who spoke Russian were constantly reprimanded by the older generation for not communicating in Yiddish and for abandoning their community and customs. The struggle to reverse the impact of twenty years of Soviet policies was, not surprisingly, a lost battle; the changes that the Minsk Jewish community had undergone were too far-reaching to reverse in such a short period. Moreover, the very changes that made the Jewish community less cohesive, such as the abandonment of Yiddish in favor of Russian and the adoption of non-Jewish customs, behavior, and interethnic social networks, had enabled numerous Jews to escape the ghetto and survive the Holocaust on what Jews called "the Russian side," thus making coping less attractive and viable.

A discussion of coping among the native Jews of Minsk would not be complete without touching on one of the most sensitive topics in the literature on occupation and reactions to it—and this is the subject of what is often called "horizontal collaboration;"[35] that is, sexual relations between German servicemen and non-German, in this case Jewish, women. In my view such relations did not constitute collaboration, but were instead a form of coping. Sexual relations and affairs between Germans and Jews were strictly forbidden, but they took place nonetheless. Sexual violence remains one of the most understudied topics in Holocaust research,[36] even though survivors' testimonies describe quite a few instances of it. In some cases the relationship was consensual. Thus, Sima Margolina's neighbors Ania and Liza befriended two German servicemen, originally from Belgium. The soldiers would visit Ania and Liza in the ghetto, while Margolina's cousin stood guard, making sure that no one interrupted their meetings.[37] The details of the story are corroborated in the testimony of the cousin, Samuil K.[38] Eventually the soldiers helped their Jewish female friends to escape the ghetto. Another story of a love affair between a Jewish ghetto inmate and a German officer, Captain Willi Schultz, will be described in chapter 6. For young and attractive Jewish women, having consensual sexual relations and love affairs with Germans was sometimes a life-saving behavior.

Compliance was more common among the German Jews than Soviet Jews, though it remained a rare mode of behavior. Whereas life in the USSR taught people how to get around rules and work through unofficial channels, German Jews were known for their scrupulous obedience to rules and laws. Soviet Jews were extremely compliant when it came to political issues, but in the economic realm their obedience evaporated. "Russian Jews—they had Soviet training (*po-Sovetski naucheny*) that if it is forbidden, then it is in practice allowed, while these [German Jews]—they obeyed laws like fanatics," lamented Samuil K.,[39] who had suggested to a German Jew that they escape together to the partisans, only to be refused. "The word 'forbidden' was a law for them," one of the native ghetto inmates said of German Jews. "They were very disciplined, these Germans."[40] The German Jews believed everything, claimed Mikhail Treister. "When told to pack, they just packed and went."[41] Some German Jews simply could not force themselves to believe that their compatriots were capable of killing civilians in large numbers, even after hearing stories of violence from the Minsk Jews.[42]

The recollections of a handful of German Jewish survivors of the Minsk ghetto support the claim that compliance was indeed chosen by some of them. Like their Soviet coethnics, German Jews also emphasize the importance of work, a key pillar of coping. Quite a few bartered their belongings for food or jumped at opportunities to get better job assignments. At the same time, none of their accounts mention hideouts, which existed in almost every house in the Soviet ghetto, and very few recall stealing food.[43] Henry R. from Hamburg still found it amazing "how people could take it—they just stood there waiting to be pushed in to the gas van. [They were] standing for hours in line to be loaded in to gas vans, knowing what gas vans mean."[44]

In the Minsk ghetto, the German Jews who survived did so mainly due to external factors rather than because they had actively selected some form of noncompliance. According to Henry R., a part of the ghetto where the Hamburg Jews lived had been scheduled for destruction, but a German officer who was also from Hamburg saved it. He was sent to the front as a punishment.[45] Hayim Bar'am from Berlin gave up on what was perceived as a great opportunity to increase one's chances of survival: "In spring 1942," he recalled, "the German ghetto was required to provide fifty drivers. And being a driver—there are so many chances here. . . . I had a driver's license, but in 1938–39 the Jews were required to give them back and I'd never really driven a truck . . . so I did not see myself as a candidate" for the job.[46] Bar'am's account is even more illuminating when compared to the numerous stories of Soviet Jews who, in order to survive, claimed that they had skills that they did not in fact possess in order to jump on any and every opportunity.

Evidence of German Jews' more widespread compliance comes mainly, though not only, from the testimonies of Soviet Jews, and it is quite possible that their recollections are heavily colored by ethnic stereotyping and preexisting perceptions of Germans' supposed obedience. The few existing testimonies of the "Hamburg ghetto" survivors themselves do show that among Central European Jews coping was the predominant strategy. But it is also undeniable that compliance might well have had more appeal for German Jews than for their Soviet coethnics. Forcefully removed from their homes and transferred to a foreign, hostile land where they did not know anyone, did not speak the local language, and could not fall back on preexisting support networks, their options were more limited than those of the local Jews. Under such impossible conditions compliance was often the only possible strategy.

KRAKÓW

The Jews could not be lions because they did not have an army, so they had to be "foxes on the lookout for hidden opportunities. . . . What we had to do was save as many lives as possible." These words from Mietek Pemper's memoir summarize quite well the most common behavior strategy of the Kraków Jews, namely coping.[47] In this section, I discuss the coping strategies adopted by the Kraków Jews and demonstrate that they, too, were often shaped by pre-Holocaust ties and experiences. I will also show that while people with higher levels of integration into Polish society had an advantage when it came to evasion (see chapter 6), coping with German persecution inside the ghetto was easier for people who had closer connections with other Jews before the war.

As in Minsk, very little evidence of widespread adoption of the compliance strategy can be found in Kraków. The main exceptions date to the early period of German occupation, when anti-Jewish measures such as looting and beating were still viewed as temporary aberrations. In Minsk, mass murder began almost immediately, but in Kraków the situation was different, and initially the belief that obedience to German orders was the most prudent option seemed reasonable.

Some fell back on history, noting that anti-Semitic violence notwithstanding, the Jews had survived for centuries. When the ghetto was established, Else D. and her family did not even think of escaping or hiding. "We were optimistic—what else can [the Germans] do? Jews lived before in ghettos."[48] (Here it should be recalled that a de jure ghetto had existed in the Kraków metropolitan area for centuries and was officially abolished only in 1867, so the word "ghetto" itself did not carry especially threatening connotations.[49] Jews had complied with similar regulations in previous centuries, and there was little reason not to do it again.)

There were also Jews in the city who initially believed that the German authorities had a legitimate right to issue orders, and that these orders ought to be obeyed by the subject population. "I said—we lost the war, the conqueror has the right," recalled Max H.[50] But as persecutions escalated, compliance became less popular. Some relied on their previous experience with or under German (rather than simply German-speaking Austro-Hungarian) rule; others believed that any attempt to break the rules would be either futile or too dangerous.

When Irene F. tried to convince her parents to get false papers, her father, a lawyer who had worked for many years in Germany, objected and told her she was crazy. Her parents, according to Irene F., were very legalistic, and such blatant a violation of rules was inconceivable for them.[51] Eliezer Cukier's father grew up among ethnic Germans. "My father . . . being a *yekke*[52] was told to show up (for expulsion), so he showed up," Cukier recalled.[53]

Another reason to opt for compliance was the belief that disobedience or attempts to escape or to somehow work around the rules would be futile. Yoel Wolf was on the list of young males who were to be deported from the ghetto to a labor camp. Luckily, he managed to escape the deportation. When he told his aunt about this "miracle that just happened," the aunt demanded that he immediately show up for deportation because the Germans "have order, they will find out that you lied and we all will suffer."[54] According to Yitzhak Bar-Meir, who came from a very religious family, people in his social milieu disapproved of Jewish resistance, because disobedience would endanger the ghetto's survival prospects.[55]

Finally, compliance was the default option when people gave up, or when all other options became or were seen as impossible. The parents of Rina Treibicz persisted in believing the Germans when they told them that if they worked they would be allowed to live, so they did nothing to hide or escape.[56] Some "thought that [by] being passive they could somehow remain alive," recalled Ester Manheim.[57] Gizela Markowitcz simply did not have the power to disobey. "They sent me . . . and I went. Without any thought, without any resistance . . . I was always so weak." During the deportation from the ghetto Markowitcz was ordered to give her newborn baby to the Germans, who told her that the child would eventually be allowed to join her in the labor camp. She believed them and complied, never to see her son again.[58] But for those who wanted to retain at least some semblance of control over their fate, compliance quickly became an untenable option. Coping, and more specifically a proactive approach to securing good employment, procuring food, and getting on Schindler's List became the modal behavior.

The Kraków ghetto Jews "have only one way to save ourselves, and this way is work," claimed ghetto commissar Gutter.[59] In the Płaszów camp to which the remaining ghetto Jews were relocated, Pemper, the dexterous Jewish secretary of the camp commander, went to great lengths to convince his boss to redirect production from textiles, which were an important, but dispensable addition to the German war effort, to armaments, which were a crucial contribution that would decrease the likelihood of the camp's liquidation. In this, the Kraków ghetto was not different from most other ghettos, which subscribed to the "salvation through work" philosophy. It was a strategy eventually doomed to fail, but in Kraków it allowed more than a thousand Jews to live until the moment when they were taken under Oscar Schindler's wing.

On an individual level, employment and food were the top priorities. In this Kraków differed somewhat from the Minsk ghetto, where mass shootings started almost immediately after the German occupation of the city, making hideouts another essential part of successful coping. There were hideouts in the Kraków ghetto, but they appeared only relatively late and even then were uncommon (see appendix 2). Unlike living conditions in Minsk, conditions for the majority of Kraków's Jews were rather tolerable, at least until deportation. "The first month in the ghetto we felt a certain amount of relaxation because the immediate danger had passed," recalled Helen R.[60] The ghetto had stores full of delicacies, restaurants, coffee shops, a cabaret, and a stand-up comedy show. There was, according to Frederic B., a semblance of normal life.[61] For younger people life was "almost normal with the exception of not going school," remembered Yehuda Maimon.[62]

"We are healthy and have enough to eat. I hope that we will survive," wrote Dola Stark to her brother in December 1940.[63] A number of families in the ghetto even had enough food and living space to keep pets,[64] something completely unimaginable in Warsaw or Minsk, where even the mice were devoured.[65] "Initially life was not that bad at all.... It was difficult, but I never went hungry," recalled Alexander A.[66] Tushia Z., on the other hand, does recall being hungry. The reason was that her father did not have a job. A well-known journalist, he had lost his source of income and was ill-suited for physical labor. Tushia was employed, but her salary was insufficient to support the entire family.[67] Having a job often was of little help in obtaining food, because wages were abysmally low, official food rations insufficient, and black market prices extremely high. "The [official] rations were not enough to live on, but too large to [make one] die," recalled Henry E.[68] The main value of employment was that it was considered the best insurance policy against expulsion during the early period of the German occupation, and against deportation to the death camps after 1942. "You had to have a job. If you tell the Germans that you don't have a job, they either kill you, or send you away," summarized Victor L.[69]

Not everyone could find a job. Some were too young or too old, others did not have the necessary skills. The Kraków Jews came up with several ways to overcome this problem. One way was simply to have a fake work card, as Victor L. did.[70] Another was to lie about one's age. The mother of Aneta W. knew that people who did not work would not survive, so she "raised" Aneta's age and arranged a job for her in her workplace. To make Aneta W. look taller, and therefore more fit for work, her mother made her wear a coat with a high hood.[71] Reena F. falsified her birth certificate to make herself older so she could work and obtain a permit to stay in the ghetto.[72] While young people tried to look older, old people did their best to appear younger. Dr. Ludwig Zurowski, a Polish physician, supplied Tadeusz Pankiewicz's pharmacy with hundreds of liters of hair-dying liquid. "The old and gray who were considered useless for labor and therefore most in danger of extermination became, due to the proper cosmetics, *arbeitsfähig*, fit for work," wrote Pankiewicz.[73]

In special danger of expulsion, and later on deportation and killing, were members of the intelligentsia and those employed in the provision of services, which became unnecessary under the new regime. Knowing that he was not fit physically for manual labor, Mietek Pemper quickly learned German stenography. Max H. was a beautician before the war, a profession that would not contribute much to the German war effort. Realizing this, he took a risk by volunteering to work as a barber in the epidemic hospital. As a hospital employee, Max H. was spared deportation until the very liquidation of the ghetto, while virtually all other Jewish barbers were expelled from the city in 1940.[74] High school teacher Leopold P. lied about his profession and was allowed to stay in the ghetto.[75] Victor L., who knew nothing about electricity, claimed that he was an electrician.[76] David W. registered as a mechanic even though he had no idea what mechanics was or what mechanics did.[77]

Such cases were unusual, however. More often than not, if they were to find employment or to improve their lot, people had to rely on their prewar ties and networks, and here relations with other Jews were more important than those with Poles. Meir Bosak, who was trained as a historian, applied for the necessary worker ID, claiming that he was a metalworker. The certificate had to be vetted by a German official who was assisted by a Jewish policeman, and the policeman happened to be Bosak's schoolmate.[78] According to Anna N., "If you knew someone who could know somebody in the employment office . . . then you did alright."[79] Even in the ghetto jail those who had families in the ghetto or connections with the Jewish police could get sufficient food. Prisoners without family in the city starved.[80]

Food, even if largely available, was nonetheless a source of major concern. Edith W. had "several primary things to think about": what she would have for dinner, what she would eat for breakfast, and how not to die.[81] For many, the only way to obtain food was from the black market. "We lived off buying and selling whatever we could find," recalled Alexander A.[82] David R. did not look Jewish and had a faked Polish ID, so his father started sending him to different towns to work as a go-between, assisting Jews from different places in business transactions.[83] Isaak W. spoke flawless German, so he also became a broker between Jewish and German networks, connecting Jews from the ghetto who wanted to sell their belongings with Germans who were interested in buying what they had to offer.[84] Leopold P. described his occupation as a freelance black market agent. "I was running around the ghetto, trying to smuggle food."[85] Julian M. worked in the lamp factory outside the ghetto. One of the ingredients used for lamp production was a certain type of poison, which Julian M. stole, smuggled into the ghetto, and sold to people who preferred suicide over deportation.[86] Victor L. sold cigarettes on the black market with the help of an SS man.[87] In addition to the black market, food could be obtained through intra-Jewish networks. The brother of Moshe B. worked in food distribution, so he helped with extra food from time to time.[88] Raymond F.'s sister worked in the communal kitchen, so her family had sufficient food.[89]

Finally, another key priority for many Jews was to find employment in Schindler's factory. That Oscar Schindler took good care of his Jews was well known in Kraków. "There was only one real hope [for survival]—Schindler," claimed Henry S. who applied for employment in Schindler's factory, but was sent to Auschwitz instead.[90] Schindler gave people hope and encouraged them, and this gave his workers the power to carry on. "Schindler promised us that as long as we work for him, we will survive," recalled Edith W. Initially, however, her friends did not believe him, for "how can you believe a German?"[91] But Edith W. had confidence in Schindler, and she was not disappointed. Naturally, people were willing to invest considerable efforts in becoming a "Schindler's Jew." Some used bribery, but for others social ties and prewar intra-Jewish connections paved the road to rescue. Marcel Goldberg, a notoriously corrupt Jewish policeman who played an important role in putting the Schindler List together, knew Leon K. from high school, so Leon K. was put on the list.[92] The cousin of Else D.'s husband worked in the employment office, and she arranged for his family to be on the list.[93] Goldberg was also a friend of Rosalie S.'s father, so she was sent to Schindler's camp, and "it was like heaven."[94] Iaakov W., who spent several days at the Schindler factory sub-camp in Płaszów, described the people there in very negative terms. According to him, they were people with con- nections (*protektsionerim*); many from the Jewish high society of Kraków. They disliked Iaakov W. and made him feel very unwelcome.[95]

Stories of bribes and corruption are never pleasant; especially when one's inclusion on the list more often than not meant the death of someone who was not as lucky or not endowed with either connections or money. Nonetheless, it seems that in Kraków, because of its lack of strong com- munity institutions and leadership, coping had to be an ostensibly indi- vidual and private survival strategy. This strategy, Primo Levi aptly argues, was employed in circumstances outside the traditional moral universe, and therefore it cannot be evaluated against conventional standards of moral- ity.[96] "Everyone concentrated on his own survival," attested Josef R.[97] "You did not trust anybody," admitted Miriam H.[98] Yet at critical moments it was almost impossible to survive inside the ghetto without external help, and the larger one's intra-Jewish support network was, the easier it became to endure life both politically and psychologically. Yitzhak Bar-Meir had no documents and therefore no legal status. He had to go into hiding, but as he came from a very religious family and an exclusively Jewish milieu, he chose to hide *inside* the ghetto, not outside of it. When he was caught by the Jewish police, Bar-Meir's contacts with other prominent Jews allowed him to walk away.[99] On the other hand, people who had completely assimilated into Polish society and cut themselves off from the Jewish milieu suffered greatly.

On top of the physical hardships, the ghetto presented an additional dif- ficulty for assimilated Jews, because they lacked a social circle of friends and acquaintances. Whereas many social Jewish organizations, first and foremost youth movements, intensified their activities in the ghetto and provided their members with an extraordinarily rich and vibrant social and spiritual life, those who had not belonged to Jewish organizations before the war felt isolated. All Polish-language signs and public inscriptions in the ghetto were replaced with ones in Hebrew/Yiddish letters, and this added to their feeling of loss and alienation.[100]

In their long correspondence with an uncle in the United States, teenagers Genka and Lusia Wimisner did not discuss friends, and most likely they did not belong to any Jewish groups.[101] Erna H. came from an assimilated family and considered herself "a very good Pole." She found life in the ghetto strange and harsh, not least because she "was not used to living among Jews."[102] The experiences of these young women contrast quite sharply with the accounts of people of their age who were part of Jewish organizations before the Holocaust and who usually found life in the ghetto emotionally and intellectually stimulating. Moshe B. and his friends engaged in mock trials of Dostoyevsky's *Crime and Punishment* heroes.[103] Sonia W. studied Latin and philosophy and claimed that she got "one of her best educations in the ghetto."[104] Religion and education thrived inside the ghetto walls, even though Jewish schools were officially closed.[105] These cultural resources were for the most part unavailable to assimilated Jews. For many of them, the only way to socialize was to get together at Pankiewicz's pharmacy, which became an informal social club for assimilated Jews.

When it came to interpersonal relations with the Germans, many testimonies describe quite cordial relations with German employers and civilian supervisors, especially during the early stages of Kraków's occupation. At the same time, only a few testimonies (and certainly fewer than in Minsk) describe Germans helping Jews to obtain food, probably because the food situation in the Kraków ghetto was not as desperate. I also could not find any reference in the testimonies to real or alleged love affairs and consensual sexual relations between Jews and Germans in the city. According to several testimonies, there was one such case in the Płaszów camp, but the details are not entirely clear. It is quite possible that in Kraków, the capital of the General Government, such a transgression was simply too risky for the Germans. Another potential explanation is that, given the much larger number of German women in Kraków than in Minsk, German males were less likely to engage in romantic and sexual relations with Jews.

BIAŁYSTOK

In this section, I discuss the coping strategies adopted by the Jews of Białystok and demonstrate how these were jointly shaped by the realities of the Holocaust, such as Judenrat policies, and the nature of Nazi persecution, as well as by pre-Holocaust networks and relations.

In many respects, coping was virtually the only strategy available to the vast majority of Białystok Jews. While the Judenrat and its leaders engaged in public collaboration and preached compliance, it became increasingly difficult to survive by faithfully following Nazi orders and living on the food rations provided by the authorities. The evasion option, as will be shown in the next chapter, was also largely unavailable due to the nature of ethnic relations in the city and the very low levels of Jewish integration into Polish society. Thus, coping and trying to outlive the Nazis inside the ghetto was the key mode of behavior still open to the vast majority of the Jews. Moreover, in Białystok, a cohesive and robust Jewish community in which most members subscribed to an exceptionally strong, city-centered Yiddish-speaking *Białystoker* identity,[106] the mechanisms for coping were easier to organize and maintain than in the more internally fragmented and socially and linguistically diverse Minsk and Kraków ghettos.[107]

Throughout the ghetto's existence, Barasz's cooperation with the Germans made coping a viable and attractive strategy. In Białystok, many people went hungry, but no one died of starvation. Judenrat public notices instructing the public to burn potato peels (which were considered a delicacy in the starving Minsk ghetto) are the best evidence that the food situation was tough, but not desperate. Judenrat meetings protocols indicate that until their confiscation by the German authorities in early 1942, there were at least fifty-five privately owned cows in the ghetto.[108] Finally, the ghetto also had communal vegetable plots, the so-called Barasz Gardens. Cultivated by members of the Zionist youth movements who underwent agricultural training as part of their preparation for immigration to Palestine, the plots provided Judenrat institutions, such as the hospitals, orphanages, and public kitchens with produce that was largely unavailable to inhabitants of other large ghettos. Those who had money could patronize coffee shops and restaurants and consume luxury items inside the ghetto walls.[109] The health situation was also tolerable. In the Białystok ghetto there were no epidemics of typhus like those that decimated the Jewish population of Warsaw. The generally good state of public health was in part a legacy of two years of Soviet rule. According to one of the ghetto physicians, Dr. Tobia Tzitron, the ghetto had universal health care services, organized on the Soviet model of hospitals, outpatient clinics, and separate sanitary services tasked with disease prevention.[110]

Given an extremely hostile outside world and a rather tolerable existence inside the ghetto, being inside the walls was initially a source of optimism and security. When the ghetto was enclosed, the Jews were happy because they felt protected, recalled Hadasah Levkowitcz.[111] Chaim Mielnicki, who was targeted by Polish nationalists for his collaboration with the Soviets, also felt safe in the ghetto. "[T]he ghetto was self-contained, in the sense that it was exclusively Jewish, and that inside its walls, at least we didn't come in contact with any Polish or Nazi fanatics," he recalled.[112]

As the Jews' food stocks and savings dwindled, the problem of supplementing the rations provided by the Judenrat became increasingly acute. The only solution was to find independent sources of supply. For some, their workplace became such a source. The mother of Celina H. worked as a housekeeper for a German officer. "It was the best possible job" because she was able to bring food to her family in the ghetto. Sometimes people who worked outside the ghetto were able to trade valuables for food.[113]

The majority of those employed in factories did not enjoy such opportunities. For these families the black market became the solution. "Jews needed food, which Poles had; Poles needed goods, which Jews had," aptly summarized Charles Zabuski.[114] The cemetery, located by the ghetto fence, became the main venue for these Polish-Jewish transactions. The increasing demand for food was answered as well by the emergence of groups of smugglers, who made black market activities their main occupation. Some of these were professional criminals who knew the trade. For others, previous contacts with the Polish population came in handy. Interethnic ties were minimal in the city before World War II, so any connections helped and those who could act as brokers between the Jewish and Polish communities found plenty of lucrative business opportunities. Harry Bass knew quite a few Poles in the city and this, he testified, helped him a lot when he snuck out of the ghetto to exchange goods for food.[115] He never considered himself or his family integrated into Polish society, so hiding among the Poles was out of the question, but his contacts were more than sufficient for business. Yekutiel S. was one of the few Białystok Jews who attended a Polish school and therefore spoke good Polish. He made a living engaging in black market activities. Disguised as a Pole, he bought potatoes and firewood at the city market, where they were cheap, and smuggled the products back to the ghetto.[116] Shamai Kizelstein, the son of a city council member under the Poles, exchanged his bicycle for a sack of potatoes and at times was able to sneak hats, which were highly sought after by Polish peasants, out of the ghetto to exchange them for food.[117]

Not surprisingly, many smugglers were Jewish refugees from outside the city. Some engaged in black market activities because they spoke better Polish than most Białystok natives; for others, who were unregistered and "illegal" in the ghetto and therefore could not apply for factory jobs, this was the only possible source of income. Jack R. who came to Białystok from nearby Brańsk and had Polish friends outside the city, used to smuggle food into the ghetto.[118] Charles Zabuski's brother-in-law, a refugee from Warsaw, did not look Jewish and spoke good Polish. Pretending to be a Pole, he snuck out of the ghetto and went to a place where many Polish-Jewish transactions took place. When Poles from the countryside came to the city to trade with the ghetto, he scolded and shamed them for selling food to Jews while Poles were starving. The peasants, ashamed, sold him their produce at a low price.[119] Avraham K. had smuggled himself to the Białystok ghetto from the neighboring town of Tykocin and was therefore "illegal." He was appalled by how badly the refugees were received in the ghetto. "If I only knew how they would receive us there, I might have tried to hide among the non-Jews," he admitted. For him, becoming a smuggler and trading on the black market was the only available way to make a living. "I took risks but I didn't have a choice. It was not hard to get stuff out of the ghetto, it was much harder to smuggle things into the ghetto," he remembered.[120]

Obviously, not every ghetto inhabitant could afford to buy things on the black market, and therefore those who had been wealthy before the war had substantially better chances of not going hungry. The father of Michel Mielnicki owned two buses in interwar Poland and the family had savings, including U.S. dollars. "Amazing stuff, Yankee currency—for one [U.S.] dollar we could buy seven kilos of black market bread or several kilos of potatoes," he remembered. These savings also helped the family after it was sent to the Prużany ghetto. "When suitable work was not available we had our cache of American dollars to fall back on."[121]

This widespread smuggling outraged Barasz, for it compromised the impression he so desperately wanted to create of a compliant, productive, and hard-working ghetto. More than once the Judenrat appealed to the ghetto population to refrain from widespread smuggling, or at least to not provoke the Germans by smuggling what were considered luxury items; the Jewish police also at times went after smugglers. During a town hall meeting with the ghetto public on November 9, 1941, Judenrat member Limon tried to shame other Jews by saying that instead of going to work they went out to do business, and they didn't realize that by doing so they could endanger the ghetto as a whole.[122] To increase the ghetto's productivity, Barasz urged Jews to understand that they were living in extraordinary times. He berated doctors who were willing to grant sick leave: "They claim that anyone who is infected with tuberculosis cannot work. Certainly! But there is a danger here that the man will die not from tuberculosis, but from not working!"[123] None of these efforts helped, because while Barasz and the Judenrat were preoccupied with the long-term survival of the community, the ghetto's inhabitants focused mainly on meeting their most basic and immediate needs.

In addition to the physical risk of being identified on the streets and arrested, or being beaten by German sentries, the smugglers (especially those with legal status in the ghetto) also faced an uneasy trade-off between immediate gain and long-term security. Smuggling brought food and money, while working was perceived as the best insurance policy against deportation. The majority preferred the latter. "It was clear to all that [having a worker ID] was like having permission to live," recalled Eva Kraczowska.[124] Thus, many people exerted great efforts to find employment. Once a group of Jews was recruited to fix a roof, remembered Charles Zabuski. "Never in my life had I held a hammer in my hand and I didn't know anything about roof repair, but the desire to live and sustain my family gave me a burst of courage; I declared myself a roof expert and I forgot to be afraid. I didn't know then that in the years ahead I would preserve my life again and again by claiming to be expert at several other 'careers'."[125]

Not all jobs were created equal, and employment in factories that produced goods considered essential for the German war effort was seen as the surest key to safety. The February 1943 Aktion, during which factory employees were spared, only reinforced this impression. Joe D., who worked as a plumber in the SS building, was not issued an "essential worker" permit and had to hide during the Aktion.[126] Irene S. opened a school in the ghetto and taught kids "everything from Latin to physics." Such a job could not protect her from deportation; she survived the February 1943 Aktion only because her father was a clerk in the Jewish police. After the Aktion, Irene S. immediately got a factory job.[127] As so many ghetto Jews sought employment in factories, the employee rosters soared, but notwithstanding Barasz's efforts to make the ghetto a model of efficiency and diligence, production was as much a show as it was real work. The Jews were not compensated for any additional effort and time, and therefore had every incentive to get a job, but then to work as little as possible. In addition, they also understood perfectly well that appearance was more important than actual output. "We were turning all the machines' engines on when it was needed and when it was not. It was a real festival, just to make an impression that we work really, really hard," testified Kraczowska.[128] Zachary A. also recalled turning on all the machines when the German supervisors visited the factory floor.[129] Some scholars would view these shirking efforts and "weapons of the weak"[130] as passive resistance, but I contend that they were an integral part of the coping strategy and simply helped the Jews to expend as little energy as possible, and not an effort consciously to disrupt German production. There were deliberate sabotage efforts as well, but these I classify as resistance rather than coping.

Employment choices and opportunities, which frequently determined who lived and who perished, often depended on prewar experiences, networks, and ties. Chaim Mielnicki had worked for the Soviet political police from 1939 to 1941. He did not register in the ghetto because he feared that his presence would become known to the Germans or Poles. What saved the Mielnicki family was that Chaim's cousin, Pejsach Mielnicki, was a Judenrat member. Pejsach Mielnicki took care of him, even though he likely disapproved of his relative's collaboration with the communist security services.[131] Shamai Kizelstein looked for a job inside the ghetto. A factory clerk who knew his parents helped him find employment. Bernice S. knew German, and "it came in quite handy.... My knowledge of the Gothic script gave me a job as a secretary.... It was an unusual thing for a Jewish girl" to work as a secretary outside the ghetto, and this allowed Bernice S. to help her family.[132] Yekutiel S. pretended to be a carpenter because his father had a carpentry shop.[133] Zachary A. had studied engineering in a technical university in Danzig and therefore registered as a mechanic. His German boss realized that he was not really a mechanic, but kept him anyway— Zachary A. was his only employee who spoke German.[134]

Indeed, the number of German-speaking ghetto inmates was not large. That, as well as the minimal interactions that took place between Germans and Jews both inside and outside the ghetto, also meant that interpersonal relations between the two groups were much more limited in Białystok than in Minsk and Kraków. Ghetto folklore preserved a story (and eventually a song) about a young Jewish woman, Cesia Wajntraub, who fell in love with a German officer. Wajntraub's lover tried to save her, but was eventually put on trial for this transgression. Emotionally moving though it is, the story is most likely a legend.[135]

Finally, hideouts, an essential component of the coping strategy, were built all over the ghetto. Because escape to the Aryan side was not a viable option in Białystok, the choice ghetto Jews eventually had to make was either to hide or to comply with deportation orders, which in the vast majority of cases meant the gas chamber. During the final liquidation of the ghetto, the Jews mostly complied, but in February 1943 those who could not rely on their factory jobs to protect them from deportation hid. "The most important issue each family faced was to obtain enough food, and the next was to have a place to hide in the event of an Aktion," recalled Luba Olenski.[136] "[T]wenty thousand people in the hideouts—impossible to find them," Mordechai Tenenbaum wrote, describing the February 1943 Aktion. Tenenbaum's Dror movement built one of the largest bunkers in the ghetto. Thirty-five meters long, 1.5 meters wide, and a good 4 meters below the ground, it was equipped with a ventilation system, water, and electricity. "A real catacomb," noted Tenenbaum proudly. Many other hideouts were no less sophisticated. For some, building hideouts became a source of income. Thus, Hashomer Hatzair members built hideouts for rich people in the ghetto and with the money they gained bought weapons from the Poles.[137]

For Abraham O., taking his family to the forest was not an option, so he decided to build a bunker in which they would be able to survive for at least six months. In it they hid during the ghetto liquidation, determined not to go outside no matter what. "We lived like rats in a hole," is how Abraham described life in the bunker.[138] Eva Kraczowska and Jay M.'s family hid from August until November 1943. "We waited until the very last," Jay M. testified, but eventually they could survive no longer in the ghetto, and nothing good awaited them on the Aryan side of the city. They escaped to the partisans.[139] Jay M.'s sister, Selene B., refused to go to the forest and remained in hiding with her mother. They were eventually discovered by an ethic Pole combing the ghetto area for abandoned Jewish valuables and betrayed to the Germans.[140] Liza Shtrauch spent twelve weeks in a hideout, but then was arrested and sent to the Stutthof concentration camp.[141] When hiding became impossible, people preferred to give themselves up rather than go to the Aryan side. "One day I got up in the morning and the house was empty," remembered Esther G.[142] She hid in the attic, but eventually decided to give herself up, and was deported to Auschwitz. For reasons discussed in greater detail in the next chapter, none of those people seriously considered trying to hide among the Poles. When coping inevitably failed, the Jews of Białystok were doomed.

Were there Białystok Jews who opted for compliance? I could not find any testimonies that report such behavior until the final days of the ghetto's existence. There are, in my view, two reasons for this. First, the mass murder of Jews in the city started on the very first day of the occupation, so from the beginning it was clear to all that blind, total, and willful compliance with German orders was very likely to end in death. The second and a more important reason is that from the early stages of German rule, almost absolute control over internal community life was given to the Judenrat. Whereas insubordination against the Germans was feared (even if carried out none-theless), working around rules set up by the internal Jewish leadership was not. A consequence of the Białystok ghetto being a cohesive community was that its inmates, unlike those in Minsk and Kraków, were in no real danger of being turned over by the Jewish police to the Germans for smug-gling, stealing food, or other minor offenses. Transgressions were by and large dealt with internally and leniently, so for individual Jews, breaking and bending rules made absolute sense when the situation required.

The lack of compliance, however, does not mean that compliance was not demanded or expected. As discussed in the previous chapter, the sur-vival strategy adopted by Białystok ghetto Judenrat leader Ephraim Barasz was to make the ghetto indispensable for the German war effort. The vi-ability of this strategy heavily relied on the Jews' willingness to follow or-ders and support Judenrat efforts; any act of insubordination could, poten-tially, make the Germans question the utility of keeping the ghetto intact and its inhabitants alive. Thus compliance was demanded from the Jews by Barasz on more than one occasion. According to the ghetto leader, only by faithfully fulfilling the Germans' and his orders could the local Jews survive the war.

"Our goal is one: to save our souls until the end of war," claimed Barasz during a Judenrat meeting on March 22, 1942. To achieve this goal, the Jews had to "1. Follow the orders one hundred percent; 2. Be useful [to the Germans]; 3. Behave in ways that would satisfy the German authorities."[143] In a meeting with the ghetto population on April 5, 1942, Barasz urged the Jews to "faithfully and entirely fulfill the government demands." When the Jews did not follow the rules, he felt outraged, but was helpless to change the situation. Doing so would have required harming many members of the community he strove to protect.

Because it was extremely hard to survive by faithfully following Ger-man rules and regulations, compliance became the least common survival strategy throughout most of the ghetto's existence. However, on the crucial day of the ghetto's liquidation, August 16, 1943, compliance did become the modal behavior. Even though by then virtually everyone in the ghetto knew about Treblinka and Auschwitz and understood that deportation al-most certainly meant death (see chapter 3), thousands upon thousands of Białystok Jews streamed to the deportation point as ordered. The under-ground hoped that the Jewish masses would revolt, but only a few joined the uprising or tried to hide. The vast majority went quietly to the trains scheduled to take them to the gas chambers.

Why did so many people choose compliance on that fateful day? One reason was the paucity of viable alternatives. As will be discussed in chapter 6, for most people the evasion option was unfeasible. They simply did not have the required looks and social connections. The Aryan side was hostile and unwelcoming. And the option of resistance seemed just as unrealistic.

But even more consequential was the fact that during the two years of the ghetto's existence, its population had become accustomed to relying on Barasz's leadership, guidance, and judgment, even if they occasionally subverted or challenged it at the margins. So when Barasz and the Judenrat ordered the Jews to go, they went. It is quite possible that some went to the deportation point hoping that Barasz would take care of them wherever they might end up, or perhaps they simply felt lost and powerless to do anything else when the Judenrat's grand strategy, for so long believed to be the one right road to survival, collapsed literally overnight. The tragedy was that the relative success of the Judenrat's cooperation with the Germans and the strategy of coping that it promoted inside the ghetto had so mollified the majority of Jews that they were unable to react to the sudden change. In the most tragic moment of the ghetto's existence, Barasz's repeated calls to faithfully comply with all German orders were finally, for the first time, answered by the Jews of Białystok.

Concluding Remarks

This chapter analyzed coping, the most common survival strategy adopted by Jewish victims of the Holocaust, and the intimately related, but substantially less common strategy of compliance. As I showed, coping was anything *but* paralysis and passivity. It required proactive attempts to secure food, employment, and hideouts, and it could sometimes be as dangerous as open resistance. I also tried to demonstrate that even though the majority of Jews engaged in coping, important differences existed in the circumstances under which people would be more likely to adopt the strategy, and in how successful they would be in meeting their coping goals.

These differences, the chapter argued, stemmed from the varying impact of pre-Holocaust political regimes. Prewar politics determined the level of individual Jews' integration into non-Jewish society and support networks, and it affected the strength and cohesion of a city's Jewish community as a whole. In the three ghettos, people who were more plugged-in to intra-ethnic social networks were more likely to adopt coping when the city's entire Jewish community found itself cut off from the external world. Ghetto inmates who before the war were more integrated into non-Jewish society found themselves less able to rely on their prewar support networks, which remained outside the ghetto, and did not have the time, or sometimes the will or ability to establish new, intraethnic ties and relations. For those people, coping was a constant challenge, and their ability to do so successfully inside the ghetto had severe limits.

On the aggregate level, the frequency and strength of interethnic vs. intraethnic ties also shaped the cohesion of the local Jewish community. For the inward-looking, strong, cohesive, and proudly Yiddishist Jewish community of Białystok, coping worked, and worked well, but only temporarily. Had the Germans decided to leave the ghetto intact, coping would have proven a winning strategy. But when Berlin decided to liquidate the ghetto, Jewish Białystok was doomed. For the weaker, more heterogeneous and divided Jewish communities of Minsk and Kraków, coping was an even greater challenge. Some desperate grassroots attempts to recreate the previously strong Jewish community were undertaken in the Minsk ghetto, but it was too little and already too late. Yet when overall survival—rather than successful coping inside the ghetto so long as the Nazis allowed it—is considered, this was not necessarily a bad thing. For the mirror image of coping was evasion, and people who had a hard time coping in the ghetto because they had more Slavic than Jewish ties and friendships were more successful in looking for shelter and salvation outside it. When the coping strategy collapsed in one ghetto after another, the very factors that had made coping so difficult made evasion easier.

This chapter also discussed compliance, which I see as a subcategory of coping. In principle, the compliance strategy was available to the Jews. They could have quietly and submissively followed the Germans' orders, in the hope that such behavior would keep them alive. In practice, however, very few Jews voluntarily adopted this strategy, because it was apparent from an early stage that submissiveness and compliance were likely to lead to death. People who had previous exposure to German power were more likely to comply, but even among these individuals compliance was not common when alternatives were available. Compliance, the evidence from the three ghettos shows, was adopted chiefly when other strategies were seen as or became unfeasible, as in the case of some German Jews in the Minsk ghetto or during the Białystok ghetto's final liquidation. More common and reasonable as an initial strategy during the first days of the war when the Germans' intentions and behavior were unclear, it became increasingly untenable.

Those who passively complied stood no chance of survival in the ghettos. Contrary to early scholars' descriptions, passivity and paralysis were rare. Active coping, not passive obedience, was route that most Jews took. Still, the analysis of compliance is extremely important both empirically and theoretically. For if we want to understand why the Jews chose particular behavioral strategies, it is crucial to look also at what they *could* have done, but in the vast majority of cases did not do.

CHAPTER 6

EVASION

Israel G., a Jew, no longer existed. Instead, there was Vasilii Donets, an ethnic Ukrainian. That Vasilii Donets was circumcised, fluent in Yiddish, and had family in Palestine was irrelevant. The only thing that mattered was the ethnicity inscribed in his new, fake ID papers. His mother had it easier. Her name—Alexandra—was ethnically neutral; not a deadly giveaway like "Israel," and could remain a part of her new identity. A woman, she also did not have to fear the so-called "trousers test." With new documents and fluent, unaccented Russian and Ukrainian, the Donets' could now make a run for their lives from the dying Khmel'nik ghetto. Alexandra and Israel G. were not the only Jews who chose this option. This chapter explores the evasion strategy—an attempt to escape persecution by hiding, emigrating, or assuming a false identity.

* * *

We will never know how many Jews chose evasion, which I define as an attempt to escape persecution by leaving the community: hiding outside the ghetto walls, immigrating, or assuming a false identity. Even for relatively well-documented and researched Warsaw, the estimated number of Jews who went into hiding ranges, depending on the study, between 5,000 and 50,000.[1] For Poland as a whole, notes Grabowski, "historians agree today that close to ten percent of the . . . Polish Jews who survived until the summer of 1942 tried to escape extermination."[2] That there were Jews who tried to escape is intuitive, yet we are still left with several puzzles. Why did only 10 rather than 100 percent choose evasion, even when it became clear that the Nazis were engaged in systematic, total slaughter? Which factors made a person more or less likely to opt for evasion? And finally, was evasion a strategy equally distributed across different communities; and if not, what explains the variation?

Writing in 1943–44 from his hiding place outside the Warsaw ghetto, the Polish-Jewish historian Emmanuel Ringelblum was the first scholar to analyze the phenomenon in which he himself took part.[3] Ringelblum's data were inherently limited, but his observations on evasion are illuminating. The first and most important thing Ringelblum and subsequent analysts agree on is that escape from the ghetto was risky but feasible, and that there were numerous ways for Jews to move to the Aryan side. This was true for the Warsaw ghetto with its high brick wall, and even more so for the open ghettos where no physical barriers existed.[4] What bedeviled successful evasion was not the act of escape, dangerous though it was, but the perceived chances of survival after escape.

The second point on which scholars agree is that despite entire libraries of racial pseudo-scholarship produced by numerous Nazi pseudo-scientists, in Eastern Europe the Germans could not visually tell a Jew from a non-Jew.[5] Only the local population could identify evading Jews. Unfortunately—and this is a third point of agreement among researchers—wartime Polish and, to a somewhat lesser extent, Soviet societies were at best indifferent, and at worst hostile to the plight of their Jewish citizens. The exact nature of popular attitudes is still hotly debated. What is clear, however, is that the majority of Slavs, even if they did not approve of the Nazi genocide, did nothing to assist the Jews. Some were sympathetic to the Jewish plight and may have wanted to help, but they were deterred by the death penalties meted out to captured helpers. And at both ends of the distribution were the numerically small groups of those who actively tried to help or harm.

"Danger lurks at every step," wrote Ringelblum. "The landlords, smelling a Jew in every new subtenant . . . the gas and electricity account collector; next, the manager and the porter of the block, a neighbor, etc.—all these constitute a danger for the Jew" because they, unlike the Germans, could recognize a Jew and denounce her to the police.[6] In the vast majority of cases, if an evading Jew was discovered and caught by the authorities she was as good as dead.

People who tried to harm Jews did so for a number of reasons. Some were driven by ideological anti-Semitism. Others might not act against Jews as a group, but would denounce a specific person with whom they had a conflict. Still others were driven by purely economic motivations, seeing Jews as legitimate, convenient, and defenseless prey. A whole new profession of *szmalcownik* (pl. *szmalcownicy*) emerged in wartime Poland. They were street-level blackmailers who would identify hiding Jews, threaten to denounce them to the authorities, and take all their belongings. When Jews did not or could not pay, they were indeed routinely denounced. So widespread was this new trade that almost all the Warsaw Jews who tried to hide reported

encounters with the *szmalcownicy*.[7] The situation for Jews attempting evasion was similar in other cities. In the countryside, peasants would organize
a Jew-hunt (*Judenjagd*), seeking out and murdering hiding Jews, and taking
their belongings.[8] Jews who chose evasion were constantly traumatized and
felt haunted, lonely, and isolated.[9] According to survivors' testimonies, quite
a few were convinced that he or she was the last Jew in Europe.

At the other end of the spectrum were those who helped the Jews in their
quest for evasion. This was an extremely high-risk behavior, and scholars'
fascination with it became so intense that for decades the study of evasion
essentially became an analysis of rescuers. People who put the lives of their
entire families at risk to shelter and help hidings Jews were celebrated—and
deservedly so—in popular and historical writings. In Poland, they are still
often pointed to, cynically, to fend off criticism of Polish society's wartime
attitude toward the Jews. But the outcome of this focus was, inevitably, a
biased analysis of the supply side of rescue among non-Jews that paid little
regard to the actual demand for evasion among the Jews. Political scientist Kristen Renwick Monroe argues that rescuers were driven by moral
beliefs, ideological commitments, and an all-inclusive, universalist vision
of humankind.[10] Similarly, psychologist Eva Fogelman links the decision
to help the Jews to rescuers' values.[11] In Philip Friedman's *Their Brothers'
Keepers*, people who saved the Jews were driven predominantly by Christian morality and the belief that Jews and Christians were brethren.[12] Some
undoubtedly were, but new research that looks at the whole spectrum of
rescuers' behavior concludes that money, rather than altruism, was key.[13]
Jews in hiding were willing to pay, unlikely to complain, and if necessary,
easily disposed of. It is true that sheltering Jews was often punished with the
death penalty, but so were other types of behavior, such as participating in
the black market or resisting, in which, unlike in helping the Jews, the Poles
engaged in large numbers.[14]

Sociologist Nechama Tec offers a more nuanced explanation in which
rescue was determined by a combination of factors that varied from one
Nazi-occupied country to another: the level of German control over the
government apparatus; Nazi racial hierarchies that determined the treatment of local non-Jewish population by the Germans; the size of the Jewish
population; and the level of Jews' integration into the broader society.[15] Yet,
this macro-level explanation cannot explain noticeable in-country variation
in rescue and evasion patterns. Moreover, while rescue and the analysis of
rescuers are an important part of the story, the evasion phenomenon is complicated, and to fully understand it we should focus on the behavior and the
choices of the Jews, rather than their helpers.

A combination of factors determined both a Jew's likelihood of seeking the evasion strategy and the specific type of evasion she chose to pursue. Evading Jews could live "on the surface," pretending to be non-Jews, or they could go into hiding, sheltered by a non-Jew outside the ghetto.[16] Being above the ground, argued Ringelblum, required skills and features that would ensure the Jew's ability to successfully pass as a non-Jew. First, she needed money to purchase fake identity papers. Second, she needed to have a "good," that is, not typically Jewish, external appearance. Third, she had to have the ability to pass as a non-Jew culturally, behaviorally, and linguistically. Since very few Jews, the argument went, were lucky enough to possess this winning combination of money, appearance, and language proficiency, the "majority of Jews on the Aryan side [remained] 'under the surface.'"[17] Being hidden by a non-Jew most often also required money, and sometimes substantially more than being "on the surface," as well as the right social ties to find a person who would provide shelter. Therefore, it was perceived that, in the words of Antek Zuckerman, one of the leaders of the Warsaw ghetto underground, only "Jews with money, rich Jews who could pay; and, on the other hand, intellectuals who had contacts with the good Polish intelligentsia" could find shelter on the Aryan side.[18] Fearing blackmail, denunciation, and certain death, the majority of Jews were simply too scared to attempt the evasion option.[19] Quantitative analysis of evasion also supports the argument that fear and the lack of contacts prevented evasion. Varese and Yaish argue that a key component of successful evasion was directly asking for help.[20] Tammes, in a study of the Amsterdam Jewish community demonstrates that people who had closer contacts to non-Jews were more likely to evade deportation.[21]

This chapter does not disprove the above-mentioned explanations, but it does challenge some conventional wisdoms. Unfortunately, previous writings on the topic draw their conclusions from either an assortment of anecdotes and stories from all over Nazi-controlled Eastern Europe (with a heavy emphasis on Poland)[22] or from detailed in-depth studies of a single community, most often Warsaw.[23] My approach is different. By comparing evasion patterns in the three ghettos, this chapter will determine if the explanations offered above apply equally across different localities. It will also analyze which factors were the most important in contributing to the decision to evade.

If Monroe, Fogelman, and Friedman are right and Jews were indeed helped because of the *rescuers'* personality traits, psychology, and humanistic worldviews, then we should not observe any noticeable patterns in who exactly was rescued and sheltered. Tec's country-level argument precludes major differences in evasion and rescue patterns between Kraków and Białystok.

If money were paramount, then evasion should be restricted to financially better-off Jews. If, as Zuckerman argued, evasion depended on close contacts with the Polish intelligentsia, then people with lower levels of education and nonprofessionals would have had little to no chance of hiding.

Yet the chapter will show that one did not have to be rich or highly educated to have social ties with non-Jews or to be fluent in Russian, Polish, or Belorussian. The rescuers, even if guided by altruism, tended to help Jews they knew personally. It is unclear if they would have gone to the same lengths to help complete strangers. Money and a "good" appearance were indeed important aids to evasion, but it was possible to compensate for their lack. The most crucial factors—related but not identical—were the ability to pass as a non-Jew culturally and linguistically, and prewar social relations with non-Jews. These abilities, the chapter will argue, were shaped by the pre-Holocaust regimes under which each of the three cities lived. Pre–World War II politics and state policies in the areas of education, housing, and employment determined the degree of Jews' integration into broader society and the extent of interethnic relations in each community. Where governments allowed and promoted ethnically mixed schools, neighborhoods, workplaces, and political parties, the result was a more thorough integration of Jews into the society. This integration inevitably led to constant, even if not always very close contacts between Jews and non-Jews and created interethnic social networks that could later be mobilized for successful evasion. Granovetter's seminal work demonstrates that "weak ties," such as those formed in the workplace or through business and school contacts, provided people with invaluable opportunities for acquiring various benefits and reduced "interracial distance."[24] The more interethnic weak ties a person had, the higher their likelihood of choosing evasion. Conversely, a lack of interethnic social networks coupled with strong intraethnic networks allowed for easier coping (see chapter 5), but virtually precluded evasion.

The chapter will also show that existing arguments often overlook physical factors that affected escape, such as the community's geographic location, in particular its proximity to borders, forests, and frontlines. The adoption (if not always the success) of the evasion strategy was first and foremost a function of human and physical geography.

Minsk

According to Hersh Smolar, the leader of the ghetto underground, approximately ten thousand Jews escaped the Minsk ghetto, mainly to Soviet partisans' detachments in the forests. There were two ways to make it to the forest—in an organized fashion with a partisan guide, or on one's own, without knowing where the partisans were or whether they would be willing to let escapees join the unit. The Minsk ghetto was surrounded only by barbed wire, so escape, even if very risky and often lethal, was nonetheless somewhat easier than in Białystok or Kraków, which were enclosed by a fence and a wall, respectively. As in other ghettos, the main problem was not the act of escape itself, but survival afterward. Here, prewar factors and social networks came into play.

The presence of Soviet partisans in the forests around Minsk was common knowledge. According to Abram Rubenchik, "in the Minsk ghetto there was no household in which people did not talk about Staroe Selo, Lisovshchina, and Skirmontovo"—the villages in the so-called Partisans' Zone that were closest to the city.[25] No less universal was the expectation, initially at least, that as Soviet citizens Minsk Jews would be admitted and protected by the partisans. The reality did not always match these expectations. Driven sometimes by anti-Semitism, sometimes by dispatches from Moscow that claimed the Germans were using Jews as spies, and sometimes simply by the fear that women and children would hinder mobility and fighting capacity, many partisan commanders were wary of allowing Jews to join their units.[26] Yet Jews kept flocking to the forests because, anti-Semitism notwithstanding, the majority were eventually admitted. Being with the partisans significantly increased the likelihood of survival.

Successful escape required either established connections with the partisans and the ability to convince them to let one join the unit (usually by coming to the forest armed or with supplies the partisans needed) or, as an alternative, being able to survive outside the ghetto without the partisans' protection. In the areas in and around Minsk, which the Germans controlled, a Jew's ability to survive outside the ghetto depended first and foremost on how well he or she could hide their Jewish identity from the *local* population. "When I started leaving the ghetto I always removed the patch," testified Anatolii Rubin. "I wasn't afraid of Germans—not that I wasn't scared, but they just didn't recognize me as a Jew; they couldn't tell a Jew from non-Jew . . . but I've always avoided encounters with Russians and Byelorussians, because often immediately after they saw me they started screaming 'A kike! A kike!' (*Zhid! Zhid!*)."[27]

Passing as a non-Jew required certain traits. First, people who did not physically "look Jewish" had a better chance of evading enemies. A Belorussian family hid Anna S.'s cousin—she had blue eyes and did not look Jewish, so they agreed to take her in. Sima Margolina used to sneak out of the ghetto, remove her yellow patch, and simply roam the streets. One day she met an old woman who instructed Sima to follow her. "I see that you are Jewish," the woman told Margolina. "You will go with me, child. I will save you. But remember, [don't tell] anyone that you are Jewish. Not even to my husband Kuz'ma. He might, if drunk, say something. Don't tell anything to anyone, just forget who you are. . . . You don't look like a Jew—you have blue eyes, I will save you."[28] Thus, Margolina's successful evasion was possible not only because of her rescuer's attitudes, but also thanks to her non-Jewish appearance. But looking non-Jewish was not enough, one also had to blend in with the local population. "In the 'Russian area' one should be properly dressed and with a haircut," wrote Berta Bruk.[29] For people who had escaped the starvation and torment of the ghetto, a dignified appearance was not always easy to achieve. Bleaching one's hair was also popular, recalled Nina Shalit-Galperin.[30] To some extent, gender also affected one's ability to pass. It was harder for boys to pass as non-Jews, even if they had non-Jewish looks, because many male Jewish children were circumcised. At the same time, this problem was less widespread in Minsk than in Poland. Under Soviet rule, many Minsk Jews had become secular to the point of not circumcising their male offspring,[31] while in Poland even the most assimilated Jews tended to circumcise their sons. That he was not circumcised saved Boris Kukhta's life because, when he tried to register as a Belorussian, the clerk demanded that he remove his pants.[32]

Slavic appearance was an advantage, but neither a necessary nor sufficient condition for successful evasion. Social skills, such as a flawless command of Russian, or, even better, Belorussian, were more important. Those who spoke Russian, even fluent and grammatically flawless Russian, with a Yiddish accent, were in danger of being discovered every time they opened their mouths. Here, people who were educated in Russian or Belorussian rather than Jewish schools had an advantage. Lazar T. had studied in a Belorussian school and spoke very good Belorussian. This, he admitted, helped him a great deal outside the ghetto.[33] Sima Margolina, in addition to her Slavic looks, was also fluent in Belorussian, which helped her in the village where she was taken by the elderly woman. And two decades of violently secular, communist rule meant that younger people were not expected to know religious traditions and prayers, which made passing as a non-Jew much easier than in thoroughly religious Poland. Speaking the local language was often enough.

Finally, a fake ID was needed. The son of Rubin's father's ethnically German[34] friend found a wallet with the passport and birth certificate of a Slavic man named Stepanov and gave it to Rubin.[35] The combination of a passport, a "good" appearance, and flawless Russian allowed Rubin to survive the Holocaust passing as non-Jew even though he was circumcised. The ability to get a non-Jewish passport depended not only on the person's non-Jewish appearance. Connections and interethnic networks, usually an outcome of growing up, studying, working, or participating in political organizations alongside non-Jews—all policies promoted by the Soviet regime—were more important. Asja T. was well integrated into non-Jewish society. She had graduated from a Russian-language school; her older sister was married to an ethnic Russian; and her brother had a Russian girlfriend. After a year in the ghetto, Asja T.'s prewar Russian neighbor managed to get her a certificate stating that her house had burned down, meaning that she did not have any documents. With blond hair and the certificate, she was able to successfully pass as a non-Jew.[36] Toward the end of the war she was sent to Germany as a Belorussian forced laborer and survived. Sophia Fridland's survival story is similar. Her prewar friend gave her a birth certificate with which she was able to leave the ghetto and eventually go to work in Berlin, where no prewar acquaintance could recognize her as a Jew.[37] Daria Dadasheva's friend was a painter and forged her non-Jewish ID papers.[38] Valentina Svoyatytskaia looked Jewish, but she had many non-Jewish friends who helped her obtain a fake passport and hide when needed.[39]

For children, having a non-Jewish nanny—yet another indicator of the family's integration into non-Jewish society and its participation in interethnic social networks—often turned out to be lifesaving. Yakov Etinger, the son of a prominent physician, was hidden by his nanny. The night before November 7, 1941 Aktion, Etinger's nanny snuck into the ghetto, told the family that German troops were surrounding the area, and convinced them to escape and hide with her relatives. Later, Etinger's mother contacted a prewar friend, a Belorussian, and with his assistance managed to get a new passport, which stated that Etinger was his nanny's son, and therefore, a Belorussian as well. With this passport, he escaped and went to live with his nanny.[40] Raisa Ledvich was also hidden by her Belorussian nanny, Antonia Zhur.[41]

Those who could not or did not want to live as non-Jews or hide outside the ghetto had only one option if they wanted to escape—to flee to the partisans in the forests. Pre-Holocaust relations were also crucial to this strategy. Vera B. left the ghetto for the partisans' zone without any connections with the underground. No unit was willing to take her in; the partisans would take in unarmed males, but not females. However, in one unit she met a person she knew from her university studies. This person helped her to stay—and she was later taken to a safe area.[42] Lazar T. and his father escaped to the area where their family had lived before moving to Minsk. "Dad asked around, and after a couple of hours we were in the partisan unit."[43]

Many wanted to escape, but could not do so because they had to take care of small children. Khasia Pruslina, an underground member, went to college with a certain Orlov, who worked in the education department of the city administration. The underground contacted Orlov and he agreed to provide Jewish children with faked documents and to enroll them in orphanages outside the ghetto. The underground even had a special group that coordinated activities to save children.[44] One of the children placed in the orphanage was Pruslina's own daughter. For the child, this was an opportunity to survive, while it enabled Pruslina to devote herself entirely to underground work.[45] Katya Tokarski decided to leave her daughter Valentina, who did not look Jewish and spoke proper Russian, on the Aryan side no matter what.[46] Valentina survived, sheltered by the Gromovs, a Belorussian couple. When the Gromovs heard rumors that the Germans were going to search their neighborhood for hidden Jewish children, they escaped to the partisans where Valentina's adoptive father was killed in a firefight with the Germans.

For those who had no underground connections, getting to the partisans was not an easy task. Although most people knew about the underground, only a few were able to contact it.[47] Moisei Gorelik and his friends lacked the necessary contacts. They escaped the ghetto, wandered the countryside looking for the partisans, and were forced to return when they found none.[48] Gorelik's story is anything but exceptional. A number of testimonies mention people who tried to reach the partisans but either could not find them or were not admitted to a unit and had to return to the ghetto. Esfir Movshenson wanted to escape but had no idea how to go about leaving.[49] "Everyone thought only about how to escape to the partisans to stay alive," recalled Vera S.,[50] but not everyone had the ability to reach them.

Some, knowing that partisans were more likely to admit people who came to the forest with weapons, did everything they could to arm themselves. Others tried to obtain additional things that the partisans might need or want. After her uncle escaped to them, Nina Shalit-Galperin started looking for ways to get herself to the forest. "Anyone who had connections escaped," she claimed. A person she met in the ghetto told her that if she brought a pair of leather jackboots to the partisans' commander she would be admitted to the unit. She immediately purchased the boots on the black market.[51] Raisa Khasenyevich came to the forest with a typewriter.[52] Vera B. stole salt at her workplace and smuggled it into the ghetto. With the money she hoped to buy a grenade.[53] But even in these circumstances, social connections could compensate for a lack of proper underground credentials, weapons, or needed merchandise. Berta and Lialia Bruk were able to get to the partisans because their former maid worked for the underground. Although unarmed, they were admitted.[54] Reuven Liond, a refugee from Poland, was admitted because he was from the same small town as one of the partisans' couriers.

Many, unable to get what the partisans needed, gave up on the idea. "I didn't have the connections that would help me to join," wrote Rakhil' Rappoport.[55] Others were saved by a stroke of pure luck. Leonid Okun' was charged with leading people linked to the underground to the partisans. Once he was told by his commander to get a certain Dr. Lifshits out of the ghetto. Okun', however, made a fatal mistake, and instead of Dr. Lifshits, a male surgeon, he brought Dr. Lifshits, a female gynecologist. This mistake saved the "wrong" Dr. Lifshits and her family, but it cost Okun's mother, sister, and her family their lives. Okun' had planned to bring them to the forest, but his commander was angry with him and refused to even discuss the issue. When Okun' finally got the commander's permission, he discovered that his family was no longer alive—someone had tipped off the Germans about Okun's resistance activism and they had been executed.[56] The situation improved when Jewish partisans' detachments, especially Unit 106 under the command of Shalom Zorin, were established. Zorin's unit had a family camp where Jewish women, children, and elderly people were housed, and where no one was turned down due to their inability to procure weapons or other desirable goods.

Unlike their Soviet coethnics, German Jews could not pass as Slavs or rely on non-Jewish contacts in the city, and therefore only a handful chose evasion. Realizing that he could not hide in Minsk, Fred Alexander, who worked at the city's railroad station, decided to return to Germany. With the help of a friendly German railroad official, who gave him a swastika-adorned armband, Alexander jumped on a Reich-bound train with wounded soldiers. He managed to reach Berlin and eventually ended up in Switzerland.[57] Escapes to the partisans were also extremely rare. We know of only five cases of attempted escapes from the Hamburg ghetto to the partisans. Two were thwarted and the outcome of a third is unknown, but the remaining two were successful.[58] In one case, a Jew from Czechoslovakia was able, with the help of the underground, to join the partisans. Unlike most residents of the Hamburg ghetto, he knew a Slavic language and therefore could communicate with the locals, even if only in a limited way. The second, an extremely unusual case of successful escape, is the story of Ilse Stein.

It begins with forty-six-year-old Captain Willi Schultz, who supervised Jewish workers in the former Soviet Belorussian Government House, which during the war housed various German military offices. Hayim Bar'am, a Jew from Berlin who worked under Schultz, described him as an anti-Semitic sadist;[59] Raisa Gitlina also described Schultz as an anti-Semite.[60] Elizaveta (Lea) Gutkovich, a Soviet Jew who worked in the Government House boiler room, mentioned being beaten by Schultz.[61] One day, after an Aktion in the "Russian" part of the ghetto, a group of German Jews began working in the Government House. "Schultz went to look at [the] German Jews, and suddenly stopped by one young woman and shook her hand," recalled Gutkovich. "And I think to myself: 'That has never happened before—Schultz shaking hands with a Jew.'" Gutkovich, who spoke German, befriended the young woman, eighteen-year-old Ilse Stein from Frankfurt. Shortly after that Schulz assigned Stein to oversee German Jews, while Gutkovich was put in charge of the Soviet Jews as Stein's deputy.

Eventually, Schultz admitted to Gutkovich that he was in love with Ilse and wanted to save her. When Schultz's friend, a military pilot and a former communist, came to Minsk, it was suggested that they should all cross the front line and fly to Moscow. The plan fell through when the pilot was sent to the front line. In 1943, after Stalingrad, Schultz assigned Gutkovich to listen to Soviet radio broadcasts and translate them for him. Unfortunately, a Gestapo agent caught Gutkovich listening to the radio. This was an offense punishable by death, so Gutkovich decided to immediately escape to the partisans with the help of another coworker, a Belorussian who had connections to the underground. Realizing that he would not be able to save Ilse alone, Schultz asked Gutkovich to take him and Ilse with her. Working with the underground, Gutkovich and Schultz were able to arrange a truck, weapons, and permission for a group of Jews to leave the ghetto in order to load coal at a train station near Minsk. The next day a German officer and twenty-five Jews escaped to the partisans. From there, Schultz and Stein were taken to Moscow. Several months after that Schultz died, to the best of our knowledge after contracting meningitis.[62] Stein and most of the people who escaped with her survived. Her story, no matter how captivating, is much the exception. For almost all other Hamburg ghetto Jews, the evasion option was unavailable. They lacked contacts, did not know the area, and, because they did not speak Russian, could not even ask villagers for directions to the partisans.

A more general question that arises from the massive scale of escapes to the partisans is whether such an act should be more properly described as resistance, rather than evasion. As I demonstrate in this chapter, and will show further in chapter 7, there were two primary types of people who escaped to the partisans: those for whom escape to the forest was a continuation of their anti-Nazi struggle in the ghetto, and those who had not previously been in the underground. The second group escaped to the forest primarily because they perceived it to be their best chance for survival. They also tended to escape later, in late 1942 and 1943, when partisan units were already well organized and controlled large swaths of territory in the forests surrounding Minsk. While many of these people fought German troops after being admitted to partisan units, fighting Germans was an *outcome* of their flight to the forest, rather than its motivation. Instructive in this regard are the ways in which Minsk ghetto survivors discuss revenge.

Former members of the underground and partisan groups frequently invoke revenge as an impetus for action in testimonies and memoirs. Yet an important distinction exists within this group: people who had been active in the underground often cited the desire to avenge the destruction of their family, friends, and the Jewish community as their reason for joining the partisans; people who were not involved in the ghetto underground often reference revenge as a factor in their narratives only after they joined the partisans. For them, survival and evasion were the key motivators; the desire for revenge, even if important, arose only later, when an opportunity to exact it unexpectedly became a reality. This distinction, however, should be taken with a grain of salt—it is possible that underground members wished to underscore this particular aspect of their activities, and that both the desire to fight and the desire to survive were in fact equally compelling. At the same time, when people say that they escaped first and foremost to survive, thus minimizing the heroism of their actions, they may be doing so out of humility.

For the Jewish partisans revenge meant killing as many Germans as possible. Killing German soldiers in combat blended revenge with military necessity; the vengeance component was most explicitly manifested in partisans' treatment of German POWs. German soldiers, when captured, often begged for mercy, sometimes showing photographs of their wives and children. This strategy usually backfired, with devastating consequences for the luckless captives, for often the Jewish partisans they confronted were the only survivors in their entire families, and the Germans' actions aroused resentment in them rather than compassion. A German POW's fate was especially bleak if he was taken prisoner by a purely Jewish group. In Zorin's Jewish partisan unit, Germans were "torn to pieces, beaten to death. We didn't even waste a bullet on them," admitted Leonid Okun'.[63] When Arkadii Krasinskii's unit ambushed a Belorussian collaborationist police patrol and captured a German soldier who accompanied them, a partisan who had lost a wife and three children in the ghetto grabbed a saw and literally took the German apart.[64] "We tore them to pieces (*na kuski razorvali*), kicked them to death," recalled Moisei Gorelik.[65] Jewish police servicemen who worked for the notorious Special Operations Unit (see chapter 4) were killed as well. Rank-and-file Jewish police who were not known as avid collaborators were generally spared.

At the same time, survivors rarely talk about the revenge they exacted on Belorussians who had mistreated, deceived, or betrayed them. After liberation, Boris Kukhta came, armed with a grenade, to the house of a person who tried to denounce him to the Germans, but in the last moment Kukhta decided not to kill him.[66] Leonid Okun's desire for revenge was especially fierce. Okun' had once been deceived by a Belorussian family that gave him whitewash instead of flour in exchange for boots. Later, his mother gave all the valuables that the family still had to a Belorussian woman who promised to lead Okun', still a child, to the partisans. The women took the boy into the forest and abandoned him there. Luckily, a partisan patrol stumbled upon him. After the liberation in 1944, Okun', fifteen years old by that time, insisted on joining the Red Army and became the youngest Soviet soldier to be twice decorated with one of the highest Soviet military honors—the Order of Glory.[67] He returned from combat with a clear intention to shoot the people who had mistreated him, but they were gone. When he was interviewed for the WWII veterans' testimonies project in 2007, Okun' was still upset that while he was able to exact his revenge on the Germans, the Belorussian offenders went unpunished. Okun's story also highlights an observation made earlier in this section—that escaping to the partisans on one's own, without underground connections, was an extremely costly and risky endeavor. Okun' survived by luck. Many others did not.

Kraków

The exact number of Kraków Jews who escaped or tried to escape Nazi persecution is difficult to estimate, but the qualitative evidence suggests that the evasion strategy was widespread in that city's ghetto, probably more so than in any other large city in Poland. The main reasons for this were Kraków's proximity to the Slovak and Hungarian borders and, more importantly, the city's historically higher levels of Jewish integration into and contacts with non-Jewish society. In this context, however, it is important to stress that integration does not necessarily imply assimilation; in Kraków, even the most religious Jews spoke Polish and often sent their children to state schools, all the while ostensibly clinging to their traditions, ways of life, and even to the external marks of Jewish appearance, such as beards, sidelocks, and traditional garb. Relatively few Jews in the city had strong family or friendship ties with ethnic Poles, but the number of those who had many "weak ties," the kind usually formed in business and educational settings, was substantial.

As discussed in chapters 2 and 3, evasion among Kraków Jews, especially males, began in the first days of World War II. Most escapees tried to reach Lwów, the other major urban center in Galicia, which in the meantime had been occupied by the Soviet Union. To their dismay, the refugees found living conditions under the Soviets quite harsh. "Streets were full of aimless refugees from the west. Every step of the way I met friends from Krakow [sic] who were completely lost and didn't know what to do with themselves," recalled Maria Epstein, herself a Kraków refugee.[68] "No food, no supplies, and only the pictures of Stalin everywhere," recalled Al B.[69]

Not surprisingly, when in 1940 the Soviet authorities announced that those who had come to Kraków from German-occupied Poland could register to return to their homes, numerous Jews immediately jumped at the opportunity. The problem was that the Germans were less than enthusiastic about admitting more Jews to the territories they controlled, and they did all they could to block the Jews' return. The Soviets, at the same time, viewed those who preferred German rule over their communist paradise as potential, if not actual traitors. The refugees' predicament was subsequently solved in a typically Soviet manner—most were deported to Siberia and Central Asia, where the majority survived the war. Some, however, managed to smuggle themselves back to Kraków. Celina R.'s grandfather "paid a fortune" to bring the family back. "It was a big mistake, but we didn't know that yet," she recalled.[70] The mother of Aneta W. pretended to be an ethnic German seeking repatriation. Hers was an extremely dangerous course of action, but it was also her only chance to get back home.[71] Victor P. managed to obtain false identification papers and simply boarded a train to Kraków. His main fear was that fellow passengers might recognize him as a Jew. The solution he found was as bold as it was simple—being a graduate of a Polish (rather than Jewish) school, Victor P. knew all the anti-Semitic slogans and started proclaiming "anti-Semitic propaganda" on the train. People applauded him, and he got to Kraków safely.[72]

Escape to Soviet-occupied areas was common, but it was not the only way to evade Nazi persecution. Many Kraków Jews tried to leave Poland altogether. This option, however, was available mainly to people who had either the means or the exceptional connections to do so. Joseph Hollander owned a travel agency, so when the war started he was able quickly to obtain a Romanian transit visa and escape to Italy. From there, via Portugal, he and his wife reached New York. Hollander's next task was to rescue the rest of his family. Initially, the family tried to get to the United States. "Many people have registered themselves for emigration overseas. In order not to blame ourselves later we are thinking about doing the same," Hollander's brother-in-law wrote him in August 1940. Some family members even began taking English-language lessons.[73] When they registered for immigration to the United States, however, the waiting list numbers (not to be confused with immigration quota numbers) they received were 43,711 and 43,712, meaning that years would pass before they would even be considered for inclusion in the immigration quota list.[74] The United States was a coveted destination, but the desire to escape Poland was so great that any country would do. When Hollander managed, through his travel agency connections, to provide his relatives with Nicaraguan travel papers, they were ecstatic. It mattered little that they knew next to nothing about Nicaragua. A week after receiving the documents they were still trying "to locate the place on the map" and had been "consulting the dictionary to learn about the language and the people."[75] Unfortunately, the German authorities did not allow the family to exit Poland, and all of them perished. Yitzhak Ganani's father thought of purchasing Guatemalan passports, but nothing came of the idea.[76] Thirteen-year-old Yisrael Buchbinder had also heard stories about people going to South America and in the middle of the journey changing their destination to Palestine, so he started a hunger strike at home demanding that his father obtain a South American country's travel documents.[77]

Zipporah S.'s family happened to have Turkish passports—many years before the war the family had moved to Poland from Turkey. However, the passports were no longer valid and could not protect them in Poland, so the family decided to leave the country altogether. The grandparents, hoping that Turkish documents, even if expired, would help them to cross the border simply boarded a bus bound for Hungary. They were stopped on the border and shot. The rest of the family then decided to cross the border on foot with a local guide, and they succeeded in evading German border patrols.[78]

As the venues for legal immigration were extremely limited and constantly shrinking, most people who crossed the border did so illegally. This was an extremely risky undertaking that required, in addition to courage, considerable amounts of money or connections with the right people, or preferably both. Celina S. had a Polish friend who helped her obtain false Polish papers. Another friend of her father's assisted her in illegally crossing the border to Slovakia. Then, through Hungary and Romania, she managed to get to Palestine in 1944, when the war was still in full swing.[79] After his father was arrested by German authorities and sent to a camp, Leon K. made an (ultimately unsuccessful) attempt to smuggle his mother and sister to Hungary. He could do this because his father had left the family considerable amounts of money.[80] Louise J., discussing her relatives' attempt to smuggle themselves to Hungary, mentioned that they could do so only because they had the money.[81] Chana Barsuk's family also escaped to Hungary with the help of money and Polish friends.[82]

Those who could not escape the Nazis altogether had to devise other strategies. In Kraków, as in other places, to successfully hide among the Poles one had to have at least some money to pay for false documents, and preferably an appearance and habits that were not too Jewish. A shortage of money or Jewish looks could, however, be compensated for by prewar ties with sympathetic Poles. These were absolutely crucial, because people who went into hiding outside the ghetto would have to rely on preexisting social ties and networks. In Kraków interethnic social networks were more common than in virtually all of the other major cities in Poland, with the result that the evasion strategy had greater appeal there than elsewhere.

False documents were not cheap, and their quality varied greatly. For that reason, the more affluent a family was, the better their chances of acquiring "good" documents. Yet this was not a fool-proof strategy—for even very costly and well-forged documents could sometimes present those who carried them with problems. Some were purely aesthetic, and, given the stakes, trivial: Miriam Peleg recalls a Jewish woman who felt deeply offended when she got an ID with the surname Zając, "hare" in Polish.[83] Irene F. obtained a birth certificate and high school transcript with the name Danuta Milewska. "It bothered me that [Milewska] was an F-student," she recalled.[84]

Other problems were more substantial. For example, some legitimately Polish surnames sounded too similar to Jewish ones and therefore put the people who used them in unnecessary danger. Some places of birth, initially quite popular, eventually became too dangerous to be put on a fake ID. Before the German invasion of the USSR it was considered a wise strategy to list Eastern Poland as one's place of birth on fake documents. The logic was that if people who carried these IDs were arrested as suspected Jews, it would be impossible to check the local archives, which were now in the Soviet occupation zone. This strategy became useless after the German invasion of the USSR in June 1941; now people who were supposedly born somewhere in Ukraine or Belarus were exposed to a double danger—the veracity of their documents could be checked against the originals in local archives, and their level of knowledge about their supposed birthplaces could be easily tested.[85]

Money was not the only means of obtaining false documents; ties to friendly Poles were a safer and cheaper way. The parents of Victor P.'s ethnically Polish classmate, a cavalry officer who was killed in 1939, gave him their dead son's ID papers. When it became clear the he could not use them because he looked very different from his classmate, another Polish couple gave him the documents of their missing son, who happened to resemble Victor. He did not pay a penny for either of these IDs.[86] An ethnically Polish friend of Celina P.'s parents managed to get her false Polish documents.[87]

Those who did not look Jewish had a certain advantage. "[I looked like an] eighteen-carat German, and many Germans like fourteen-carat Germans," joked Marcel W.[88] His non-Jewish looks helped him survive on Aryan papers. David R. was blond and spoke good Polish, so it was not hard for him to pretend to be a Pole. His father bought him Aryan papers.[89] The family of Aneta W. was split—her mother and brother did not look Jewish and escaped to the Polish part of the city, while Aneta W. and her father, who had typical Jewish features, stayed in the ghetto.[90] Josef R. recalled that it was possible to find a hiding place for his mother, who did not look Jewish, but not for other members of the family.[91] Maria B. was once urged by a Pole: "Take your [Star of David] armband off; you don't look Jewish, why don't you hide among us"?[92] Others used cosmetics to hide their Jewish appearance. "My mother dyed my hair blond," recalled Sonia W.[93] But this proved only a partial remedy as the "hair was acceptable, but the nose was not." To cover typically "Jewish" noses people might pretend they were suffering from a toothache and wrap their face in a scarf.[94] Even more important than looks was behavior. Jews, the popular wisdom went, could easily be recognized outside the ghetto on account of their sad eyes and their habit of acting like a hunted animal. They constantly looked around nervously, and even without the Star of David armband behaved as if they did not belong on the city's streets. "Only the one who went through what we went through can understand what it meant to me to go to the train station [passing as a Pole]. All of us, whoever looked at our eyes saw fear. Obviously I threw my armband away but I was instinctively checking all the time if I had it because a Jew who was caught without an armband was shot on the spot," recalled Szoszana Budik.[95] "You need to make sure not to stick out in anything," recalled Edith Katz of her time in a Polish school when the family lived outside the ghetto on fake documents. Her younger brother eventually quit school because, being circumcised, he could not use the bathroom.[96] Nerves of steel and chutzpah were therefore assets. Miriam Peleg grew up in the countryside, the daughter of one of the few Jewish farmers in the area; she spoke flawless Polish and did not look Jewish, but what finally convinced her to obtain Aryan papers was an encounter with her brother's friend (her future husband) Mordecai, who moved around Poland with a bicycle registration permit as his sole ID.[97]

External appearance was important, but the ability to culturally and behaviorally pass as a Pole was essential. Not speaking proper Polish was at least as dangerous, and likely even more dangerous, than looking typically Jewish. Chawka R., a courier for the Jewish underground, recalls how she accompanied Antek Zuckerman, one of the leaders of the Warsaw ghetto resistance, during his visit to Kraków. Zuckerman "looked like a Polish nobleman—tall, blond, with a thick moustache. But with Polish he had a problem" because he spoke with a heavy Yiddish accent. The courier's job was to accompany Zuckerman and to assist him in situations that might require verbal contact with ethnic Poles.[98] But even those who spoke perfect Polish were often helpless and therefore vulnerable when it came to religion and traditions. In Jewish schools, Christian traditions and rites were not taught, and in state schools Jewish students were either excused from attending (Catholic) religious classes or were taught religion separately by a Jewish teacher. In quite a few families Jewish children had Polish nannies who took them to Sunday Mass as the only way to combine work with church attendance, but otherwise even the most acculturated Jews were largely clueless about many things that ethnic Poles took for granted.[99] In a telling example that appears with minor variations in numerous testimonies, Regina L. was once asked about the day of the saint after whom she was named.[100] She did not have an answer, and realized—rightly so— that not knowing such a basic thing would immediately expose her non-Christian origins. She quickly bought religious texts and made sure she and her sister know the prayers by heart. Sometimes the danger of being exposed came from other, nonreligious issues and stereotypes that separated Jews and Poles. Avraham Blum escaped the ghetto and, passing as a non-Jew, sold cigarettes at the train station with a group of Polish teenagers. Once the group discussed what they wanted to be when they grow up. "A dentist," Blum said. His friends immediately shouted "*Żydowski zawód!* (A Jewish profession!)."[101]

As explained above, evasion had a gender component, because in Kraków even assimilated and nonobservant families circumcised their male children. For women it was therefore easier to pass as Poles, because they did not face the threat of a "trousers test," which was an immediate and deadly giveaway. But even circumcision, it appears, could be "cured." Professor Jan Lachs, a renowned gynecologist and expert in the history of medicine, managed to come up with a procedure that, if "applied over several months made it impossible to detect the presence of a past circumcision." The procedure, according to Pankiewicz was commonly used in the ghetto, but I could not find testimonies that mention it, possibly because of the topic's sensitivity.[102]

Having non-Jewish looks and speaking flawless Polish were benefits, but people could survive on the Aryan side even if they looked Jewish and did not speak flawless Polish. One option was be to find a hiding place outside the ghetto. This could be done with money. Jews hiding outside the ghetto often paid exorbitant amounts to rent hiding places. In such business relationships, many (though certainly not all) landlords and paid helpers kept their part of the bargain, but there was also a real danger that eventually the hiding Jews would be robbed by their helper, abused (financially, physically, or sexually), betrayed to the Germans or the police, murdered, or simply kicked out.[103] Jakob Lieberman and his siblings feared that this might be their lot when their money ran out, so they conspired to kill the Pole who was charging astronomical prices for shelter and food to prevent him from denouncing them to the Germans. Luckily, things never got to that as they were able to get assistance from *Żegota*, a Polish underground agency tasked with helping Jews in hiding (it is described in greater detail below).[104]

Jews were obviously well aware of all these evasion options, and therefore people who could find or afford hiding places with non-Jewish friends and acquaintances were more likely to try their luck on the Aryan side regardless of their looks. That Jews would seek help from the Poles they knew is unsurprising. What is remarkable is how often Jews were sheltered and helped—a potential death penalty notwithstanding—not only by close friends, but also by Poles with whom they had only tenuous social ties—because they were store patrons, former coworkers, pre–World War II household help, schoolmates, apartment building janitors, or friends of friends.

Thus, Shmuel Rotbard and his sisters were hidden by their father's prewar business contact, an officer in the Armia Krajowa, the Polish nationalist (and generally quite anti-Semitic) underground.[105] In the meantime their property was in safekeeping with another Polish acquaintance.[106] Helen R.'s sister arranged for their mother to hide with Polish friends.[107] Henry E.'s brother-in-law, the manager of the Catholic Church movie house, was able to hide in a convent.[108] When Joseph B. was hiding outside the ghetto, a Polish woman who before the war had washed floors in his family's house brought him food.[109] Rena R. hid her daughter with their Polish maid.[110] "Thanks to my father we had many Polish friends. If not for Polish friends I would have not survived," claimed Victor P.[111] Yet it was not only his father's close friends who helped Victor P. As mentioned earlier, the family of his classmate gave Victor their son's ID and then arranged for new documents when it became clear that the son's ID would be of little value to him. A prison guard, who happened to be another ethnically Polish schoolmate, assisted him in getting out of jail when Victor was arrested. "We knew many Polish people in Kraków," recalled Regina L.[112] Her brother's friend, who served in the Polish police, helped Regina's mother and sister-in-law go into hiding after they escaped the ghetto. The maid of Regina's parents' friend hid her and her sister. Irena Gurewicz's nanny got her fake ID papers and sheltered Irena's baby brother.[113] A Polish acquaintance who was secretly in love with Chana Barsuk's mother arranged a hiding place for the Barsuk family on the outskirts of the city.[114] Some of these Jews were assimilated and had more connections with Poles than with Jews, but others were not. Some were religiously ultra-Orthodox; others were secular Jewish nationalists. Due to the specific circumstances and local history of Kraków, many lived and operated in what was largely a Jewish milieu and social network, but it was never *exclusively* Jewish. And simply having a non-Jewish neighbor, client, or domestic helper often made all the difference.

This very partial list of Kraków Jews who were actively assisted by their Polish acquaintances is by no means intended to suggest that the phenomenon was universal. Often Jews seeking help were harmed, cheated, or turned down by their prewar friends, colleagues, and employees. The most common reaction was simple indifference. But the larger point remains— people who were better integrated and had more contacts with non-Jews were more likely to pursue the evasion strategy and had a higher likelihood of survival than those who had no friends or spoke broken Polish.

Having friends and social connections could sometimes be a double-edged sword, however. Stanisław Taubenschlag came from a totally assimilated family and did not even consider himself Jewish. Knowing that he could count on numerous Polish friends, he chose evasion, easily obtaining false documents under the name Count Kozłowski. Because the family had cut off their ties with the Jewish community, very few Jewish informers could recognize Taubenschlag on the street, and most ethnic Poles, even those who knew him, considered him one of their own. Yet sometimes Taubenschlag's family's prominence in Polish society put him in danger: he was once denounced by a student whom his father, dean of the Jagiellonian University Law School, had failed on an exam.[115] Even more benign encounters with prewar acquaintances could be quite dangerous. "People like shop girls, waiters, and above all, daily helps of my relatives. . . . It was them whom I feared most, not because they were hostile, but on the contrary, because of the warmth of their loud greeting in the street whenever they met me: 'I am so happy that you are alive, Miss Marysia!'" recalled Miriam Peleg.[116] To avoid the potential danger of being recognized on the street, many evading Kraków Jews simply took their fake IDs and left the city. Some, like Bruno Shatyn,[117] moved to the countryside, others fled to Warsaw, which could offer the anonymity of a big city that was harder to obtain in Kraków. The most daring, but ultimately safest choice was to volunteer to go into the den of the beast—the German Reich.

Paradoxically, it was much safer for Jews to hide as Polish forced laborers in Germany than in Poland, where numerous paid and voluntary collaborators could instantly recognize a Yiddish accent or a typically Jewish behavioral trait. For those impersonating Poles in Germany, moreover, having non-Jewish looks was a bonus, not a requirement. Yet even there people who were better integrated into Polish society had better chances of succeeding. To go to Germany, one did not have to *look* Polish, but one did have to speak Polish. Recognizing this fact, Victor P. even started a "business" smuggling Jews to Germany. He would find Poles who had been ordered by the German authorities to go to Germany as forced laborers, take their IDs, and arrange for Jews who spoke flawless Polish to go in their stead.[118] Because Berlin was supposedly "free of Jews," he decided that it would be the safest place for his clients. The only problem was the Allies' air raids on the city. While arranging his brother's transfer to Germany, Victor P. therefore had to take special measures to ensure he would be employed in a relatively safe suburban community.

Victor P.'s story is not unique. Anna N. spoke flawless Polish, so after she managed to get false papers, she signed up to go to Vienna as a Polish laborer. There she worked as a maid for the family of a Nazi official. "This was the ideal way to get away," she recalled. In Vienna there were many residents from all over the former Habsburg Empire, including Southeastern Europe, so "my looks were not that different."[119] Alex G. realized that "the writing was on the wall." He looked Jewish, so staying in Poland was out of question. Instead, he obtained fake ID papers and volunteered to go to Germany. He and his future wife also ended up in Vienna, where they had a comfortable life that included visits to the famous city's opera.[120] Irene F. was told by the Polish family that helped her to escape the ghetto that her hair was too dark for Poland, so she decided that the best way to hide would be to go to Germany.[121] Eugenia Ruter and her Polish rescuer helped two of Ruter's acquaintances who had escaped from a labor camp. They both were provided with fake IDs, and the one who looked more Jewish almost immediately went to Warsaw and there signed up for work in Germany. The other, whose looks were less Jewish, stayed in Kraków for a longer period but eventually went to Germany as well.[122] Sylvia F. escaped the Płaszów camp after she was deported from the Kraków ghetto, and volunteered to go to Austria. She survived the Holocaust, but her memories of Vienna are less pleasant than those of others because she felt in constant danger of being exposed. In the ghetto and the camp she at least did not have to pretend to be ethnically Polish.[123]

Finally, Kraków housed a branch of the Polish Council to Aid Jews, more widely known under the code-name Żegota, which was affiliated with the Polish Government in Exile. The task of Żegota was to assist Jews in hiding with money and documents, and not surprisingly the Kraków Żegota office was one of the most active. The organization began operating in Kraków late in 1942 and assisted hundreds of Jews in hiding. What is more important for my argument, however, is the way in which this organization began operating in the city. The Polish effort to help Jews in hiding originated when several activists of the Polish Socialist Party (PPS) bonded together to assist Jews whom they knew or who were members of the PPS.

A discussion of evasion in Kraków would not be complete without citing one particular case of clandestine German support for Jewish escape efforts. Lieutenant Oswald Bousko,[124] originally from Vienna, was a German police officer in the city. In his youth Bousko became a devoted Nazi and according to Pankiewicz, who knew him, "considered Hitler a God." After the German takeover of Austria, Bousko's views of National Socialism underwent a dramatic transformation and he became a fierce opponent of the Nazi regime. The main focus of his anti-Nazi activism was assisting Kraków ghetto Jews in their escape. In the summer of 1944, Bousko deserted the German army, but he was eventually court-martialed and executed.[125]

BIAŁYSTOK

Up to fifteen thousand Jews escaped to the forest from Minsk, and hundreds of Kraków's Jews hid in and around the city. By contrast, the number of Białystok Jews who chose evasion was miniscule. Among those who tried, only a handful survived. This situation can be partly attributed to the ghetto's enclosure—it was much easier to escape the Minsk ghetto because it was surrounded by barbed wire, while there was a wooden fence around the ghetto of Białystok. The Kraków ghetto, however, was surrounded by a combination of a brick wall and a wooden fence, and this did not seem deter Kraków Jews from escaping. Furthermore, as in Minsk, there were large and thick forests not far from Białystok, and until the very end of the occupation the German presence in the countryside was limited. We know that despite the existence of physical barriers, it was possible to leave the ghetto, for quite a few survivors explicitly stated that they could have fled, but decided against this option. It is also undeniable that the Białystok ghetto was well organized and that material conditions there were much better than in Minsk, though they were not substantially better than in Kraków. The evidence suggests, rather, that the lack of widespread evasion in Białystok should be attributed not to material conditions, topographic factors, or physical barriers created by the Germans, but mainly to sociopolitical factors—the city's history of toxic interethnic relations that resulted in very limited Jewish integration into the broader society and a paucity of interethnic social networks.

As mentioned previously, successful evasion required a combination of favorable circumstances. Money was often needed to pay for hiding places and a non-Jewish appearance was an advantage. However, even more important than being rich or not looking Jewish was the level of integration into non-Jewish society: the ability to speak the local language, familiarity with Christian culture and traditions, and, most crucially, social ties and friendships with non-Jews. Many Jews in Białystok were destitute, but the city's Jewish community also had a sizable middle class and a number of wealthy people. Some had lost significant portions of their wealth under the Soviets, but the fact that the ghetto had thriving restaurants, and that many quite expensive products were smuggled in from the Aryan side speaks for itself. Nor do we have any evidence that Jews in Kraków or Minsk looked any less Jewish than their coethnics in Białystok. It was not money or facial features, but the level of integration that explains why so few Białystok Jews chose evasion.

Białystok was a polarized and segregated city with hostile interethnic relations. Most Jewish children had virtually no non-Jewish acquaintances, let alone friends. Boris Penski played only with coethnics because in his neighborhood "there [was] nothing but Jewish kids"; Polish youths would go into the area only to start fistfights.[126] Many Białystok Jews did not even speak proper Polish. Unlike the Austro-Hungarian monarchy in Kraków, the Russian Empire did not promote ethnically integrated schools in Białystok, and the differences between the cities persisted throughout the interwar period when both were a part of the Polish state. Hana Birk attended a Jewish school where Polish was taught only a few hours a week, "like English in Israeli schools."[127] Zvi Yovin spoke only Yiddish and Hebrew at home, and his Polish was very weak; a fact that he did not regret.[128] In many well-educated families the situation was no different. Tobia Tzitron was a physician from a prominent local family. He knew German much better than he knew Polish, even though he lived most of his life in the Polish state.[129] Overall, few Jews in the city were fluent in Polish, and those few were mainly from middle- and upper-class families.

Even the Jews who spoke Polish well had few, if any, non-Jewish contacts. Quite telling in this regard is the case of Eva Kraczowska. Her father was a physician and a Polish army officer. The family spoke Polish at home and attended Polish schools. Yet these schools were Polish only in their language of instruction—all of the students were Jewish. Kraczowska had no non-Jewish friends. The family did not even have non-Jewish neighbors.[130] Given such a high level of residential segregation, it is hardly surprising that Jews often feared simply passing through ethnically Polish neighborhoods.[131] Mixed neighborhoods did exist in the city,[132] but they were rare. Even families that in most other cities would have considered themselves well integrated into non-Jewish society did not see themselves as assimilated in Białystok. Harry Bass's father was the secretary of the local chapter of the Polish army veterans' organization, and therefore had numerous contacts with Poles. Yet according to Bass, the family was "maybe [at] a footstep to the Gentile community," certainly not a part of it.[133]

The toxic relations between the Jewish and Polish communities in Białystok proved detrimental to the survival chances of many Jews after the

German occupation of the city. In purely practical terms, it was possible to escape the ghetto. Many people went out to work in the factories, others engaged in smuggling. If it was possible to smuggle cattle across the ghetto fence (and it was),[134] humans could certainly have gotten out as well. As in other ghettos, the key challenge was not to escape, but to survive afterward. The Aryan side was perceived to be threatening and hostile, and indeed much more so than in Minsk and Kraków.

Some people tried to escape after the February Aktion, recalled Lipa A.,[135] but it was "intolerable outside" (*bahutz haia bilti nisbal*). "Did you think about saving yourself?" Rachel Lahower was asked during an oral history interview. "No, there was nowhere to go," came the reply.[136] "Who would take you in? . . . There was no way of escaping . . . unless you had contacts or money" to buy Aryan ID papers, argued Irene S.[137] Given that Irene S. was one of the few who spoke perfect Polish and did have Polish acquaintances, her remarks are a good indication of how desperate things really were. Even money, lots of it, could not always buy a way out. Before the ghetto's liquidation, Menachem Rivkind's aunt wrote him from Białystok about her plans to hide on the Aryan side and told him that she doubted that the Poles "will want to help, and despite considerable effort, no place has yet been found." Rivkind was a wealthy industrialist, a son-in-law of the Judenrat Council chairman Rabbi Rosenmann, so money was likely not a concern. Yet they could not find a place to hide,[138] a problem rarely encountered in testimonies from Kraków or Minsk. Even when such a place was eventually found, salvation was anything but guaranteed. Masha Weinstein paid an ethnically Polish nurse who worked with Weinstein's husband, a physician, to hide their daughter. After just a week they had to bring the girl back into the ghetto because the nurse's neighbor was threatening to denounce her to the Germans. The child was eventually sent to Auschwitz and gassed.[139] In the Holocaust context as a whole, Weinstein's situation was tragically common. What is unusual, though, is how rarely such stories are told by Białystok ghetto survivors. Evasion and denunciation are correlated; the paucity of denunciation accounts indicates how rarely the evasion strategy was chosen.

Some, though probably very few—the exact numbers are unavailable— tried to escape Białystok's ghetto during the first stages of its existence. Dr. Karshman, a Judenrat member, left Białystok and fled to Warsaw.[140] A handful of others could have escaped, but chose not to. Shortly after the Nazis occupied the city, Moshe Goldschmidt was assigned to work for a rear unit of the German army. When the frontline moved further to the east, the unit had to follow. Its officers came up with the idea of changing Goldschmidt's name to Max, registering him as belonging to the *Volksdeutsch* category (a person of German background), and taking him with them. Goldschmidt did not want to leave his family and refused the offer.[141] Yehiel Shedler worked outside the ghetto and met a Polish girl, with whom he had a relationship. The girl wanted to hide him, but Shedler refused.[142]

The number of people trying to escape increased towards the end of the ghetto's existence. Most were caught and killed—some by Germans, some by local Poles. Chasia Bornstein-Bielicka, a resistance member who lived outside the ghetto, rented a room from a Polish family that was convinced she was a Polish peasant girl. She often heard the landlord telling his son how he and his comrades in the Polish nationalist underground caught hiding Jews, took their eyes out, and brought them back to the ghetto.[143] Fanya, Shmuel Iwry's sister, tried to hide their parents in a cave outside the ghetto, but they were betrayed and shot. During the ghetto's final liquidation she realized that evasion was impossible and took poison.[144]

Many made desperate attempts to escape when it was perceived as the last chance to survive, sometimes jumping off the trains carrying them to death camps. The vast majority perished, either hit by the moving trains, shot by German guards, betrayed, or killed by local Poles. In March of 1943, George Turlo, a non-Jew, took a train from Białystok to Warsaw. "During the first portion [of the journey]," he recalled, "the train was stopping very often on the rail tracks, and a putrefied smell, stench, was coming from the outside. And I saw the German soldiers pouring the gasoline on some bodies along the track. And somebody told me this was the latest convoy from [the] Białystok ghetto to . . . Treblinka."[145] Only a few were lucky enough to survive the jump. Those who did had to navigate a hostile and unfamiliar terrain—physical, but more importantly also human and social. Gedaliyah Wender was ten years old when his father threw him and his sister out of a train bound to Treblinka; his mother jumped as well. His mother and sister were badly wounded in the jump, and it was clear they would not survive. In the last moments of her life the mother had to prepare her son for independent survival—she taught him how to say "bread" and other essential words in Polish, because Gedaliyah had no knowledge of the language whatsoever.[146] With no ability to communicate with the local population, Wender roamed the countryside until he was hired by a friendly Pole as a farm hand and converted (temporarily) to Christianity. Esther Cohen also survived the jump. She was fluent in Polish and ended up in the house of a local priest who promised her that if she converted to Christianity he would find a safe place for her. However, in the Białystok context, speaking Polish did not imply any familiarity with Polish traditions, and the young Esther feared that the baptism ceremony might be painful. She refused. "Had the priest been smart and told me the story of the baby Jesus . . . then I would have wanted to convert," she admitted.[147]

Even those who were better prepared than Wender and Cohen had a hard time finding a safe haven. Aryeh Kaminski was born in a small town near Białystok, could speak a local dialect of Polish, and was familiar with Christian traditions. After being deported from the Białystok ghetto, he jumped off the train and managed to get to a Polish village. There he was welcomed so long as he was perceived to be a Pole, but when his Jewishness was discovered Kaminski was attacked and chased away.[148] The villagers' behavior is not surprising. Polish-Jewish relations in the Białystok region were notoriously poor, and in very recent history there had been widespread, bloody massacres of Jews by their Polish neighbors in the area.[149] Even in politically more moderate Western Galicia, a Jew's chances of survival while hiding in the countryside were slim.[150] In those rare cases when Polish peasants of the Białystok countryside did voluntarily help, their assistance went to people they knew and with whom they were friendly. Jack R., originally from Brańsk, hid with a Polish farmer who had had business relations with his father before the Holocaust.[151] After staying with the farmer during the first stages of the German occupation, Jack R. managed to smuggle himself to the Białystok ghetto, where he had relatives. Urged by his cousin, Jack R. went back to his farmer friend and stayed with him until the liberation. Anschel Schneider, originally from Choroszcz, a small community ten miles from Białystok, hid for some time with Polish farmers who were friends of his family. Even though these Poles belonged to a right-wing, virulently anti-Semitic underground organization, they were willing to take the risk of hiding a Jew they knew personally.[152] Felicja N. was born in Warsaw to parents who had moved there from Białystok.[153] In 1939 she escaped to her grandparents in Białystok and lived with them until the German invasion of the Soviet Union. Her great-grandfather owned a sawmill in a village near Białystok and had befriended one of the local Polish families. The families, according to Felicja N., had known each other "for ages." Eventually, Felicja N. managed to escape the Białystok ghetto and reach the friends' village. The family hid her without ever asking to be paid. Interviewed in 1991, she refused to reveal the names of her saviors—first, because they were humble people, and second, because they still feared the reaction of other people in the village.[154]

Shifra Gotlib came from a wealthy family that employed an ethnically Polish maid. When she gave birth to a baby boy in the ghetto, Gotlib did not circumcise the child and smuggled him to their maid, who sheltered him until the liberation.[155] A story like Gotlib's would be quite unremarkable for Kraków, where Jews were often assisted and saved by their Polish domestics, but it is highly unusual for Białystok. Jennifer Marlow has emphasized the importance of Polish maids and nannies for successful evasion, pointing out that nannies familiarized their Jewish charges with the Polish language, traditions, and culture, which later helped them to successfully pass as Poles. Quite a few nannies were willing to risk their lives to help their former employers.[156] But whereas in Kraków numerous Jewish families employed Polish domestic help, very few did so in Białystok, thus inadvertently blocking a critical pathway to successful evasion.

Celina H. and her twin sister were among those who spoke Polish thanks to their nanny. They were not locals—the sisters had been born in Warsaw after their mother moved there from Białystok. In 1939 the family escaped to Celina's grandparents and found themselves in the Białystok ghetto after the German invasion of the USSR. To compensate for not having ties to local Poles and not being a part of local interethnic networks, a number of other advantages were required. Luckily, theirs was an affluent family and could pay for shelter outside the ghetto. Being females, the girls were not circumcised, and they did not look typically Jewish. When it became increasingly dangerous to stay in the ghetto, Celina H.'s mother bought her and her sister Polish documents and hid them, in exchange for payment, with a Polish peasant.[157] However, the ability to pass as Poles was more important than the right looks, and here their impeccable Polish came in handy. It is doubtful that they would have been taken in had their Jewishness been apparent every time they opened their mouths. Similarly, Maria Dworzecka, who was born just three days prior to the German invasion of the USSR, was saved by a combination of looks and connections. Her mother, who was originally not from Białystok and did not look Jewish, managed to get fake IDs and escape the city. Even though Dworzecka does not know much about her mother, who was killed in a car accident in 1948, the source of the IDs is not hard to guess—the family had been active in the ethnically mixed communist underground of interwar Poland.[158]

Even after the ghetto was liquidated, there were people who still resisted moving to the Aryan side. They remained in bunkers and cellars for months with almost no food and water because coming out of hiding was perceived as suicidal. Eva Kraczowska and Jay M. hid together from August 16 until

November 1943.[159] "We waited until the very last," recalled Jay M., and then they escaped to the forest.[160] Interviewed separately, in Israel and the United States, neither of them broached the possibility of trying to move to Białystok's Aryan side, even though Polish was Kraczowska's mother tongue. Without Polish acquaintances and ties, her linguistic skills were useless.

Unlike Kraczowska, Zachary A. did have Polish acquaintances even though (or rather, because) he was not a city native and had arrived in Białystok only after the war began. During the last days of the occupation, the brother of a Polish friend hid him.[161] Miriam Grosman, the sister of underground leader Chajka Grosman, was helped by the family of her non-Jewish friend Olla, with whom Grosman had worked during Soviet rule. A former Polish colleague offered to help Berta Sokol'skaia escape, but in the end she refused because she was not willing to leave her family behind.[162] As in Minsk and Kraków, ties to non-Jews, when they existed, could be mobilized for help. The tragedy was that only a few Jews in the city had such ties.

In Białystok there was also a group of young Jewish women who lived on the Aryan side, working for the ghetto underground and the Jewish partisans in the forest as couriers and smugglers of weapons and provisions. They were engaged in resistance, not evasion, for living on the Aryan side was for them not an act of escape but an assignment they had been given by the ghetto underground. Yet this group gives us a good indication of who was perceived as capable of surviving outside the ghetto. Their memoirs and testimonies are important and inform our understanding of what it meant to be a Jew in hiding on the Aryan side of Białystok. The most striking feature of this group of about a dozen young female Zionists and Communists is that, besides Chajka Grosman, none of them were originally from Białystok. The majority came from Grodno, only fifty miles away, but a town with much higher levels of Jewish integration into Polish society. All spoke good Polish, but they discovered that speaking the language was not enough to successfully pass as a Pole. Chasia Bornstein-Bielicka, a left-wing Zionist, was well integrated into Grodno's Polish society. She went to a Polish school, had Polish friends, and spoke flawless Polish with a local accent. But she had no knowledge of Christian prayers and traditions. "Only much later I became aware that my Polish name [in false documents] 'Halinka' is after St. Helena. [But] which St. Helena—there are two."[163] Lisa Chapnik, a Communist, was Bornstein-Bielicka's schoolmate. When she attempted to move her niece out of the ghetto to join her on the Aryan side, the first thing she taught her were Christian prayers, because as a Jew, the girl knew none. This didn't help—the niece was denounced and taken to the Gestapo. Even though Chapnik managed to obtain her release, the girl had to return to the ghetto, where she perished.

Bornstein-Bielicka also describes how exactly Chapnik had managed to move to the Aryan side. Bornstein-Bielicka worked as a maid for a German official, a devoted Nazi. Once a female neighbor of her employer, also a German, told Bornstein-Bielicka that she was looking for a maid and asked if she knew someone. Bornstein-Bielicka considered this a perfect job—"working for the Germans, as far as possible from the Poles." The person chosen by the underground for the job was Lisa Chapnik.[164] Ania Rud came to Białystok with her husband via Grodno. She lived on the Aryan side even though she did not look typically Polish. To "improve" her external appearance, she had her hair dyed. While she was on the Aryan side, her husband, who also did not look Polish, had to remain in the ghetto because it was considered too dangerous for circumcised males to be outside the ghetto.[165] This precaution was well warranted for the danger was real, yet it had not prevented substantial numbers of Jewish males from successfully pursuing the evasion strategy in both Kraków and Minsk.

Finally, a story told by Bornstein-Bielicka demonstrates that the Germans were well-informed about the pervasive antipathy of Białystok Poles toward the Jews. After working as a maid for a Nazi official, Bornstein-Bielicka tried to get a job with Otto Busse, a German painter who was known in the ghetto for his friendly attitude toward his Jewish employees. During the job interview, Busse mentioned his former secretary, a Jew who had been deported, and Bornstein-Bielicka replied that she knew this person from elementary school and thought highly of her. Later, after Bornstein-Bielicka revealed to Busse her true identity, Busse admitted that he had hired her because of this one remark during the interview—never before had he heard Poles in Białystok saying good things about Jews.[166] Of course, it is quite possible that because Busse was a German, Poles were simply scared to say positive things about Jews around him, but the story nevertheless says something about the nature of Polish-Jewish relations in Białystok. Other German rescuers in the city were textile factory managers Artur Schade and Otto Beniske (the name also appears in the sources as "Beneschek"). Schade was the manager of a factory in which Mina Dorn's father was the foreman. Schade once asked his foreman to find him a Jewish cook because he "couldn't stand the Poles." Dorn took the job. After the ghetto liquidation she and her cousin Mery Mendelson were hidden first by Beniske, for whom Mendelson worked as a maid, and then by Schade.[167] Schade's willingness to save his Jewish maid is noble and brave, but his was hardly an all-inclusive, universalist vision of humankind. Schade clearly harbored ethnic prejudices, but in his case they were primarily directed against Poles, not Jews.

Concluding Remarks

In no other survival strategy is the difference between Minsk, Kraków, and Białystok more pronounced than in that of evasion. In the three ghettos success at evasion depended upon the same set of factors: money, looks, the ability to culturally and behaviorally pass as a non-Jew, the existence of non-Jewish contacts, and the availability of safe havens. It was not necessary to possess all of these advantages; having even one item on the list could lead to successful evasion, but the more boxes the escaping Jew could check, the better his chances. The first two factors were present in roughly equal measure in all three ghettos. In every city there were Jews who could pay, and the Jews in Kraków did not look more Slavic than their coethnics in Minsk or Białystok. What explains the substantial differences in evasion patterns across the three ghettos are the remaining factors—the Jews' ability to successfully pass as Slavs, their involvement in interethnic social networks, and their access to safe havens. These, in turn, were shaped by the pre-Holocaust political regimes under which each city lived.

In Minsk the escaping Jews could reasonably expect help if they reached the so-called "partisans' zone," while in Kraków they could try to cross the nearby border to Hungary and Slovakia or volunteer to go to Germany as Polish laborers. In Białystok, until the last stages of the occupation, there was no substantial presence of partisans in the forests, and the border was far away. As for trying to go to Germany while passing for a Pole, I have not encountered even one testimony discussing such an attempt from Białystok. It is possible that given their virtual inability to pass as Poles, Białystok Jews never tried this option, especially given the tolerable—at least until February 1943—life conditions in the ghetto. Maybe they were simply not aware of the possibility, or perhaps the special legal status of the Bezirk Bialystok played a role. Whatever the reason, this variation supports my argument that a focus on local-level factors is more productive than a country-level analysis for the understanding of evasion patterns.

The importance of local-level analysis becomes most pronounced when we look at the key factors that determined the choice of evasion over coping. The factors that made coping a more successful and attractive strat-egy reduced the likelihood of evasion and vice versa, so that to an extent the two strategies were inverse images of one another. The robust and cohesive Jewish community in Białystok made reasonable (by Holocaust standards) life conditions possible and gave the city Jews fewer reasons to try to escape as long as the ghetto existed. In the Minsk and Kraków ghettos, which had much more fractured and substantially weaker pre–World War II Jewish communal institutions, coping was chaotic and thus individual Jews were more likely to seek evasion. At the individual level, gender also affected the attractiveness of each strategy. It was easier for males to find jobs inside the ghetto, while females had an advantage in passing as non-Jews. But even more crucial than gender was the ability to culturally pass as a non-Jew and the extent of the individual's social networks.

In Minsk and Kraków many Jews could pass as Russians, Belorussians, and Poles; in Białystok they could not, and they were fully aware of this fact. In Minsk, the Jews' chances were even better, because Soviet rule had partially succeeded in its efforts to obliterate the religious aspects of Slavic-Jewish differences; in Kraków, as many Jews quickly discovered, their knowledge of Polish language and poetry counted for little against their ignorance of Catholicism, the key component of Polish identity. The more numerous contacts between Jews and non-Jews in Minsk and Kraków increased the number of their potential helpers outside the ghetto, something that the Białystok Jews could not take advantage of simply because interethnic so-cial networks were largely nonexistent in the city.[168] The Jews in Minsk and Kraków did not have to become assimilated to achieve that goal. Even quite limited contacts, the so-called "weak ties,"[169]—to non-Jewish families who lived in the same apartment building, to Polish patrons of Jewish stores, or to Belorussian schoolmates—greatly increased the likelihood of choosing evasion. The analysis of the three ghettos clearly demonstrates the limits of arguments that focus predominantly on rescuers, their ideals, and their psychological profiles. What Jews did during and especially *before* the war had a much stronger impact on evasion and rescue.

It might be tempting to blame the lack of widespread evasion in Białystok on the city's Jewish community. Why had they failed to learn Pol-ish? Why had they not developed closer contacts with the Poles? We who have the benefit of hindsight can see the fundamental flaws in this line of argument. We know what ethnic polarization did to the city. Białystok Jews could not have anticipated such effects. In the grand scheme of things, the integration of minorities and interethnic relations are to a very large extent dependent on regimes and their policies, rather than on the private actions of individuals.[170] The Austro-Hungarian authorities in Kraków and their Soviet counterparts in Minsk achieved higher levels of Jewish integration by using a combination of incentives to foster interethnic social networks. They opened opportunities for social, educational, and economic mobility, and applied state pressure, especially in the realm of primary and secondary education. In Białystok, the Russian Imperial government and their Polish successors did none of this. Thus, for the Białystok Jews, integration into non-Jewish society was neither beneficial nor expected. It is also useful to re-member that in 1918, interethnic relations in Minsk were not that different from those in Białystok. However, twenty years of brutal but efficient Soviet social engineering had completely reshaped interactions and ties between the Jewish and Slavic communities. It is very likely that had Białystok been under Soviet rule for twenty years it would have come to resemble Minsk. Soviet rule in Białystok, however, lasted only twenty months, and this was clearly not enough time to change the city's ethnic relations.

CHAPTER 7

RESISTANCE

Initially, there were rumors. Some people saw, or said that they saw, people in the forests not far from Khmel'nik. They carried weapons, spoke Russian, and claimed to be Soviet partisans. The news prompted some young and middle-aged males in both the ghetto and the non-Jewish part of the town to act. Israel G. knew most of them; two, Alexander Schwartz and Chayim Tsyprin, were close friends of his parents. Israel G. knew about the underground's attempts to obtain weapons and hide them in the synagogue, but neither he nor his family had ever taken part in the resistance. Israel was too young, and resistance was not considered a proper occupation for women with children, such as Alexandra G. Israel's father did resist, but not in the ghetto. In fact, by that time he was not even alive, having been killed in action during the Red Army's retreat in the fall of 1941.

The underground's plan was to collect as many weapons as possible and escape to join the partisans. Some eventually did, but most were arrested and shot by the Germans when their weapons cache was discovered. Why and how the Germans got wind of the underground—whether it was because of bad luck, a mistake the resisters made, or due to a denunciation—we do not know.

* * *

Jewish resistance has historically been one of the key foci of Holocaust research, due largely to the desire to counter accusations that Jews were passive, complacent, and went "like lambs to the slaughter." Holocaust historians, especially those based in Israel, have focused attention on the Jews' resistance to persecution. It is true, those scholars contend, that *armed* resistance was infrequent, but equating resistance with violence is unnecessarily restrictive. The Jews, this line of argument goes, had almost unanimously engaged in *amidah* ("standing up against" in Hebrew), or unarmed resistance. Taken to its logical extreme, this scholarship eventually came to suggest that anything the Jews did to prolong their lives and not to be killed by the Germans could be described as resistance. For example, Yehuda Bauer viewed resistance as

> smuggling food into ghettos; mutual self-sacrifice within the family to avoid starvation or worse; cultural, educational, religious, and political activities undertaken to strengthen morale; the work of doctors, nurses, and educators to consciously maintain health and moral fiber to enable individual and group survival; and, of course, armed rebellion or the use of force (with bare hands or with 'cold' weapons) against the Germans and their collaborators.[1]

The problem with this approach is that very different types of individual and collective behaviors, such as self-sacrifice within the family, commitment to one's professional duty, and armed rebellion are lumped together into one analytical category. As a result, our ability to understand the phenomenon becomes limited at best. In this book I adopt a narrower view of resistance. I define "resistance" as involvement in organized activity aimed at harming the personnel and property of the perpetrators of mass violence. Resistance can consist in armed acts and involve violence of some sort or in unarmed and nonviolent acts, such as printing underground media and providing intelligence to the perpetrators' enemies. The smuggling of food, self-sacrifice within the family, and the work of doctors and educators belong to the previously discussed, and no less honorable category of coping, which I analyze in chapter 5.

The historical record shows that open resistance to extreme forms of oppression is "rare yet hardly unprecedented."[2] Uprisings and rebellions did take place in Stalin's Gulag camps, on slave ships, in POW camps, in high security prisons, and in other extremely oppressive environments.[3] Over the last several decades, social scientists and historians have devoted substantial effort to trying to understand where and under what conditions such resistance is likely to break out and what sort of people are more likely to join in such high-risk activity. Many influential studies emphasize the importance of mental factors such as identity, self-respect, honor, pride,[4] emotions,[5] perceptions of threat,[6] and commitment to a goal.[7] Other works prioritize physical factors that make the outbreak of violent resistance more likely, such as rough terrain.[8] Still others focus on grievances,[9] the presence of mechanisms designed to overcome the collective action problem,[10] social networks,[11] or tipping points after which mobilization becomes widespread.[12]

This literature, however, often ignores the events that follow initial mobilization and fails to consider why some resistance movements end up being more successful than others. Holocaust scholarship is no exception. When it comes to Jewish *armed* resistance, the most intense attention has traditionally been devoted to ghetto revolts, especially to the one in Warsaw. This heavy focus on the Warsaw ghetto uprising is understandable, given that it was one of the Holocaust's defining moments. But the Warsaw ghetto uprising, for all its importance, is not representative of the whole phenomenon of Jewish armed resistance to the Nazis. Indeed, in numerous respects it was an outlier. As this chapter will demonstrate, not all Jewish resistance groups wanted to stage ghetto rebellions, and among those that did, not all succeeded.

The goals of this chapter are threefold. First, by analyzing Jewish resistance organizations in the ghettos of Minsk, Kraków, and Białystok, I will explore the whole ideological and political gamut of such groups. Second, I will argue that people with a history of pre–World War II political activism were significantly overrepresented in the resistance. Third, I will focus on why some resistance groups failed early on, while others managed to put up a sustained fight. The chapter will link this difference in resistance groups' trajectories to the varying levels of skills these groups possessed, and will show how such skills were shaped by pre–World War II political regimes and patterns of state repression in Poland and the USSR.

The existing scholarship on Jewish armed resistance tends to the conclusion that identity and emotions were the key motivating factors. Jewish resistance—the "war of the doomed"[13]—was a minority strategy. Few people engaged in it. They were both males and females and only a handful had military training. Most were young, though some middle-aged Jews took part as well. Jewish resisters, argues Michael Marrus, were driven by the desire "to defend the honor of the insurgents and their people. In effect, this was a fight for the future, for the historical record."[14] When the Warsaw ghetto uprising broke out, its commander, Mordechai Anielewicz, wrote that the dream of his life "has risen to become a fact. . . . Jewish armed resistance and revenge are facts."[15] Dolek Liebeskind, one of the leaders of the Jewish resistance in Kraków used similar language. "We are fighting for three lines in the history books to make the world know that the Jewish youth did not go like lambs to the slaughter," he proclaimed. But what was it about Anielewicz and Liebeskind specifically that made them willing to spend their energies on such a high-risk enterprise, one that eventually led to their deaths, rather than on personal survival? I will argue that these resisters' pre-Holocaust political activism shifted their focus from personal to collective good and made them prioritize collective survival—even if only a symbolic survival in history books—over their personal physical survival.

Anielewicz and Liebeskind were driven by the same desire, but their behavior differed. Whereas the Warsaw ghetto rebelled, the Kraków ghetto did not. Numerous forms of underground activism were possible, and not every leader of the Jewish resistance was lucky enough to see their dreams of rebellion become reality. A successful transition from initial mobilization to a sustained violent resistance, such as a large-scale ghetto uprising is a possibility, not a certainty that can be taken for granted.[16] Practitioners of both insurgency and counterinsurgency know this, but scholars generally overlook this crucial point. "Nascent movements are extremely vulnerable, and many if not most are crushed before they have a chance to grow beyond small cells," argues the U.S. Army Special Operations Command (USASOC) overview of human factors affecting underground movements.[17] Some Jewish resistance groups, I will show, were better positioned to carry out sustained anti-Nazi violence than others. This difference was shaped by an important, intuitive, but often overlooked variable, namely the *skills* to organize and mount such resistance.

All underground movements have two crucial components: operational capacity and operational security.[18] An organization's operational capacity determines its ability to successfully fight the government. Operational security consists in an organization's ability to withstand the authorities' efforts to suppress or eradicate it. The paramount concern of all clandestine groups is to maximize secrecy and minimize exposure to the government's security services. In practical terms, operational security is the ability to outfox the security services by establishing secure communication channels, procure weapons without being detected, maintain well-hidden meeting places and munitions caches, produce high-quality forged identification documents, and identify and neutralize informers and infiltrators. Jewish resistance groups that possessed operational security skills were able to engage in sustained resistance; those without such skills were swiftly eliminated by the German security apparatus.

How could Jewish resisters obtain these essential skills, and why did some possess them while others did not? Here, as with other questions of Jewish behavior, pre-Holocaust political regimes played the key role. A crucial pathway to acquiring the necessary skills lay in past exposure to pre–World War II state repression. In places where before the German takeover some Jews had been selectively repressed because of their political or social activism, those Jews now possessed the necessary skills; in places where there had been no pre–World War II state repression or the repression had been indiscriminate, the skills did not exist.

In the case of selective repression, when people are targeted because of what they do (e.g., political or social activism), they have a choice between ceasing their activities or sticking to their ideals and risking punishment. To avoid punishment activists will either go fully underground or will adopt a semi-clandestine lifestyle and be forced to learn operational security skills.[19] Because repression is selective, the rest of the population does not have to worry about its safety. The general populace has no incentives to go underground and, by extension, acquire operational security skills. Indiscriminate repression works differently. The threat is distributed throughout a much larger group, and hence overcoming the collective action problem and organizing an underground becomes much harder. The incentive structure changes only when the threat becomes imminent, lethal, and immediate.[20] Prior to that point, organizing resistance and going underground exposes the first movers to an increasing, rather than decreasing, risk of punishment. Yet when the danger is already immediate and lethal, aspiring but unskilled resisters will be unlikely to survive, because they will not have enough time or opportunity to learn and adapt.

The three ghettos on which I focus exemplify this variation in patterns of pre–World War II state repression and demonstrate the impact each pattern had on subsequent Jewish resistance to the Nazis. Minsk, a part of the USSR, was subject to the indiscriminate repression of Stalin's Great Terror in the late 1930s. Initially targeting the Party's top brass, the terror soon spread to the entire society, "leaving almost no one untouched.[21] From 1918 to 1939, Kraków and Białystok belonged to Poland, where state repression was selective, targeting only one group in which Jews were active—the communists.[22] Polish communists went underground in 1919; the authorities viewed the party as a subversive organization, and its members were put on trial, sentenced to long prison terms, and incarcerated in the Bereza concentration camp. Communists who ceased their political activism went largely unmolested by the authorities. Those who persisted had to adopt a clandestine lifestyle to avoid arrest. In September 1939, Kraków was occupied by Germany, whereas Białystok, a part of Eastern Poland, was taken over by the USSR and remained in Soviet control until mid-1941. During that time Soviet authorities initiated selective repression of non-communist political organizations. This selective repression, which I discuss in greater detail in chapter 2, forced several Zionist political youth movements to go underground and operate clandestinely.

The following pages will discuss Jewish resistance in the three ghettos, who the resisters were, what goals they strove to achieve, and whether they succeeded in their endeavors.

Minsk

The Minsk ghetto was a hub of underground resistance, but it was resistance of a kind that differed substantially from the Jewish underground in the other two ghettos. In Minsk, the underground was almost purely communist. Consequently, this defined how the Minsk ghetto's underground organized and fought, what it wanted to achieve, and which people it mobilized for the struggle.

As discussed in chapter 2, early twentieth-century Minsk had community-based Jewish self-defense structures, and before the 1917 Revolution, the Minsk Jews' support for the Communist Party was limited at best. As late as the early 1920s, Zionism and Bundism were the most popular ideologies among the city's Jews, and until the late 1920s a Zionist underground, though a numerically small one, existed in the city.[23] However, twenty years of Soviet policies and the purges of the late 1930s, in which numerous former Zionist and Bund activists were targeted, were sufficient to render any non-communist underground impossible, indeed unthinkable.

Almost immediately after the city was occupied by the Nazis, numerous small and uncoordinated underground initiatives emerged. They were directed mainly by idealistic Communist Party youth branch members and low-level communist cadres. As Epstein points out, in August and September 1941 members of these groups "tended to use the word 'resistance' rather than 'underground' to describe their activity, because they belonged to informal, autonomous groups, and for the moment were not thinking of going beyond that."[24] Anatolii Rubin recalled his older sister's behavior during the early days of the ghetto: "[S]he went out, brought leaflets . . . young people would gather in our house . . . and they, with their Komsomol training, organized, sang anti-fascist songs. . . ."[25] Mark Taits and his two friends, all teenagers, got together to save Soviet POWs. When the ghetto was not yet surrounded by barbed wire, Germans would march columns of POWs through it. The POWs were lightly guarded, so Taits and his friends would open the front door of one of the buildings along the POWs route, allowing some of the prisoners to sneak out of the column into the building. Taits and his friends then gave the POWs civilian clothes and showed them the way to the forests.[26]

Seventeen-year-old Masha Bruskina was a devoted communist. At first she lived with her mother in the Minsk ghetto, but later she moved to the Aryan side, dyed her hair, and assumed her mother's maiden name, Bugakova. She probably joined an anti-Nazi resistance group a few weeks after the German conquest of Minsk. Volunteering as a nurse, Bruskina cared for wounded Soviet soldiers and helped them to escape by smuggling civilian clothing and medication into the hospital. When prisoners were healthy enough, other members of the group led them into the forests. This was a poorly coordinated initiative by devoted communists who had every intention to resist but lacked the sophistication and experience needed to successfully conduct underground work. Bruskina and her comrades were quickly captured by the German security services and hanged.[27]

Some older communist cadres also contemplated resistance. However, as disciplined party members who had lived through the horrors of Stalin's Great Terror, they knew that, as the Russian saying went, "no initiative goes unpunished," and simply could not bring themselves to create any organizational structure without an explicit order from above. Moreover, they were confident that the local Communist Party bosses must have authorized some trusted members to stay in the occupied city to organize resistance. Creating an independent underground without permission would be tantamount to a usurpation of other peoples' rightful privileges. The attitude of communist refugees from Poland—people who were repressed in their homeland and had worked for many years in the underground—was different. Less accustomed to rigid party discipline, these people were willing to act without supervision by party elites. Moreover, they had the necessary skills.

Among the Polish-Jewish communists was Hersh Smolar, a high-ranking activist with decades of underground work under his belt. After escaping from Białystok to Minsk, Smolar found himself in the ghetto, living under the alias Efim Stoliarevich. In the ghetto, Smolar encountered other communist cadres, whom he knew and trusted—Notke Wainhoyz (Wainhauz) and Yakov Kirkaeshto. In addition, Smolar was "biographically available"[28] for high-risk activism. Single and without dependents to support, he could devote himself to full-time underground work. Eventually, a small underground organization was formed under Smolar's leadership. Later he was also put in touch with another group of communists, led by Nohum Feldman. There were only Soviet Jews in this group. While Feldman and his associates were determined to fight the Germans, they did not think of themselves as an organization because they were not authorized by the party to set up any formal structures. When Smolar told Feldman about his group, the first thing Feldman wanted to know was: "What do you mean you formed an organization? *Who gave you the right to do that?* Who gave you the order to form an organization?"[29] Eventually, in August 1941, the Jewish underground was formed with Smolar as its leader.

Shortly after this encounter, Smolar was also introduced to Isai Kazinets, the informal leader of a group of young communists on the Aryan side. Kazinets was Jewish, but he had a fake passport and his Jewish origin would remain unknown until after the war. Like Feldman, Kazinets wanted to know who had authorized Smolar to act. Smolar's reply was "a mute gesture"—he pointed to his heart.[30] Yet, Kazinets, a disciplined party member, simply could not accept the notion that a fellow communist would start an underground without the explicit authority to do so. Ironically, this misinterpretation contributed to the establishment of the city-wide resistance. Smolar, who was perceived by Kazinets to be a high-ranking communist official, unable to reveal his true status, was surprised to discover that in the city underground he had been assigned a *nom de guerre*: "Skromnyi" ("Modest" in Russian). Still confident that Soviet government agents were also operating somewhere in the city, the resisters—just to be on the safe side—chose to name the underground the "Second," or "Auxiliary" City Committee, thus ceding primacy to the "authorized" underground. Which, of course, never existed.[31]

How was the Minsk ghetto underground structured and what were its goals? The available data are somewhat contradictory, because Smolar published the history of the underground twice—in Moscow in 1946, and then in the West in the 1980s. In the first version, the organization consisted of only Communist Party and Komsomol members, and its key goal was to fight the Germans as a part of the larger communist anti-Nazi struggle. In the second, saving the ghetto from destruction and leading Jews to safety in the forest became the main priorities, and membership in the underground was open not only to communists, but also to former Zionists and Bundists who had been recommended by trusted members.

Initially, the ghetto underground's leadership consisted of Smolar, Wainhoyz, Kirkaeshto, and Feldman. Later Kirkaeshto and Wainhoyz were killed but new members joined and assumed key roles. The most important of these was Mikhail Gebelev. Like other underground leaders, Gebelev was a devoted communist. In 1924 he had already risen to the rank of Komsomol leader in his small hometown of Uzliany. From 1937 to 1939 Gebelev studied at the Communist Party's school for propagandists and worked as a low-level party cadre. His wife and children had escaped the city before the German takeover, and this made Gebelev more available for resistance work. Another prominent underground member, Israel Lapidus, had worked before the war for the Communist Party's district committee (*obkom*). When the war began, he joined the Red Army as a political officer. After German troops surrounded and wiped out his unit, Lapidus returned to Minsk and joined his family in the ghetto.[32] Ziama Okun, Anna Machiz, the siblings Khasia and Matvei Pruslin—all Communist Party members and activists before the war—were also prominent in underground activities. The underground adopted the organizational structure of *desiatki*—groups of ten, in which the rank and file knew only the members of their own group. We know the identity of all desiatki leaders, as well the names of many of the more than three hundred underground rank-and-file members. Virtually all of the leadership and other prominent members of the resistance were Communist Party and Komsomol members and activists.

Not all the ghetto communists automatically joined the ranks. For instance, despite the fact that before the war Tatyana G. had been secretary of the Komsomol cell at her factory, she was able to join the underground only because she was friends with an underground member.[33] She had blond hair and did not look Jewish, and was thus assigned to be Mikhail Gebelev's messenger. She was lucky—many people, including party members, tried to find their way to the underground, but failed. For non-communists it was extremely hard to join the resistance. "In every household people are talking about the underground, but no one knows how to get in touch with it. This is especially hard for us, Jews from Poland. People are extremely cautious with us because many Polish Jews serve in the ghetto police and behave cruelly towards the population," lamented Yakov Greenstein.[34] Eventually, Greenstein and his wife were able to find and join the resistance, but only because one of the underground's key members happened to be their flatmate.

Polish-Jewish communists, however, even if their numbers were small, were crucial for the survival of the resistance thanks to their previous underground experience. Operational security rules were sound and tight. Abram Astashinskii,[35] an underground member, admitted that initially he had no idea who the organization's leaders were, because the flow of information and contacts between the resisters was kept to an absolute minimum. The only information the German security services were ever able to get on Smolar was one of his several aliases.

The situation in the city underground outside the ghetto could not have been more different. Soviet communists "hadn't the slightest idea of the elementary rules of illegal political work," lamented Smolar.[36] They had no relevant prior experience whatsoever, and some "thought it was beneath them to hide their involvement" in the resistance.[37] For instance, the underground leadership kept written minutes of their meetings. Even more dangerous (and eventually fatal) was the behavior of the leaders of the underground's military council, high-ranking officers in the Red Army. These people had substantial military training, but no knowledge of underground work. They set up their headquarters across the street from the German security services building and persisted in prewar work habits, such as having secretaries and maintaining written logs of their schedules. "Their long years of legality were evident at every step," complained Smolar.[38] The city underground paid dearly for these operational security failures. The leadership and several hundred rank-and-file members were captured and killed by the German security services. The movement was eliminated and attempts to resurrect it were unsuccessful.

While the city underground perished, the ghetto underground—which had fewer resources and was, because of its Jewishness, in much greater danger—survived. The collapse of the city underground brought the existence of the ghetto underground to the Germans' attention, as some arrested non-Jewish members of the city underground revealed the names of their ghetto comrades. Many Jewish resisters were captured as a result in a massive German onslaught, but the ghetto underground remained intact. Numerous German attempts to apprehend Smolar failed as well, and he eventually left Minsk to join the Soviet partisans in the forest. The ghetto underground continued to operate until the majority of its members had relocated to the forest prior to the ghetto's destruction.

One of the key goals of the ghetto underground was to assist the incipient partisans' units in the forest, providing them with warm clothing and medicines, even though such items were desperately needed in the ghetto as well. The ghetto shoemaking workshop sent most of the footwear it produced to the partisans.[39] Essential medical supplies, testified ghetto hospital physician Anna Karpilova, were shipped to the forest whenever needed.[40] The ghetto hospital also became the underground's informal headquarters after Smolar started working in the hospital's boiler room. Germans refrained from entering the building out of a fear of infectious diseases, and Smolar made full use of this fact. Mark Taits, a doorman in the ghetto hospital testified: "I didn't know what Smolar did there; I just knew that no one was allowed into the boiler room—there [Smolar] was the boss."[41]

After Soviet partisan units had been organized around Minsk, the underground began smuggling trusted operatives into the forests. At this early point, it was impossible to get to the partisans without being active in the underground. Even underground members' families did not receive preferential treatment. In the Aktion of March 2, 1942, Gebelev lost his father, siblings, and their families. Could he have saved them? According to Gebelev's daughter Svetlana, he could have, as he had access to the fake and blank passports and identification forms that the underground used. He also could have smuggled the family out of the ghetto. In fact his relatives, according to some accounts, asked Gebelev to help organize their escape. He refused. For Gebelev, the cause of the underground trumped the well-being and even the survival of his own kin.[42]

Underground activism eventually came to affect resisters' entire families. Children, even if not actively involved in underground work, were nonetheless endangered. Frida Reizman's father led an underground weapons assembly squad. "I often slept on grenades and pistols because they were hidden underneath my mattress," she recalled.[43] Notke Wainhoyz kept the underground's printing press in his attic and recruited his sister-in-law for the dangerous task of distributing the resistance's leaflets.[44] The father of Yekaterina Perchonok-Kesler was a resistance member. Arrested by the Germans in April 1942, he was taken away in the direction of the city prison and never seen again. Three nights later, several Germans broke into the family's apartment and killed everyone who was there. Adjacent apartments were untouched, suggesting a targeted assault. Yekaterina Perchonok-Kesler had spent the night elsewhere and she survived.[45]

Although the underground operated inside the ghetto, its members saw themselves as participants in a broader communist, rather than strictly Jewish, endeavor. Khasia Pruslina received a fake passport from Smolar and was ordered to organize an underground cell outside the ghetto in the Russian part of the city. She was the only Jew in her cell and never questioned the assignment. "I was of a much better use [for the underground] on the Russian side," she claimed.[46] Whether one was in the ghetto or outside was purely a practical matter—a person was posted where he or she could contribute the most to the underground as a whole. Had Pruslina been told to go back to the ghetto and expose herself to the German killing squads, she would undoubtedly have done so.

Yaakov Greenstein's memoir is one of the very few that explicitly discuss the collective choices made within the underground. Sara Goland, an underground activist who brought the Greensteins to the resistance once told him: "In the ghetto, our only option is . . . the struggle of people sentenced to death, and in the forest we can do great things and assist the Red Army to expel the invaders-murderers from our land."[47] For the underground, violent action inside the ghetto was simply not an option. Discussing the Jewish collaborators, Greenstein writes: "We could have killed the traitors any time we wanted. We didn't do it because a terrorist action could have harmed our ability to carry out our duties." This strategy contrasts sharply with that of the Jewish undergrounds in many other Polish ghettos, such as Kraków's, where killing Jewish collaborators was the resistance's top priority. The possibility of internal ghetto rebellion does appear in Greenstein's account. "If we had no other option, we would have thought about doing something in the ghetto," he argues. However, approval from the Soviet partisans was required for such a rebellion to take place, for "any action in the ghetto . . . not approved by the higher command [would] be perceived as provocation."[48] In my data, this is the only instance of a ghetto uprising being explicitly mentioned by a Minsk underground member, and it is significant that this option is voiced by Greenstein, a refugee from Poland and a Zionist in his political convictions.[49]

Some scholars, however, see the Minsk ghetto underground as more Jewish than communist. "During the war," writes the historian Dina Porat, "[Jewish communists] began to see their connection to and responsibility for the Jewish people as more important than their ties to the Party outside the ghetto."[50] While I disagree with Porat's overall claim that in the ghetto the "Jewish" aspect of a resister's identity trumped the "communist" element, it is undeniable that both played an important role, if only because the war experiences of Jewish communists differed from those of their Slavic comrades. The Minsk ghetto underground, while ostensibly communist, did invest efforts in saving Jews *qua* Jews, especially after it became clear that the ghetto's days were numbered. The most notable expression of this attempt to save as many Jewish lives as possible was the creation of Jewish partisan detachments that, unlike non-Jewish units, had both military and civilian components. The most important of these detachments was "Unit 106," commanded by Shalom Zorin, who had fled the Minsk ghetto for the forest in late 1941. The unit consisted of a large family camp where Jewish children, women, and males who were unfit for combat—mostly Minsk ghetto escapees—were housed, as well as a fighting squad that protected the family camp and engaged in other missions.

It is therefore useful to compare Zorin's unit with a similar partisan detachment that was organized by Tuvia Bielski and his siblings. Unlike the "106," which consisted mainly of Soviet Jews, Bielski's unit, which later became the subject of Nechama Tec's sociological study[51] and the Hollywood movie *Defiance*, was composed mainly of Jews from Eastern Poland. The structure of both units was similar, and they shared the same goal—saving as many Jews as possible. Both were officially part of the

Soviet partisan movement. Yet despite these similarities, there were important differences between the two groups. "Our commander Zorin was more communist than Jewish, while the Bielski brothers were just the opposite," remarked Arkadii Krasinskii.[52] According to Leonid Okun, in Bielski's unit communist political officers were no more than window dressing—in practice, the detachment was independent.[53] This was not the case in the 106, where Khaim Feigelman, the unit's political officer and a low-ranking communist cadre before the war, organized extensive ideological training.[54]

If mistreated by other partisans, the Bielskis were willing and able to strike back. "[The unit] had 'sharp teeth' and had first-rate cutthroats (*otbornye rebiata-golovorezy*), Polish Jews who did not suffer from excessive sentimentality," recalled Okun.[55] Tatyana Boiko and Moisei Gorelik, who were quite familiar with both units, described the Bielskis' group as more independent, entrepreneurial, and nationalistic than their Soviet counterparts in the 106.[56] Though he tried to keep a degree of autonomy in his relations with the Soviet partisans' central command, Zorin was substantially more constrained in his actions. Okun, Zorin's personal messenger, recalls instances when Zorin was deceived by other units or when he was not informed about German troops operating in the area, but had to "suck it up."[57] And even though saving Jewish lives was indeed the Jewish partisans' goal, Jewish partisan commanders were sometimes as severe with their subordinates as were their non-Jewish, often anti-Semitic counterparts. Israel Lapidus, one of the Jewish partisan commanders, ordered the execution of another Jewish partisan, one Mishka Baran, for his refusal of an order to carry a milk jar; Zorin also executed a Jewish partisan who blatantly violated the security rules.[58]

Among the German Jews, we have no evidence of any resistance activity. According to Walter Brauner, the Soviet Jews, because they knew Russian, could cooperate with the partisans, but this "had nothing to do with us [Central European Jews]." Eric Floss was not even aware of the existence of the underground in the Soviet part of the ghetto.[59] The "Hamburg ghetto" did have young males and people with military training and combat experience, and some of its inmates had been politically active before the Second World War. Yet there are numerous reasons why a resistance movement was unlikely to arise in the "Hamburg ghetto," among them the Germans' lack of language skills and local contacts. The fact that the German Jews were also deficient in the skills needed to organize and lead such an effort also undoubtedly played a role.

Kraków

Anti-Nazi resistance groups began to organize in the city shortly after the German takeover. Made up predominantly of ethnic Poles, they engaged in the distribution of anti-Nazi propaganda, underground newspapers, and transcripts of British radio broadcasts, and they gathered intelligence for the Polish government in exile. Some Jews took part in these activities, but their numbers were small. Many of the groups did not welcome Jews, and even when Jews did want to contribute to the resistance effort, most did not have the proper contacts or connections. Marcel W. was a Polish patriot who wished to join the underground, but he had no idea how to do so, because he did not know any Polish underground members.[60] Unlike Marcel W., Mietek Pemper was a member of an underground group, and thanks to his typing abilities, took an active part in the production of underground leaflets. Pemper's underground activism was short-lived, however. He resigned when anti-Semitic diatribes started to appear in the publications he was helping to produce.[61] Norbert Githeim was in the Polish underground for much longer than Pemper. A Polish Army reserve officer, he knew and was known by the underground's leadership, which saw to it that his family was given fake documents and relocated to an ethnically Polish working-class suburb. However, when Githeim was killed by the Germans, the underground notified his wife and children that it could offer them no further assistance. They returned to the ghetto.[62]

The city's Jewish underground crystallized at a relatively late stage in the ghetto's history. Eventually, two Jewish resistance organizations emerged in Kraków—the *Iskra* (Polish for "spark") and the Fighting Organization of the Jewish *Halutz*[63] Youth (*Organizacja Bojowa Żydowskiej Młodzieży Chalucowej*), more widely known as the *Hehalutz Halochem* (Hebrew for "Fighting Pioneer"). The emergence and conduct of both groups can be directly traced to their leader's pre–World War II political activism and exposure to state repression.

"One evening I hear a knock on my door," recalled Shlomo Sh., who later became one of the Iskra commanders. "It was Heszek Bauminger, he told me that he was my instructor in the [Zionist] youth movement, but it took me some time to recall who he was."[64] Both Shlomo Sh. and Bauminger were born into religious Zionist families and had been active in the religious-Zionist *Hashomer Hadati* youth movement; Bauminger was the instructor (*madrich*) of a group to which Shlomo Sh. belonged when he was twelve. Both subsequently left the movement. Shlomo Sh. moved to

Akiva, the largest Zionist youth movement in the city, while Bauminger became a Marxist and joined the Socialist Zionist Hashomer Hatzair, becoming the head of its Kraków branch in 1939. When World War II broke out, he was drafted into the Polish army and eventually became a POW. He was able to make his way to Soviet-occupied Eastern Poland, however, where he worked as a truck driver. According to most sources, during his stay in the Soviet Union, Bauminger abandoned Zionism and became a communist.[65] Unlike most refugees, he took Soviet citizenship, and when Germany invaded the USSR, joined the Red Army. In the fall of 1941, Bauminger once again found himself a POW, this time in eastern Ukraine. He escaped the prison camp and returned to Kraków. On his way home Bauminger witnessed mass shootings of Jews in the German-occupied USSR. He reached Kraków before the first major wave of deportations to the death camps, at a time when most Jews did not yet fear total extermination. Bauminger of course knew perfectly well what the Germans were capable of and was determined to fight back. In the early summer of 1942, Iskra, the first Jewish underground in Kraków, was established.

Initially Iskra consisted of Bauminger, Shlomo Sh., and several of their friends. Because neither Bauminger nor Shlomo Sh. were active in Jewish youth movements at that time, recruitment efforts were based on personal ties and incentives, and there was no precondition of membership in a political party or movement. "We started to organize people in cells of five (*hamishiyot*) and to convince someone to join we would tell him that if he brings four more people he would become a cell leader," recalled Shlomo Sh.[66] Iskra's membership was open to all political affiliations. At the same time, even though prewar political activism was not a requirement for membership, the majority of the organization's members were active in various political organizations, most often the Communist Party or the Hashomer Hatzair. Based on the recollections of the few Iskra members who managed to survive the Holocaust, the historian Yael Peled-Margolin reconstructed the organization's roster. It is probably incomplete, but most likely includes the majority of this numerically small organization's members. Only a third of the Iskra fighters had not taken part in the activities of political organizations prior to the Holocaust.[67]

In addition to Bauminger, a key role in Iskra's activities was played by Gola Mire. Mire was born to a religious family, but as a teenager became active in the Hashomer Hatzair. In the early 1930s, she moved further to the left and was expelled from the movement. She then joined the Polish Communist Party and its underground. In 1936 she was incarcerated for organizing an illegal strike in one of Lwów's factories. According to Mire's cousin Rivka Kuper, when World War II began she escaped from prison and made her way to Soviet-occupied Eastern Poland,[68] where she met Bauminger. When Germany invaded the USSR 1941, Mire was married and expecting a baby. Her husband, also a devoted communist, left the city to join the Red Army. Because of her advanced pregnancy, Mire could not join him and eventually gave birth to a boy. When Mire's relatives in Kraków discovered her whereabouts, they immediately sent an ethnic Pole to bring her and her son to the city. Shortly after their arrival to Kraków, the boy died. Ideologically committed, skilled, and no longer having to take care of her baby, Mire renewed her contacts with Bauminger and quickly became one of Iskra's leading figures.

Under Mire and Bauminger's leadership, Iskra emerged as a small but well-organized group that engaged in anti-German sabotage and carried out nightly stealth assaults on off-duty servicemen. The organization's name, "spark" in Polish, likely comes from the group's first major action: setting fire to the garage where the SS stored its trucks.[69] Under Mire's influence Iskra also merged with the armed wing of the communist Polish Workers' Party (PPR), the *Gwardia Ludowa*, becoming its Jewish (and arguably most active) unit in the city.

For rank-and-file Iskra members, the main goal was to fight the Nazis. They were indifferent as to whether they were doing it with the communists or the Zionists,[70] but for Bauminger and especially Mire this question was important. "Gola was a declared communist and she always pushed for action," explained Shlomo Sh.[71] To Mire's dismay, however, the PPR was unpopular among the local population, and it had few weapons. Thus, a high profile action necessitated a trade-off of a kind familiar to leaders of underground violent groups, between increasing operational capacity and, by involving more people, potentially compromising operational security.[72] Iskra's manpower was simply insufficient for a large-scale operation, so Mire decided to join forces with the Zionist underground organization, the *Hehalutz Halochem* (HH).

HH had its origins in Akiva, the largest of Kraków's Zionist youth movements. As befit the city's tradition of political moderation and relative tolerance, the movement was neither radical nor Marxist in its political outlook, rejected violence, and focused mainly on cultural and educational activities. Akiva had more than a thousand members in the city, many of them of middle-class background. In the immediate prewar years the movement worked closely with Irene Harand, an Austrian anti-Nazi and human rights activist. Many of Harand's publications were reprinted in Akiva's newspaper, edited by Szymek Draenger. Shortly after the city was occupied, Draenger and his fiancée, Gusta Davidson, were arrested by the Germans and imprisoned in the Tropau camp. In late 1939 the couple was released, but the experience of the camp left a tremendous impression on them. When Draenger returned to his Zionist activities in 1940, it was clear to him that the Jews would have no chance of survival if they continued to be passive, and he shared this opinion, quite vocally, with other Akiva members. At this stage in the movement's development, however, its leaders were not thinking about armed resistance. Instead, they prioritized smuggling as many people as possible out of Poland.

Another top priority was to continue Akiva's educational activities, which became even more important after Jewish students were forbidden to attend schools. The focus on education was not unique to Akiva; most mid- and large-sized Jewish youth movements supported educational activities. Finally, the older movement members tried to continue preparing for agricultural life in Palestine's *kibbutzim*. Thanks to one of Akiva's leaders, Dolek Liebeskind, a senior employee of the German-authorized *Żydowska Samopomoc Społeczna* (ŻSS), a Jewish social help organization,[73] the movement received permission to operate a farm in Kopaliny, where many activists eventually moved. The bucolic life in Kopaliny was quite pleasant and movement members were spared the crowded conditions and food shortages of the ghetto. The farm lasted until the fall of 1942. As news about mass killings and the deportation of entire communities started to reach the farm, Akiva leaders realized that the threat had become both lethal and immediate, and the decision was finally reached to launch an armed resistance.[74]

The farm was liquidated and its residents returned to the ghetto. Most had lost their families in previous deportations and therefore did not have to financially support their parents or younger siblings. The youth movement, and by extension, the underground, became their new family. Initially the HH included only Akiva members, but later other Zionist youth movements, most importantly Dror and Akiva B, a splinter movement of the original Akiva, joined. Dror's leader Avraham Leibowicz (Laban), in addition to being a political activist, was known before the war as a protector of the Jewish children in the religious school from which he had graduated. The school was located on the outskirts of Kraków in a working-class neighborhood, and the Jewish students in their traditional garb were often beaten up by the locals. "When we walked with Laban . . . we were safe," a former student recalled.[75] At the same time, this tough brawler and political activist could not refuse Shifra Lustgarten (in those days she was called Elza Lapa) when she asked for money to buy candy before going on a dangerous mission. "I want to eat [my favorite] candy before I die," Lustgarten said. The underground was strapped for cash, but Laban, who was in charge of HH's finances, simply couldn't say no.[76]

Laban played an important role in the underground, but Akiva members were the core of HH. Unlike Iskra, which recruited members on the basis of personal ties, in the HH pre–World War II movement membership criteria were strictly applied. The organization's roster is available.[77] Out of ninety-seven members, only six did not belong to a Zionist youth movement. One of these six was a physics teacher who prepared explosives, and three additional non-youth-movement members belonged to the Young Jewish Writers' club, with which the resistance cooperated.

As an underground organization, HH encountered several problems. Because the Zionists had not been subject to state repression in prewar Poland, its members had no idea whatsoever about the basics of underground work. The "policy of secretiveness created great anxiety among the conspirators. . . . Practically overnight they had to make this tremendous leap of transforming a nonviolent cultural group" into an underground, admitted Davidson Draenger.[78] Worse still, they lacked the time needed to learn and adjust to operational security rules, which they constantly violated—a pattern openly recognized and lamented by Davidson Draenger,[79] the surviving HH fighters,[80] and the more conspiratorial Iskra members.[81] For instance, "no sooner did two [underground members] meet than others would start joining them, and soon they would all [go] walking down the street."[82] "They knew that it was not safe to meet in large groups, and that it was a problem, but they couldn't do anything about that—emotionally they couldn't keep distance from one another," recalled Shlomo Sh.[83] In the underground "we remained a youth movement and behaved by and large like a youth movement," admitted Yehuda Maimon.[84]

Another, related problem was that the HH people did not have fighting experience. The leaders acknowledged this weakness and, as a result, the moderate, centrist Zionist group connected with the communist PPR.[85] Mire, whom some HH leaders knew as an accomplished underground activist even before World War II,[86] was able to convince the two Jewish undergrounds to join forces and conduct a major anti-German operation, which later became known as the Cyganeria bombing. The two groups did not, however, formally merge, and Mire was not in a position to impose operational security rules on HH.

Preparations for action moved forward nonetheless, and on November 25, 1942, Akiva's last meeting took place in the ghetto. Dolek Liebeskind outlined the group's goals: "We are fighting for three lines in history," he announced, to make sure the world knew that the Jewish youth "did not go like lambs to the slaughter." After that meeting the underground members left the ghetto and dispersed to hiding places throughout the Aryan section of the city. The operation the movement was working on was scheduled to take place in less than a month.

Paradoxically, while the HH activists involved in the Cyganeria bombing wanted the world to know that the Jews were fighting back, the plan was to conduct their main operation disguised as ethnic Poles (even though there was not a single ethnic Pole among the fighters). Moreover, in addition to bombing several German coffee houses and a cinema frequented by German servicemen, the plan was to raise Polish national banners over the Vistula river bridges and to lay wreaths on the monuments of Polish national poet Adam Mickiewicz and independence struggle leader Tadeusz Kościuszko.[87] Neither Germans, nor Jews, nor Poles were supposed to know that it was Jews who had killed Germans in Kraków. The HH leaders feared that if they conducted the bombing as Jews, the ghetto would immediately be eliminated; to be able to openly fight as Jews, they would have to wait until the Germans themselves decided to liquidate the ghetto. The leadership of the Warsaw ghetto Jewish underground, with which the HH was in contact, tried to talk the organization out of acting outside the ghetto and urged them to prepare instead for an armed uprising inside the ghetto walls. Mire, most likely under pressure from her PPR superiors, pushed for immediate action and, as a communist, likely put little emphasis on the ethnic component of the struggle. "The timing [of the operation] was to a large extent determined by Gola Mire who pushed for action here and now," recalled Shlomo Sh.[88]

Realizing that without Mire the HH stood little chance, its leaders reluctantly agreed to the plan. "It was quite painful that we could not conduct the Cyganeria action as Jews," recalled Rivka Kuper, the only surviving member of the HH leadership.[89] Yitzhak (Antek) Zuckerman, a leader of the Warsaw ghetto underground, even made a dangerous trip to Kraków disguised as a Pole to try and convince the HH to abandon its plans. His timing could not have been worse—unbeknownst to Zuckerman, the bombing was scheduled for the day after his arrival.[90] From their perspective, the HH leaders feared that if they waited any longer, the organization would simply be eliminated by the Germans before they had managed to do anything. These fears were justified—the ghetto Jewish police became aware of the HH underground, tried to apprehend, and eventually arrested several (though not all) of its key members.[91] Only the Germans' racially motivated policy of not arming their Jewish collaborators prevented the HH's swift elimination prior to the Cyganeria bombing.

On the evening of December 22, 1942,[92] the fighters of the HH and Iskra bombed the Cyganeria coffee house. It was at the time packed with German servicemen. A number were killed and many more wounded. The exact number of German dead is unclear, with estimates ranging from seven to seventy. The most widely cited estimate is twelve, and the nature of the attack makes this number plausible.[93] The bombings of other targets failed. Unfortunately for the Jewish underground, it was betrayed from inside and most of its combatants were swiftly arrested. Liebeskind was killed in a shootout with the German police. Zuckerman was wounded in the leg, and had to flee, bleeding, back to Warsaw.

The circumstances of this betrayal give vivid proof of HH's inexperience, naiveté, and failure to internalize the rules of operational security. The traitors were two members of the group, Julek Appel and Natek Waisman. Waisman probably should not have been admitted to the underground to begin with—his sister was a close friend of a well-known Nazi informer whom the HH had tried to assassinate.[94] Yet in spite of this, he was allowed to join, according to Kuper because he had been an Akiva member before World War II. Appel, who worked in a German mechanical shop, was also known as a Gestapo informer among his coworkers.[95] During the early days of HH, both Waisman and Appel had been arrested by the Germans but later released, most likely after agreeing to serve as informants. "Gola [Mire], who was an experienced underground person . . . warned us: 'If the Germans let them go, be very careful with them,'" recalled Kuper. "[But] we, naïve as we were . . . did not really hide anything from them. Especially not from Waisman, whom we knew for a long time."[96]

After the Cyganeria bombing, Germans raided HH's main hideout, dooming the organization and with it Bauminger and Mire, who were in constant contact with HH. Iskra's operational security rules were tighter, its members were dispersed among several hideouts,[97] and the organization was not betrayed from inside. Therefore, many members escaped arrest or were arrested because they were thought to be Polish, rather than Jewish resisters—often a distinction that meant the difference between life and death. The German security services' report on the capture and killing of the underground leaders correctly identifies the heads of the HH, and incorrectly identifies those of Iskra, yet another indication of the level of German information on these two groups.[98]

Even though the German authorities were well aware of the real identities of the people who conducted the bombing, the belief that the ghetto would be liquidated in retaliation proved incorrect. The Germans in fact did everything they could to conceal the very fact of the attack.[99] The prevailing assumption of both the Jews in the ghetto and the Poles on the Aryan side was that Polish nationalist underground fighters were responsible for the bombing. One rumor went even further, claiming that the Soviets parachuted special forces into the city. For the Jewish underground, on the other hand, the situation was desperate—a large number of resisters were arrested and thrown into the Gestapo's Montelupich prison, both organizations were decapitated, and credit for the operation went to ethnic Poles. Hella Rufeisen-Schüpper, an underground courier who lived outside the ghetto on Aryan papers, was afraid that she might be the last living person to know the truth. Driven by this fear, she revealed her Jewish identity to a random Polish co-traveler on the train from Warsaw and begged him to tell the story behind the bombing if he managed to survive the war.[100] Needless to say, it was a desperate, potentially suicidal move. Revealing her Jewish identity to a stranger, even one who looked fully trustworthy, could easily have cost Rufeisen-Schüpper her life.

Miraculously, a handful of the arrested underground members managed to escape on the way to their execution. They joined forces with those few members who had succeeded in avoiding arrest and hid in the forests around Nowy Wiśnicz, thirty miles from Kraków. Most were killed or arrested by the Germans; others by the Polish nationalist underground. A handful managed to survive until liberation; two—Elza Lapa and Szymek Lustgarten—were hidden by a friendly non-Jewish family.

Obviously, not every Akiva member joined the underground. Some were simply not invited because they were considered too young for underground work. Ida L., who belonged to the younger Akiva cohort, recalled how she and her friends used to get together to sing and chat. Only later did she learn that in the other room older members were conspiring against the Germans.[101] Frederic B. and William S. were invited to join, but refused.[102] The former did not believe it was possible to fight the Germans because they had spies everywhere, the latter was not "biographically available" as he had a family to take care of. There were also others who were not biographically available for underground activism.[103] Not every person with a history of political activism joined the underground, but the resistance was certainly dominated by politically active Jews.

When it comes to evaluating the conduct of both resistance groups, we should remember that even though both Iskra and HH were largely incapacitated by the Germans, the trajectories of the two groups diverged. Iskra managed to put up a sustained fight for about a year and was destroyed after conducting a large-scale action that promoted the group leadership's broader political goals. Had they not been pressured by the PPR to conduct the bombing, Iskra could have probably survived for much longer. The HH's fate took a different turn. The group managed to exist for only three months, conducted a single anti-German action, and was eliminated because German collaborators had penetrated its ranks. Bombing was also not a strategy that the HH chose for itself—both the target and the method were imposed on them. HH members had more than enough determination and courage to fight the Nazis, but as they had not experienced state repression prior to World War II, they lacked the necessary skills that might have transformed their initial, short-lived mobilization into sustained resistance.

BIAŁYSTOK

Shortly after the German occupation of Białystok, a joint Polish-Jewish communist underground was established. Its key goal was to assist the Soviet Union in its struggle against the Nazis. The initiative came from Tadeusz Jakubowski, an ethnically Polish local communist who hid in the ghetto before moving to Warsaw. Besides Jakubowski and a handful of other ethnic Poles, virtually all of the underground's members were Jewish. In December 1941, the "Organization of Workers and Peasants for War against the Invaders," which later became known as the Anti-Fascist Committee, was established.[104] It should not surprise anyone, notes Sara Bender, that the communists were the first movers in the resistance. All other movements and organizations had been disbanded by the Soviets. Several Zionist youth movements in the city had gone underground to evade the Soviets, but they were leaderless. Shortly after the Red Army occupied Białystok in September 1939, many of the local Zionist youth movements' activists, most notably the city's Hashomer leader Chajka Grosman, escaped the city and moved to Wilno, which until 1940 belonged to a still-independent Lithuania. Furthermore, because the Communist Party had been subject to state repression in interwar Poland, its members possessed a tested toolkit of resistance strategies. The Białystok communists were thus in a good position to launch a resistance effort immediately after the German occupation.

As in Minsk, the initial impetus for the establishment of the underground was a desire to help Red Army soldiers who had been taken prisoner by German troops.[105] According to the historian and underground activist Szymon Datner, many young Jews willingly joined the resistance—and they included people of both sexes who belonged to every political stream. It was the older members, however, who had been communist activists and had a substantial amount of critical underground experience.[106]

Around the same time, in German-occupied Wilno, where numerous Zionist youth movements' members had gathered during the Soviet occupation, these organizations renewed their activities openly. Prior to the Soviet occupation of Lithuania, Zionist youth movements had established in Wilno what later became known as the *Koordinatsia* (Coordination)—a joint body that coordinated their activities. The main goal of the Koordinatsia was to arrange for the immigration of as many activists as possible to Palestine. Under Soviet rule, the Koordinatsia ceased to exist, because the Zionist youth movements went underground and operated independently of one another (*kol ehad iashav bepinato vepaal besheket*).[107] Following the German occupation of Wilno, it was decided to resume the Koordinatsia's activities. One of the first things the Zionist youth had to do was to determine their response to the mass killings that had begun immediately after the Germans took over the city. According to Nisan Reznik, a Koordinatsia member from the *Hanoar Hatzioni* (The Zionist Youth) movement, opinions were divided. Hashomer Hatzair, led by the poet Aba Kovner, a Wilno resident before World War II, argued that the shootings in Wilno were part of a larger plan to kill all the Jews under German rule and that is was therefore necessary to immediately organize resistance. Dror, led by Mordechai Tenenbaum, a refugee from Warsaw, argued that the conditions in Wilno were unique, and that the solution was instead to try to relocate as many young Zionists as possible to safer havens.[108] Reznik believes that at that time Tenenbaum most likely did not favor armed resistance inside the ghetto.[109]

To achieve the goal of saving Dror members, Tenenbaum established contact with Anton Schmidt, an anti-Nazi German NCO, and with Schmidt's assistance devised a daring plan of smuggling them from the Latvian port city of Liepaya (Libau) to Sweden over the frozen Baltic Sea. When the plan fell through, Tenenbaum chose what he considered to be the second best refuge—the Białystok ghetto, which was relatively safe at that time. Some Dror members decided to stay in Wilno,[110] and some Hashomer members eventually also left for Białystok. Having transferred about a dozen Dror activists from Wilno to Białystok, Tenenbaum left the city and moved back to Warsaw. Even though he looked Jewish, he managed to arrange false documents for himself. His new identity was that of one Josef Tamaroff, a Muslim Tatar. Tatars usually had black hair, dark eyes, and were circumcised, and this was therefore a perfect arrangement that allowed Tenenbaum to move rather freely around occupied Poland. The key danger in having Tatar documents was the need to be familiar with the traditions and religion of Islam—which Polish Jews generally were not. However, Tenenbaum, who had studied at Warsaw University's Institute of Oriental Studies, likely knew more than most.

Meanwhile, the Jewish underground resistance movement FPO (*Fareynikte Partizaner Organizatsye*) was organized in Wilno. FPO members took in the whole political spectrum, from the communists on the far left to Revisionist Zionists on the right, and together they began preparing an uprising (which never materialized). One of the FPO members was Chajka Grosman, who prior to the war had been the leader of Białystok's Hashomer Hatzair chapter. It was decided that Grosman should return to her hometown to organize resistance among the Zionist youth.

Upon arriving in Białystok, Grosman discovered that there was a communist underground already operating in the city. They were not interested in fighting inside the ghetto, however, and saw their main goal as smuggling as many young fighters as possible to the forests, where they could better help the Soviet Union win the war. Hashomer's key mission, on the other hand, was fighting for Jewish honor and resisting the Nazis inside the ghetto. Furthermore, while the Białystok communists were willing to consider cooperation with the Marxist Hashomer Hatzair, they steadfastly refused to have anything to do with the less radical Dror, let alone with right-wing Revisionists.

To influence the communists Grosman had to travel to Warsaw, where she approached Józef Lewartowski, a leading Polish communist of Jewish origin, and urged him to support the creation of a joint underground of all political forces. While sympathetic to Grosman's goal, Lewartowski was not in a position to help. Białystok, he argued, was now legally a part of the Soviet Union, and he therefore had no authority over the comrades there.[111] In addition to attempts to influence the communists, Grosman also invested considerable effort in bringing her partner Edek Boraks to Białystok. Boraks was an experienced Zionist underground activist under the Soviets, and Grosman hoped that he would oversee the military aspects of resistance activities. After Grosman returned once more to her hometown, the previously leaderless Hashomer Hatzair members in Białystok began organizing into a resistance force.

Later on, the communists and the Hashomer were able to reach a compromise according to which both fighting inside the ghetto *and* guerilla warfare in the forests would be goals of the resistance movement. In August 1942, what would later become known as Anti-Fascist Front A was established. Its members were the communists, the Hashomer Hatzair, and a faction of the Bund. Not everyone was happy with this arrangement. A communist group led by Yudita Nowogrodska opposed the idea of fighting inside the ghetto, split from the unified underground, and created their own organization with the mission of sending people to fight in the forests.

What the Front A leaders probably did not realize is that by splitting up their forces (and their weapons caches) they were weakening both prongs of the struggle. When the first groups of Jewish partisans went out to the forests, very few Hashomer members joined them. A movement member, Aharon Liak, explained that there were two main reasons for this: first, the acute shortage of weapons, and second, the fact that the idea of an uprising in the ghetto was still foremost in the minds of the young Zionists.[112] Yet even though Hashomer sent very few people to the forests, those who went were its best-trained and most capable members, such as Eliyahu Vered, a Polish Army NCO and one of the few members with prior military experience. In the Hashomer Hatzair underground, Vered was in charge of training, so sending him to the forest probably reduced prospects for military action within the ghetto quite substantially.[113]

Even though a unified organization of communists and the Hashomer Hatzair was established, in practice each movement operated alone, often without knowing what its counterpart was doing. Some rank-and-file resistance members did not even know that other political groups also had undergrounds in the ghetto. This, nevertheless, should be seen not only as a sign of very loose cooperation, but also as an indicator of sound operational security rules. Several of the underground's rank and file indicated in their testimonies that they knew little of the underground's activities beyond the immediate tasks of their five-person cell and were not familiar with underground members outside their cell.[114]

In November 1942, Mordechai Tenenbaum returned to Bezirk Bialystok because the Warsaw ghetto Jewish Fighting Organization (the ŻOB) had decided to appoint him commandant of the ghetto underground. In practice this appointment did not mean much. Tenenbaum could not automatically command the obedience and support of any group in the Białystok ghetto other than Dror, his own movement. At the same time, he was a respected Zionist youth leader. He had been one of the key activists of the Koordinatsia and the Zionist underground in the USSR, where he had worked with the Hashomer activists, including Boraks and Grosman. In January of 1943, after lengthy negotiations on often hair-splitting ideological questions, Anti-Fascist Front B was established. It was an amalgam that included Dror, Hashomer Hatzair, Hanoar Hatzioni, the Revisionists, and a faction of the Bund party. Hashomer Hatzair, which was a member of both Fronts, served as a link between the organizations. Around that time Tenenbaum also started keeping a diary, which survived the war. Written in beautiful Hebrew with occasional words and phrases in Yiddish, Polish, Russian, German, and English, it provides a unique and invaluable, though inherently biased, source of data on the Białystok ghetto underground.

Also in January 1943, Tenenbaum composed an appeal to the ghetto Jews, which was scheduled for publication at the outbreak of the uprising. This document is a good source of insights into the motivations and goals of Tenenbaum and his comrades.

> Five million Jews have already been murdered; of Polish Jewry only ten percent has been left . . . We shall not go like lambs to the slaughter! If we are too weak to defend our lives—we are strong enough to defend our Jewish honor and our human dignity. We shall fall like heroes, and in our death—we will not die! . . . Don't escape from the ghetto—without weapons you will be killed. After you fulfill your national duty [of fighting inside the ghetto]—go armed to the partisans. The arms you can get from every German in the ghetto.[115]

For Tenenbaum, as is clear from the words "and in our death—we will not die," fighting and defending their national honor was a mode of survival similar to Liebeskind's "three lines in history." It meant not the physical survival of individuals, but the symbolic, historical survival of the group. In this sense, the ghetto's Judenrat leader Barasz (see chapter 4), who cooperated with the Germans, and Tenenbaum, who resisted them, were not that different. Both thought in terms of the group and collective survival (as each of them understood it), and both were willing to sacrifice their lives to achieve this goal. For the communists, on the contrary, Jewish national honor meant little; much more important was Soviet victory over Germany.

When news of the February 1943 Aktion reached the underground, Tenenbaum and his comrades had to choose whether to "fight after the first Jew is taken out of the ghetto" or wait until the final liquidation. Even though the weaponry possessed by the underground was completely inadequate, the general mood of the activists favored rebellion. Hashomer Hatzair led the militant line; the Dror members were more hesitant, even though most of them "despised the idea of going to the forests."[116] However, at the last moment Tenenbaum backed down and ruled against rebellion. All Dror members survived the Aktion. The Hashomer was not so lucky. A bunker in which Boraks and several other movement members hid was discovered by the Germans. They were deported to Treblinka and killed there.

After the February Aktion, the underground sped up their preparations for an uprising. "Initially it was more a game than work," recalled Fina Cukiert, a communist underground member. "The work started in full strength after the [February] Aktion."[117] The main foci of Tenenbaum's activities during those days were obtaining weapons, the unification of the two Fronts, and the protection of his organization from the German security services. "Have to be careful (*tsarikh lehizaher*)," Tenenbaum wrote in his diary. "And again, conspiracy rules—as in Soviet times," he added, describing his attempts to minimize unnecessary contacts between movement members.[118]

In his effort to obtain weapons, Tenenbaum made an attempt to contact the main Polish nationalist underground, the *Armia Krajowa* (AK). Invoking the example of Warsaw, where the AK had helped the Jewish underground obtain weapons, he wondered why the same could not also be done in Białystok. The causes of AK hostility are well known and rooted in the city's immediate history—Poles accused the Jews of widespread collaboration with the Soviets and resented them for it. Tenenbaum tried to convince the AK that Jewish organizations had also suffered under the Soviets, but in this he failed. No help was extended to the Jewish underground, even though Tenenbaum described the members of his organization as citizens of the Polish state, fighting against their country's enemy and therefore deserving support.[119] While the Polish nationalist AK was unwilling to help, the communist Gwardia Ludowa was unable to do so. Because Białystok was considered part of the Soviet Union, the GL was simply not allowed to operate in this territory, and the first Soviet partisans reached the area only after the ghetto was liquidated.

Eventually, on the eve of the ghetto's destruction, Tenenbaum was able to secure the unification of both Fronts into one fighting organization. He was elected commander and Daniel Moszkowicz, a communist, became his deputy. On the evening of August 15, 1943, Chasia Bornstein-Bielicka, a member of the Hashomer Hatzair who lived on the Aryan side, snuck into the ghetto and notified her comrades that the city was swarming with troops, and that the Germans were encircling the ghetto.[120] Her information was dismissed and no one bothered to notify Tenenbaum. Barasz, the Judenrat leader who previously promised to let the underground know when the liquidation order came, also reneged on his promise. Thus, the underground lost several crucial hours that could have been spent preparing for action. By the time of the uprising, the underground had around two hundred fighters, 130 firearms, and a large cache of grenades, mostly homemade in the ghetto.[121] Most members had very little to no military training. When the time for the uprising came, Irene S., a member of the Hashomer Hatzair, was given a grenade and sent to blow up a German tank. The problem was that she had no idea how to use the weapon. "I didn't know which end to open and how to open [it]," she later admitted. Irene S. describes how she stood with the grenade, trembling, "and I hear a German voice in the back of me . . . an old [German soldier], saying 'what are you doing, *mein Kind* [my child] . . . Give [the grenade] to me. Where are your parents?' He thought I was a lost child who just picked up a grenade." The German soldier led Irene S. to her parents, who were in the deportation area. "That was my contribution to the underground at that point," she concluded.[122]

Nevertheless, despite their shortage of ammunition and limited training, Tenenbaum and his fighters fought valiantly, and the Germans were forced to use tanks and air power to put down the uprising. Contrary to Tenenbaum's hopes, the ghetto population did not join the rebellion. The majority of the fighters were killed or captured by the Germans; a handful managed to escape the ghetto. Tenenbaum's own fate is somewhat unclear. The most likely scenario is that when he and Moszkowicz were surrounded during the final stages of the fighting, they committed suicide.

The defeat of the uprising was not the end of the Jewish resistance. Two groups of underground members went on fighting the Germans from the forests around Białystok, and Grosman, together with several female comrades from the ghetto underground, continued to operate a resistance cell in the city until its liberation in the summer of 1944. This cell provided the Soviet partisans with supplies and weapons, obtained intelligence for the advancing Red Army, and even managed to convince several German officials, including Nazi Party members, to switch sides, join the resistance, and start working for the Soviets.[123] In Białystok, both the communists and the Zionists had been victims of selective repression prior World War II, and both managed to put up a sustained fight.

Who were the underground members? The vast majority were politically active young people, either communists or Zionists. Fina Cukiert, for instance, was invited to join the underground precisely because she was perceived to have been a trustworthy Komsomol activist under the Soviets.[124] People who did not belong to political organizations or did not have proper connections had difficulty joining even if they themselves wanted to volunteer. Thus Sergei Berkner, even though not a member of any political organization, was allowed to join only because his father was connected to the communist underground.[125] He was sent to the forest and survived the war. Others were approached because of their unique skills and resources. Eva Kraczowska, who came from a wealthy and assimilated (by Białystok standards) family very much wanted to join the underground but initially had little success. The communists looked askance at her wealthy background, and the Zionists saw her as too assimilated. Eventually she was admitted to Nowogrodska's communist splinter group for the sole reason that the underground wanted to use her room as a meeting place. Almost none of her friends with a similar background were in the resistance.[126] Yisrael Pranski was approached by the underground because of his prewar ham (amateur) radio hobby. A self-described "lone wolf," he refused.[127] Zalman Fain was not politically active before the war and was not typical underground material. But he had been born in the small town of Supraśl, about ten miles from Białystok, and knew the local forests. What is more, he had served in the Polish Army where he received military training. For these reasons, he was invited to join the underground and helped lead the communist fighters through the forests.[128] Fain, however, was an exceptional case. Overall, the very small number of people with previous military experience in the underground suggests that training, capability, and physical strength alone had little impact on recruitment patterns; previous political activism was much more important.

As in the other two ghettos, biographical availability also affected the decision to join, but only to a degree. For the most ideologically committed activists it did not play much of a role. Tenenbaum was biographically available for resistance, as were most other Dror members, because they did not have families in the ghetto. But many Hashomer Hatzair and Communist fighters did have parents, siblings, or children who would have benefited from their full-time employment. Where biographical availability did seem to matter more was in the case of less ideologically devoted Jews, like Rachel Lahower who did not want to join the resistance because her parents were against the idea and "back then people would listen to [their] parents."[129]

There are two questions that are crucial to the analysis of the Białystok ghetto uprising. First, was the uprising local in its origins, or was it imported from Warsaw by Tenenbaum? And second, why did the communists in Białystok agree to take part in the rebellion, even though it did not promote their main goal of contributing to a Soviet victory but instead diverted manpower and resources from guerilla warfare?

It is impossible to know for sure whether the Białystok ghetto would have rebelled without Tenenbaum. The available evidence, though, suggests a very high likelihood that an uprising would have happened even without him. "The idea of the uprising was of the Hashomer," recalled Shmuel Goldberg, a member of the communist underground,[130] and the movement had never abandoned the will to rebel. Even when Front A started sending people to the forests, very few Hashomer Hatzair members went, precisely because the organization strongly supported the ghetto rebellion strategy. Tenenbaum himself wrote that Hashomer support for an uprising was unequivocal, while the Dror members were still undecided. It was Tenenbaum who called off the uprising during the February Aktion after Barasz convinced him to do so—Hashomer Hatzair had been willing to fight at that time. Finally, most Hashomer Hatzair members in the Białystok ghetto were city natives, as was their leader, Chajka Grosman. This evidence supports the argument that the uprising was not the result of Warsaw's influence.

Why did the communists agree to the idea of armed uprising inside the ghetto? In my view, here the city's unique local history plays a key role. According to Dror member Bronia Klibanski, the communists in Białystok were in limbo.[131] They were used to party discipline and felt lost when they found themselves cut loose from instructions and guidance. The Polish Communist Party was geographically close by, but refrained from interfering because the city was perceived to be part of the USSR; at the same time, local communists had no contacts with Moscow. According to the communist Eliasz Baumetz, there were instructions from the Aryan side, but they were inconsistent.[132] The Zionists, on the other hand, enjoyed the financial assistance and backing of Barasz and were organizationally stronger than their communist counterparts. This peculiar situation faced by the Białystok communists probably made them more open to local pressures and initiatives; and that, in my view, was why they agreed to cooperate with the Zionists.

CONCLUDING REMARKS

An analysis of the Jewish resistance in the Minsk, Kraków, and Białystok ghettos reveals two clear and related patterns. First, the pre–World War II political regimes of the cities had a substantial effect on the conduct and fate of the Jewish underground. Previous selective repression created a pool of people in local Jewish communities who possessed resistance skills; indiscriminate repression did not. Second, people with pre-Holocaust political experience were more likely to join the underground.

When we examine who resisted, Jewish resistance proves not to be vastly different from other forms of high-risk activism. When the sociologist Doug McAdam studied those who volunteered for the Freedom Summer Project in the United States, he found that "participants in high-risk/cost activism are expected to (a) have a history of activism, (b) be deeply committed to the ideology and goals of the movement, (c) be integrated into activist networks, and (d) be relatively free of personal constraints that would make participation especially risky."[133] Jewish resisters in the three ghettos largely fit this description, but not completely. Almost all were deeply committed and well integrated into activist networks. Many, such as Smolar, Gebelev, Tenenbaum, and Mire were biographically available. But some who did have families to support nonetheless made the decision to participate in resistance, which suggests that biographical availability is not a necessary condition for high-risk activism. Other factors, like ideological commitment to the cause, were more important. Where biographic availability might have played a role is in the choice between cooperation and resistance. As I demonstrated in this chapter and chapter 4, both resistance movements and cooperation/public collaboration bodies were dominated by people with previous political experience. Both groups were thus driven by an underlying desire to help the community, and in two of the three ghettos there was cooperation and mutual respect between the Judenrat and the underground. Even though we do not have comprehensive data that would allow us to fully test this claim, it is plausible that is was biographic availability that determined the choice between resistance and cooperation, with age and the need to support a family steering people toward helping the community by cooperating with the Germans, rather than going underground.

Jewish armed resistance, while ultimately focused on inflicting as much damage as possible on the Nazis, took many forms. Some were symbolic and open, such as the Białystok ghetto uprising, while others were less visible, but potentially more effective. In the choice between a highly visible, but suicidal uprising for the sake of restoring national honor and the quiet, less glamorous task of gathering intelligence for the Soviets or transferring of Jews out of the ghetto, which strategy was more valuable? I do not believe that there is a correct answer. The goal of this chapter is more modest. First, I argue that we ought to analyze the whole spectrum of the Jewish underground, including those organizations that ultimately failed in their quest to resist. Second, by identifying the factors that made resistance groups more or less likely to survive and individuals more or less likely to join the underground, we will be able to put the resistance into its real empirical and analytical contexts. By doing so we will move the discussion away from both the completely unreasonable expectation of the Jews' universal resistance and a compassionate, but analytically problematic desire to demonstrate that resistance was almost everything the Jews did to survive.

When it comes to resistance, as with other types of Jewish behavior, pre-Holocaust politics were crucial. The Zionist underground in the Kraków ghetto was unable to rebel and failed early on, whereas their comrades in Białystok were able to stage an uprising. But this does not mean that the members of the Zionist underground in Białystok were smarter, more courageous, or more committed. Rather, because Białystok happened to be located east of the Molotov-Ribbentrop line, which of course was not drawn by the Jews, Białystok Zionists had the opportunity to acquire more skills than their comrades in Kraków. Had Kraków been located 150 miles to the east, we might reasonably have expected a ghetto uprising there as well. This argument applies not only to these two ghettos. In appendix 3, I conduct a large-N econometric analysis of ghetto uprisings. The data are limited and the analysis should therefore be treated as a plausibility test only, but the results do demonstrate that pre-Holocaust regimes shaped Jewish behavior throughout Nazi-occupied Poland and the USSR.

CHAPTER 8

CONCLUSIONS

"Can there be a political science of the Holocaust?" asks Charles King.[1] One of the key goals of this book was to answer this question in the affirmative. I have done so by using the theoretical and methodological tools of the social sciences to analyze one of the most overlooked aspects of the Holocaust: variation in Jewish victims' individual and collective behavior.

At the individual level, this book suggests a new typology of victims' behavioral strategies: cooperation and collaboration, coping and compliance, evasion, and resistance. I apply this typology to Jewish behavior in three important, but understudied ghettos: Minsk, Kraków, and Białystok. The comparison of the three ghettos demonstrates several patterns. First, knowledge and information about Nazi policies did play a role in the Jews' choice of behaviors. The impact of knowledge is most evident in the massive Jewish flight from Kraków that took place during the first days of the war, compared to the more limited escape attempts undertaken by Jews in Minsk. In Kraków, Jews had access to reliable sources of information on the Nazis' anti-Jewish policies, and the city was host to numerous Jewish refugees from Germany between 1938 and 1939. In Minsk, on the other hand, negative coverage of German anti-Jewish policies was silenced in 1939–41 by the Soviets, and therefore many Jews, especially those of the older generation, were swayed by memories of their positive encounters with the German state during World War I. They relied on the information available to them and decided not to flee.

At the same time, knowledge and information alone could not account for all variation in the Jews' behavior. Other factors were more important. Thus, people with a history of pre–World War II political activism were overrepresented among those who both resisted and cooperated, while Jews who were well integrated into non-Jewish society were more likely to choose evasion. Those who were plugged into predominantly Jewish support and social networks favored coping as their key survival strategy.

It was the politically active people who resisted the Nazis in the ghettos of Minsk, Kraków, and Białystok. As this book has demonstrated, the ideology that underlay a resister's political activism did not affect her likelihood of joining the resistance—individual Communists, Zionists, and Bundists resisted with equal zeal and determination. The ideology of prewar political activism did, however, affect the form of resistance—the Communists preferred fighting outside the ghetto, while the Zionists opted for uprisings inside the ghetto walls that would safeguard the honor of Jews *qua* Jews. In addition, prior political experience impacted prospects for coordination among resisters; Jewish Communists and Zionists did not always want to cooperate, even in the face of the common Nazi threat.

But politically active people not only resisted the Nazis; they were also more likely to be among those who cooperated and publicly collaborated with them. Here, however, the evidence is more mixed. The Judenrat of the Białystok ghetto consisted almost exclusively of people with previous political and public experience; in Kraków the Judenrat included both political activists and people without past experience in public life; while in Minsk the Germans prevented politically active people from joining the Judenrat due to the prevalence of communists among them. Importantly, this argument does not hold for the Jewish police, thus highlighting the need to analytically distinguish between the two bodies. In Białystok with its strong Judenrat and robust Jewish community, the Jewish police were subordinate to the Judenrat and did not evolve into a gang of private collaborators who were willing to increase their survival chances by decreasing those of their coethnics. In Minsk and Kraków, which had largely impotent, even if well-intentioned Judenrats and more diverse and divided Jewish communities, the situation was different. Both ghettos did have some honest and upright Jewish policemen, but a very large percentage were utterly corrupt and brutal toward other Jews, even when they were not supervised by the Germans.

Cooperation, public collaboration, and resistance are located at opposite ends of the spectrum—cooperation and public collaboration implied working with the Nazis, while resistance required fighting them. But we should not forget that whereas behaviors differed, the motivations behind them were similar. Both resisters and public collaborators/cooperators sought to enhance the well-being of the group, be it the Jewish community or the ideals of communism, Bundism, or Zionism. This can be seen most clearly in the case of Ephraim Barasz, the leader of the Białystok ghetto Judenrat, who tirelessly pursued a strategy aimed at saving the ghetto by making it indispensable to the German war effort, even though he believed that after the war he would be executed for collaboration with the enemy. And indeed, in both Minsk and Białystok (until the final liquidation of the ghetto) there was a degree of cooperation and mutual understanding between the Judenrat and the resistance. Although cooperators, public collaborators, and resisters opted for different strategies, their choices all reflected commitment to the welfare of the group, rather than to their private well-being.

Coping was the most common strategy adopted by Jewish victims of the Holocaust, and many clung to this strategy till the bitter end. The most likely alternative, evasion, was not available to everyone. People who were well integrated into local non-Jewish societies and were members of interethnic social networks—e.g., those who had Polish, Russian, and Belorussian friends and knew the local language and traditions—were much more likely to choose evasion than those who were not. Thus, in Minsk and Kraków, where many Jews were well integrated into non-Jewish society, evasion was widespread, because even people who looked stereotypically Jewish had a chance to survive so long as they had non-Jewish friends or acquaintances. In Białystok, where integration was extremely limited, even Jews who had blond hair and blue eyes stood almost no chance of escaping persecution. In addition, people who were not integrated into non-Jewish society but had numerous intra-Jewish ties could reasonably expect that life inside the ghetto, as long as it lasted, would be easier than life on the outside.

The factors that shaped the Jews' choice of a particular strategy are then the following: the patterns and contents of their political activism, the type and intensity of the repression they experienced, the degree of their integration into non-Jewish society, and the ethnic composition of their social networks. This book has argued that all of these factors were shaped by one crucial variable: the city's pre-Holocaust political regime. The overall menu of possible strategies was, after all, identical across ghettos, but there was variation in the distribution of strategies from one ghetto to another. The difference between Kraków's Austro-Hungarian legacy of relative ethnic and religious tolerance and the toxic interethnic environment of Białystok had tangibly different effects on Jewish behavior in each Polish city—not only when it came to evasion, but also with regard to resistance, collaboration, and coping. Thus, the "salvation through labor" philosophy (and coping more generally) had greater appeal and a higher likelihood of success in Białystok with its cohesive and well-organized Jewish community than in the more diverse environment of Kraków, where a substantial number of ghetto inmates had more in common with their prewar ethnically Polish neighbors and colleagues than with their Jewish coethnics. Indeed, the strategy *almost* worked in Białystok, where the local German authorities did their best to shield the ghetto from destruction. No such attempts were made in Kraków.[2] In addition, patterns of pre-Holocaust state repression, which differed from one city to another, affected the sustainability of resistance in the three ghettos. In places that were subject to selective repression, activists had learned skills that would allow them to more successfully resist the Nazis, whereas activists in places subject to indiscriminate repression had not.

MOVING FORWARD: SOCIAL SCIENCES AND JEWISH BEHAVIOR

Entire libraries could be filled with the books and articles that debate whether the Holocaust was a unique, possibly inexplicable event or one that can be compared with other cases of genocide and approached not only normatively, but analytically. I do not discuss the Holocaust as a whole, but when it comes to the topic of Jewish behavior, my goal is actually somewhat more ambitious. What this book has tried to do is to incorporate theories and findings from social science research on topics other than genocide into the academic discourse on the Holocaust.

The argument that people who were politically active before World War II tended to be overrepresented in resistance movements originates directly from studies of high-risk activism in other environments. Thus, Doug McAdam's analysis of the 1964 Mississippi Freedom Summer project argues that Freedom Summer participants had a history of prior civil rights activism and strong ideological commitment to the cause. They also tended to have stronger ties to other people engaged in similar activities. Participation depended as well on their "biographical availability"; that is, on their being in the right age range and not having a permanent job or a family to support.[3] Jewish resistance in the ghettos was guided by similar processes. Mainly young, ideologically committed and well-networked people, often students without families to support or steady jobs to perform were most likely to register voters in Mississippi and to fight the Germans in the ghettos.

The importance of inter- versus intraethnic social networks is also well-established in the social sciences. As Ashutosh Varshney argues, interethnic engagement has been instrumental in preventing community-level violence in India: the denser the social ties between Hindus and Muslims, the less likely riots were to break out.[4] Jeffrey Kopstein and Jason Wittenberg have identified a similar pattern in their study of anti-Jewish pogroms in the summer of 1941.[5] Thus, it is not surprising that in Minsk and Kraków, which had higher levels of interethnic integration, the Holocaust unfolded and was experienced differently than in thoroughly segregated Białystok.

Although not a unique case of mass violence, the Holocaust is the most extreme. Yet when the goal is to understand "ordinary people in extraordinary times,"[6] there is no compelling reason not to integrate the insights of social sciences into Holocaust research and to use the Holocaust to develop new arguments and refine existing frameworks. A political science of the Holocaust, this book demonstrates, is not only feasible, it is desirable.

MOVING FORWARD: LEVEL OF ANALYSIS

This book has forcefully argued for the need to look below the macro-, state-focused study of the Holocaust so as to incorporate community- and individual-level factors into the analysis. Macro-level, state-centered research has historically been, and remains the staple of genocide and Holocaust scholarship. That makes sense if the goal is to understand the onset of mass killing, its progress over time, the aggregated victims' numbers, and the overall survival rates.[7] What is largely missing from the macro-level analysis are the people who were directly affected by this horrific violence.

When macro-level scholars do discuss the victims, they usually try to identify attributes that the main victim groups (Jews, Armenians, Tutsis) share, discuss how these groups were perceived by the perpetrators,[8] or explain mass violence as the outcome of an interaction between the state and an ethnic movement or organization that challenges it. How civilians targeted by mass violence behave after it begins remains largely beyond the scope of these studies. Yet such an understanding is crucial. In each of the ghettos I studied, the overarching policies of the Holocaust interacted with local realities and conditions. Stathis Kalyvas describes civil war violence as a "joint production" of macro-level master cleavages and local-level dynamics and histories.[9] The Holocaust was no different, yet no macro-level study can explain why evasion was quite widespread in Kraków but almost unknown in Białystok. National-level indicators of Jewish integration into Polish society tell us little about factors that were literally a matter of life and death in the individual ghettos. Why was it that a black-haired, dark-eyed, circumcised Jewish male in Kraków who had studied in a Polish school stood a better chance of survival outside the ghetto than a blond, blue-eyed Jewish female from Białystok who spoke Yiddish only?

On the opposite end of the analytical spectrum is the micro-level, pioneered by the works of Christopher Browning[10] and Daniel Jonah Goldhagen[11] on Holocaust perpetrators and Scott Straus on the genocide in Rwanda.[12] Studies that adopt this level of analysis focus mainly on the choices and behavior of individual perpetrators. With some recent exceptions, such as Lee Ann Fujii's[13] and Browning's later work,[14] victims' behavior is overlooked by micro-level scholars. To a large extent, this lack of attention to victims derives from the questions in which this literature is interested: it makes little sense to focus on victims when the goal is to solve the puzzle of perpetrators' motivations. However, the lack of attention to victims in this scholarship remains a glaring omission, because the actions of people targeted by mass murder impact the outcomes of the violence. What this book has tried to show is that the guiding question of micro-level scholarship should be broadened to "What makes people involved in and affected by mass violence behave the way they do?" rather than limited to "What makes perpetrators of mass violence behave as they do?"

An especially promising direction for future research, this book shows, is the meso-level. At the broadest sense, the meso-level is the space between national-level and individual-level factors. It is where macro-level policies meet and interact with local realities and individual-level factors. Without an understanding of this essential place of intersection between the macro and the micro, our ability to analyze genocides will be significantly limited for at least three reasons.[15] First, unlike macro-level scholarship that tends to select on the dependent variable and thereby only studies examples of genocides, meso-level research often explicitly incorporates variation into research design. Second, the analysis of sub-national units creates greater possibilities for large-N and comparative analysis, which is difficult at the macro-level because of the small number of cases and the vast differences between them.[16] Third, sub-national comparative analysis can often hold national level variables constant, and by doing so enable the researcher to identify the factors that cause variation. This, I believe, is where research should be headed. The book has tried to demonstrate the promises, but also the inherent limitations of such an approach.

Moving Forward: Theory and Policy

This book's findings have several theoretical and policy-relevant implications. First, a major goal of the book was to return agency to the victims of even the most extreme political violence. In the literature, victims of mass violence are too often portrayed as, and assumed to be, powerless and passive. During the Holocaust there certainly were limits to what the victims could achieve, but both the choices people made and the reasons behind those choices impacted outcomes. These choices and reasons, I believe, can and should be studied and analyzed systematically.

Second, the study has several implications for scholarship on the Holocaust and genocide studies in general. First, the Holocaust can and should be researched not only by using the long-established tools of qualitative historical analysis, but also by adopting quantitatively oriented research designs and the statistical analysis of large-N datasets. Although nearly seventy years have passed since the Holocaust ended, the research presented here is the first to analyze data on the entire universe of ghettos, and it has yielded new findings. This fact is sufficient to demonstrate how a mixture of qualitative and quantitative methodologies can further the understanding of one of the key events of modern history.

An additional implication of this study is that the almost complete separation between scholarship on political violence and genocide studies is unnecessary and artificial; greater dialogue and convergence between the fields would benefit both. Genocide and genocidal violence can and should be studied by applying the insights, theories, and methods of political violence research. Political violence literature, in turn, would benefit from paying closer attention to genocides and mass killings, as these might provide new insights overlooked by scholars of civil wars.

This book also contains several implications for broader political science research. First, it shows that even the most basic form of political activism, such as membership in a political movement, is not only a dependent variable that ought to be explained; it is also an independent variable that affects and explains behavior, even under conditions of extreme violence. Second, it demonstrates the tangible and long-lasting effects of political regimes and state policies on human behavior.[17] The Austro-Hungarian Empire ceased to exist twenty years before the Holocaust, yet its policies and legacy still affected the worldview and behavior of the Kraków Jews. The impact of states and state legacies is not set in stone, however. In Kraków the impact of the Austro-Hungarian legacy was strong mainly because the Polish state allowed institutions and organizations created under the Habsburgs to continue in operation. As the experience of Minsk clearly demonstrates, state institutions and policies do shape identities and can have tremendous impact even rather soon after their implementation. In 1919, Minsk and

Białystok were very similar in terms of interethnic relations and Jewish integration into non-Jewish society. Yet by 1939, the differences between the two cities were stark. Less than twenty years—that was all it took for a determined and proactive Soviet state to make a huge difference.[18]

The book also has important practical and policy implications: it shows that it is possible to analyze and even to try to predict the behavior of people targeted by mass violence, and it proposes that doing so might increase our ability to help these people when violence unfolds. The emerging literature on civilian self-protection argues that the international community and humanitarian organizations should move away from the noble, but unrealistic "salvation from the outside" mode of thinking and instead help victims of mass violence to become better prepared to help themselves. To achieve that goal, knowing which types of behavior are available and which people are more likely to adopt what strategy is of crucial importance.[19] Even if the factors that I have identified as crucial in the Holocaust context turn out to be less important elsewhere, the greater point remains—people and organizations tasked with humanitarian assistance and relief can potentially identify likely patterns of victims' behavior based on preexisting factors. Knowing that certain kinds of settings and certain kinds of people are more likely to resist perpetrators, while evasion can reasonably be expected of other kinds of people in other kinds of settings, would make it possible to develop more efficient assistance and relief strategies. Given the international community's repeated failures to prevent and stop mass violence, every effort should be made to upgrade relief efforts so as to improve the victims' lot and to make their choices somewhat less choiceless.

DATA AND ARCHIVAL METHODS

This book is based on more than five hundred Holocaust survivors' testimonies in English, Hebrew, Russian, and Polish. These testimonies consist of videotaped interviews and written accounts collected by archival institutions and oral history projects throughout the world. The bulk of the testimonies I use are housed in the Yale University Fortunoff Video Archive for Holocaust Testimonies (HVT); the Oral History Division of the Avraham Harman Institute of Contemporary Jewry at the Hebrew University of Jerusalem (OHD; predominantly Projects 58, 110, 188, and 223); and the Yad Vashem Archive in Jerusalem (YVA; Record Group O.3). A smaller number of testimonies are from the U.S. Holocaust Memorial Museum Archive (USHMM) in Washington, DC; the University of Southern California Shoah Foundation Visual History Archive (VHA); and the Jewish Historical Institute Archive (ŻIH) in Warsaw, Poland. I have also accessed a number of additional archives in Israel and the US, including the Jabotinsky Institute Archive, the Massuah Institute for Holocaust Studies Archive, and the University of South Florida Libraries Oral History Program. Each of these collections contains a small number of testimonies that I used for this book.

The earliest survivors' testimonies were collected by the Jewish Historical Commission in post-liberation Poland and these are currently available at ŻIH. These written accounts are generally quite short, bare bones descriptions of what the survivor experienced and witnessed during the Nazi occupation. The collection of testimonies from survivors accelerated with the 1953 establishment in Israel of the Yad Vashem: The Holocaust Martyrs' and Heroes' Remembrance Authority. Early YVA testimonies include written biographical narratives that focus predominantly on what the survivor experienced during the Holocaust. Later, testimonies that took the form of oral, often audiotaped interviews between the survivor and a member of the Yad Vashem staff became more usual. During an interview, the Yad Vashem staff member would usually ask the survivors not only about their Holocaust experiences, but also about their lives prior to World War II. The interviewees were predominantly Israeli citizens, although citizens of other countries were occasionally interviewed as well (for instance, during their visits to Israel). In my work, I accessed the transcripts of these interviews, but not the audio files. While each interview is different, a typical transcript spans 20 to 40 pages; the longest interview I read runs to slightly more than 300 pages.

The OHD files are transcripts of interviews conducted by Hebrew University researchers for specific projects. This substantially affects interviewee selection and the interview's thematic focus. Project 110, for example, consists mostly of oral history interviews conducted by Sara Bender for her doctoral dissertation on the Jews of Białystok during World War II. Project 188, on the other hand, is predominantly a collection of interviews conducted by Yael Peled-Margolin for a dissertation on the Jewish resistance in the Kraków ghetto, and therefore centers on this topic rather than the whole range of Jewish behaviors and experiences. The OHD oral history interviews are generally more expansive than the YVA testimonies.

Finally, I used a large number of videotaped interviews, the bulk of which are housed at the Yale University Fortunoff Video Archive for Holocaust Testimonies (HVT). Opened in 1982, the HVT is the oldest archive of Holocaust video testimonies. The HVT testimonies I worked with were predominantly from survivors living in the United States, although a sizable minority came from other countries, including Canada, Israel, and post-communist states. The archive is very protective of the survivors it interviewed and does not allow the full last names of the interviewees to be published. The archive's interviewing practices have evolved since the 1980s; the early interviews often lasted for about an hour or less, while among the more recent ones it is not atypical to find interviews that last for more than three or four hours; the longest interview I watched was sixteen hours long. Yet despite the changes, the key goal of the archive's interviews remains the same—to allow survivors to *reflect* upon, rather than to simply recount their experiences. While the interviewers do try to impose a certain chronological order in which the survivor begins by describing her pre-Holocaust life, then progresses to the Holocaust period, and finally moves to the post-Holocaust era, the narratives are more free-flowing than the YVA and OHD testimonies. The survivors often jump from one topic to another, talk about what they *felt* rather than only what they *did*, and are strongly encouraged to focus on their own story, rather than on larger macro-political factors.[1]

There are both benefits and drawbacks to the use of victims' testimonies in social science research. Victims' testimonies offer a unique opportunity to analyze people's experiences, behavior, and decisions under conditions of mass violence; and they are accounts given in people's own words that rely on their own conceptualizations, not choices among several deductively derived, predetermined options, as in survey research. Testimonies allow scaling down from macro-level histories and the analysis of elites to the study of ordinary people's responses to the contexts they inhabited. Indeed, it would be impossible to conduct micro- or meso-level analysis of the Holocaust without heavily relying on testimonies. As Omer Bartov argues, "the single most important benefit of using testimonies is that they bring into history events that would otherwise remain completely unknown, since they are missing from more conventional documentation."[2] From the social scientist's perspective, in addition to rescuing from oblivion micro-level events, testimonies provide information on behavior and processes that are otherwise overlooked. Without survivors' testimonies we would know very little about important phenomena such as smuggling, the use of "weapons of the weak," the internal structure of underground organizations, and the decision-making processes of individuals. In addition, the use of testimonies and oral histories allows scholars to conduct controlled comparisons between communities, and to produce more generalizable findings.

Because the vast majority of testimonies and oral history interviews discuss not only the survivor's experience during the Holocaust, but also his pre-Holocaust life and conditions, they allow scholars to analyze the impact of pre-Holocaust factors on Holocaust-era behavior. Only from testimonies it is possible to understand how people assessed their situation and likely future; what they knew about and expected from Nazi Germany; how they decided whether to escape the ghetto or stay put. This detailed information cannot be obtained from surveys or short biographical questionnaires, but it is crucial for developing an understanding of individuals' choices.

Finally, the sheer amount of testimonies not only presents a broad picture of the events but also allows scholars in positivist traditions to isolate, control for, and evaluate the impact of a large array of potential variables of interest. When testimonies from several archives, countries, time periods, and in different languages are analyzed together, this reduces the danger of a systematic bias (i.e., the interviewers' focus on specific types of information; the numerical domination of survivors residing in a particular country or of a certain ideological predisposition) that affects the entire body of evidence. Obviously, archives and oral history projects do have their own data collection and interviewing rules and priorities,[3] but such biases are present in any historiographical work,[4] affect only a portion of the testimonies I rely on, and can be identified and controlled for.

The promises and advantages of using survivors' testimonies are tangible, but working with this type of data also presents several challenges that should be recognized and addressed. First, survivors represent only a small subset of Jews targeted by the Nazi genocide; and survivors who were willing and able to share their experiences are a subset of this subset. Therefore, the testimonies cannot be used as a random or representative sample of the Jewish experience as a whole; they unavoidably overrepresent the stories of those who survived *and* were willing to share their experiences. An inevitable outcome of this bias, which is also evident in the coding of testimonies that I conducted in appendix 2, is that we have many more testimonies from teenagers and young adults than from other age groups, because younger people were more likely to survive. A potential way to deal with this issue is to incorporate into the analysis not only what the survivors tell about themselves, but also what they say about those who did not survive (e.g., family members, colleagues, or friends). Yet, these data are always partial, relational, and usually insufficient to fully reconstruct the behavior and decision making of those who perished. Sometimes it is also possible to use Holocaust-era documents (letters, notes, diaries) of those who did not survive, but the number of such sources is small. Additionally, certain types of behavior are likely to be overrepresented in the testimonies at the expense of others. Jews who opted for compliance as their primary survival strategy were extremely unlikely to survive. Therefore, we have virtually no testimonies from those who complied, even though we know that some victims adopted this behavior. Those who collaborated with the Nazis are also unlikely to have shared their experiences because of the social stigma associated with this type of behavior and out of the fear of criminal prosecution in Israel,[5] and under some circumstances, in the United States.[6]

This inherent feature of Holocaust survivors' testimonies inevitably shapes possibilities for research methods. These documents should not and cannot be used as the basis for the large-N statistical analysis of individual-level data. Instead, scholars should rely on the testimonies to produce in-depth qualitative comparisons, for process tracing, and, when a survivor provides sufficient information on people she interacted with, for network analysis.

Scholars who work with testimonies are also unavoidably using material collected by predecessors for their own research and commemoration purposes. An important, but often overlooked (especially by social scientists) feature of working with archival materials is the need to understand the general context in which these documents were produced and the reasons for their production, collection, and preservation. Thus, heavy reliance on testimonies from Project 188 of the OHD, which was conducted for a doctoral dissertation on Jewish resistance, might easily lead to an erroneous conclusion that this type of behavior was widespread among the Kraków Jews. Early testimonies were collected during the immediate post-liberation period and are mainly concerned with documenting and providing evidence of the Nazi atrocities. For that reason they do not extensively discuss pre-Holocaust life; prioritizing those testimonies might foreclose the possibility of analyzing the impact of pre–World War II factors on Holocaust-era behavior. The fact that Yad Vashem is an official Israeli state institution and that the majority of YVA testimonies come from Israeli citizens also likely affected what was said and what was left unsaid, especially during the decades of the 1950s and 60s when the state's official narrative lionized Jewish resistance and downplayed other Jewish behaviors. Israeli citizens might also be more likely to highlight their pre–World War II Zionism and downplay—if not outright ignore—their involvement in non- or anti-Zionist movements and organizations. On the other hand, by using already existing testimonies, a researcher can be confident that interviewees did not provide her with the data she wanted or tell her what she wanted to hear because of what they knew in advance about her research.

Another potential and related limitation relates to the issue of what Fujii calls "shades of truth and lies."[7] Based on her research experiences in Rwanda, Fujii argues that in interviews with people who witnessed or were involved in mass violence, the "meta-data"—rumors, inventions, denials, evasions, silences, and other forms of nonverbal communication—are just as important as the substantive content. While it is in theory possible to pay attention to survivors' silences and body language when watching videotaped oral history interviews, the task is complicated by the fact that the researcher sees only what the cameraman decides, or is instructed to film. Moreover, many interviews are conducted in survivors' second (and sometimes third) languages. Thus, the interviewees' body language and silences might be the result of attempts to find the right words and expressions in a non-native language rather than evidence of "denials" and "evasions." For those reasons, the issue of meta-data should be kept in mind when working with videotaped testimonies, even though it can rarely, if ever, be acted upon.

Finally, the time lapse between events and the testimonies about those events is a possible source of problems. In immediate post-Holocaust testimonies, children and young adults are overrepresented among the survivors; in more recent testimonies those who were young during the

Holocaust are the only victims who are still alive and able to testify. Testimonies given decades after the Holocaust are inevitably subject also to the erosion of memory and to faulty recollection. People can simply forget or imprecisely recall what they experienced and how they behaved so many years ago.[8] While this danger is real, it is less acute in the case of so traumatic an event as the Holocaust. According to Daniel Schacter, a memory scholar, "laboratory studies reveal that emotionally charged incidents are better remembered than nonemotional events."[9] Holocaust scholars agree with this assessment. Survivors' testimonies, argues Henry Greenspan, are stable over time; the conformity between early and late testimonies is remarkable.[10] This is consistent with what I observed in comparing recollections of individuals who gave multiple testimonies decades apart, sometimes in different languages and countries. Several other researchers, among them Christopher Browning and Jan Grabowski, have also noted a high degree of consistency.[11] Furthermore, when the testimonies are used to identify certain key patterns, strategies, and modes of behavior, rather than to precisely reconstruct the unfolding of events, such distortions and omissions as may exist should not significantly affect my findings.

The passage of time can impact the recollection of events in several additional ways. Survivors' recollection and presentation of events might be influenced by post-Holocaust symbols, culture, knowledge, events, and understandings. The emergence of "communities of memory," in which survivors discuss their experiences with one another, might eventually cause different peoples' recollections to converge on a jointly produced narrative that is then internalized by everyone.[12] Commemoration ceremonies and museums, such as the Yad Vashem or the U.S. Holocaust Memorial Museum may contribute to or foster similar effects. However, the fact that the testimonies were collected by different institutions in several countries and from people all over the globe ensures that if such a bias exists, it will affect only some of the testimonies and therefore can be detected and controlled for by comparing testimonies from different countries, archives, and time periods.

In the context of this project, two of the ghettos upon which my analysis relies are relatively understudied. The exception is Kraków, where Oscar Schindler undertook his now famous rescue effort. Survivors from Kraków did discuss Schindler prior to the appearance of the movie *Schindler's List*, but the film clearly affected their testimonies. When Schindler's name came up in pre-1993 oral history interviews, the interviewers would often ask the survivors to explain who Schindler was; these requests largely disappear after the mid-1990s. Testimonies recorded after the film debuted almost always mention Schindler independently of whether the person had any interaction with him. At the same time, the majority of the testimonies that I use predate the film, and post-*Schindler's List* testimonies do not substantially differ from pre-movie testimonies in their recollection of survivors' personal histories. In other words, the film did make survivors more likely to mention and discuss Schindler, but it did not lead to a spike in the number of people who claimed to be on his List.

A way to minimize these problems would be to prioritize testimonies from the immediate post-Holocaust period. However, while this might somewhat mitigate distortions due to the transience of memory and to cultural and societal impacts, overreliance on immediate post-event testimonies could create other problems. First, as discussed earlier, immediate post-Holocaust testimonies tend to provide only scant information on pre-Holocaust life and conditions and therefore are not helpful for certain types of analysis. Second, the passage of time presents not only challenges, but also opportunities. Holocaust survivors are much more likely to discuss sensitive and controversial issues—such as sexual violence or the harming of other Jews—in later testimonies; these topics were taboo immediately after the event.[13] Indeed, over the last several decades, scholars have successfully and widely used testimonies, depositions, and interviews from later periods to analyze the behavior and choices of the Holocaust perpetrators; there is no compelling reason why the same analytical tools should not be applied to the study of victims' behavior and motivations.

Survivors' testimonies are an important and valid source of information. My starting point is that survivors are overwhelmingly doing their best to provide the most accurate account of their experiences. However, people do make honest mistakes, such as confusing dates. And occasionally, they do deliberately lie. In deciding what is an honest mistake in an overall reliable account as opposed to a falsehood that brings the testimony as a whole into question, scholars must make use of two methodological tools. First, they must approach testimonies with adequate background knowledge of the case and its historiography; and second, they must rely on a large number of testimonies from the same locality.[14] Using a small number of testimonies from different places will not help scholars spot unusual cases and raise red flags; only immersion in a large body of evidence from the same place allows a reliable reconstruction of events and behaviors. In my work I found that after reading about thirty testimonies from one locality, a general and very consistent narrative of experiences and behaviors would emerge and it would remain largely unchanged even after the number the testimonies I read had increased many times over.[15] Equipped with this general narrative, I then reread the first testimonies I had analyzed, looking for things that I might have missed.

After assembling a local narrative, I would use it to evaluate subsequent testimonies—either to provide more support for the narrative's accuracy or to identify unusual events and behaviors. Not all deviations from the general narrative are mistakes or lies; sometimes they are analytically revelatory exceptions. Even the most unusual events and behaviors were often totally reasonable and believable if viewed against the background of a person's particular situation. It is precisely the overall consistency of the general narrative that allows the scholar to recognize and intellectually exploit these behavioral divergences; the analysis of such unusual cases is just as fruitful as a focus on those that are "typical".

At the same time, some deviations are clearly mistakes or likely untruths. The evaluation of mistakes and improbabilities is only possible after substantial immersion in the empirical data, after gaining an understanding of what happened, and how it was experienced and understood. The most common mistakes I encountered were misattributions of date and place. If, for instance, a survivor claimed that he was deported from the Białystok ghetto during the February 1942 Aktion, while the Aktion in reality took place in February 1943, but the rest of his testimony did not raise any suspicions, I treated this as an honest and rather minor mistake. Such a mistake, while clearly presenting incorrect information, does not affect the overall reliability of the survivor's description of his behavior and survival strategies. A mistake in a date or a place would be very significant if my goal had been to precisely reconstruct the unfolding of events, but it is less important when the testimony is used, as I used it, to analyze general patterns of behavior.

A second, less frequent type of mistake was factually inaccurate information about people whom the survivor did not personally know, usually public figures or officials. An example of such a mistake would be a claim that the ghetto's Judenrat did something long after it had been disbanded, or that a Judenrat head or Jewish police officer was killed by the Germans, even though the historical record shows that he was not. In such cases, the key distinction is whether the survivor claims to personally have witnessed or experienced the events or whether she recounts them as a part of the ghetto's, rather than her own, history. In both cases the erroneous claim can be analytically disregarded, but if the survivor does not claim to have *personally* witnessed such an event, I will treat her testimony as reliable in so far as it relates her own experiences and behavior.

A final and very rare type of incorrect information is the case of a survivor who claims to have personally witnessed or experienced events that are not simply unusual, but utterly improbable. The most telling example of this phenomenon that I encountered was the testimony of a female survivor from Minsk, in which she talked about escaping the ghetto and spending the rest of the war in Zorin's partisan unit. The story itself is very typical; what raises a red flag is her description of what she experienced in Zorin's unit. According to her account, Zorin was a terrible and rabid anti-Semite who abused the Jews in the unit. This testimony is improbable not only because it contradicts dozens of other testimonies as to Zorin's character; for that would simply make it unusual, though suspicious. The key problem is that it is nonsensical—Zorin could not have been a violent anti-Semite because he was himself Jewish and the whole mission of the unit he established and led was to save Jews escaping from the ghettos to the forests. What likely prompted her claim about Zorin is a combination of two facts: many partisan commanders were indeed anti-Semitic and violent; and Zorin is not a typically Jewish surname. Yet, his first name— Shalom—is as Jewish as any. Any person who had even the most cursory interactions with Zorin and knew his first name would never accuse him of being violently anti-Semitic. It is clear to any informed researcher that the woman was never a part of Zorin's unit and therefore—at least in a project focused on assembling fact-based narratives—her testimony should be discarded in its entirety.

In addition, a scholar's goal in working with survivors' testimonies should be to assemble a coherent, overarching representation of sociopolitical processes, rather than to ferret out colorful quotations and "smoking guns."[16] In a project focused on uncovering broad behavioral patterns, quotes are useful when they highlight and represent general experiences, but they should not be deployed to independently prove a hypothesis. In fact, given the large number of testimonies, it would no doubt be possible to find among them "smoking guns" for almost any claim. It is the narrative that emerges from a large number of testimonies that proves a hypothesis, not this or that individual quotation, no matter how colorful.

The temporal, geographic, and linguistic diversity that these testimonies encompass adds up to a very consistent and reliable representation of life, social relations, and experiences in the Minsk, Kraków, and Białystok ghettos during the Holocaust. This representation—and the approach used to construct it—can and should be used by social scientists wishing to understand how people behave under conditions of mass violence.

DISTRIBUTION OF STRATEGIES

In this appendix I explore the general patterns of Jews' behavior and the distribution of strategies within and across the Minsk, Kraków, and Białystok ghettos. For this analysis I randomly selected and coded data from fifty-one testimonies—seventeen from each ghetto. Some of the testimonies are explicitly cited in the book, while others were analyzed but are not cited because it would have been physically impossible to cite all of the over 500 testimonies that I accessed, read, or viewed for this book.[1]

The testimonies I coded came from different archives and were given in different languages. Thirteen came from the HVT archive, 15 are from the OHD, 17 from the YVA, and 6 from the VHA. Twenty testimonies were given in Hebrew, 17 in Russian, 12 in English, and 2 in Polish. At the time when they gave their testimonies, 28 survivors lived in Israel, 13 in the United States, 5 in Belarus, 4 in Russia, and 1 in Canada. Twenty-seven of the survivors were females, 24 were males.

In appendix 1, I argue that the testimonies cannot and should not be viewed as a random and representative sample of Jews' experiences during the Holocaust and therefore cannot serve as the underlying data for large-N individual level analysis of Jewish behavior. The coding results support this claim. The average age of the survivors at the time when the Germans occupied their hometowns was 19.1 years; only two were older than 30 at the beginning of the Holocaust. Analytically, this finding is unsurprising; teenagers and young adults were more likely to survive diseases, hunger, and hard labor than older people. Those who were young during the Holocaust were also more likely to still be alive to give their testimony decades after World War II.

Another source of bias is the socioeconomic status of the survivors in my sample. Of the 47 survivors on whom we have such data, 13 belonged to the working class at the outbreak of the Holocaust, 27 were middle class and 7 belonged to wealthy families (either owners of successful factories that employed dozens of workers or large-scale traders). Given that the Jewish communities of Białystok, and to a lesser extent Minsk were predominantly working-class prior to World War II, the data show that, in addition to age, status was also positively correlated with the likelihood of survival.

In theory, a potential way to overcome these biases is to code data on other people discussed by the survivors in their testimonies. In practice, however, the data on other people that is available in the testimonies is for the most part insufficient for systematic coding. For that reason, the testimonies are much more useful for qualitative analysis that can exploit various bits and pieces of important, but inherently partial information than for quantitative large-N study.

The coded data on schooling and language demonstrate the tangible pre–World War II difference in the levels of Jewish integration into non-Jewish society in the three cities. Thus, in Białystok 50 percent of the survivors went to exclusively Jewish educational institutions where instruction was in Hebrew or Yiddish; in Kraków only a third of the survivors in my sample did. In Minsk only 21 percent of survivors were *not* educated in institutions in which Russian or Belorussian was the main language of instruction. It should be also remembered that in Białystok middle-class families often sent their children to schools in which Polish was the language of instruction, but all the students were Jewish. Among the Białystok survivors, 68.75 percent mentioned directly witnessing or personally experiencing anti-Semitism prior to World War II. For Kraków the number drops to 41.2 percent, and in Minsk to only 11.8 percent. These numbers, it should be emphasized once again, are not precise representations of the reality on the ground, but they are nonetheless useful to demonstrate general patterns.

The distribution (in absolute numbers) of Holocaust-era survival strategies within and across communities is presented in table A2.1. The strategies are not mutually exclusive; over the course of the Holocaust a survivor could engage in a number of different strategies at different times.

As can be seen from the coding of the testimonies, collaboration was an extremely rare strategy; even those people who did engage in it would not be forthcoming about such a controversial behavior. One survivor, Dora

Table A2.1. Distribution of strategies

	Collaboration	Coping	Compliance	Evasion	Resistance
Białystok	0	17	7	1	4
Kraków	0	17	0	5	3
Minsk	0	17	0	15	2

Kozin from Białystok, had several family members in the Jewish police, but she did not personally engage in collaboration or cooperation with the Nazis. Coping was the most prevalent strategy. It was the default behavior during the initial stages of the occupation, and only after it became clear that it was unlikely to ensure survival did some people adopt other strategies. Compliance was also extremely rare. In Minsk and Kraków those who complied stood no chance of surviving, and therefore the testimonies clearly underreport and underrepresent the true extent of the phenomenon, because it is certain that in each of the ghettos there were people who opted for compliance. In Białystok, all seven recorded instances of compliance were confined to the Jews' behavior during the ghetto liquidation, when many Jews obeyed the deportation orders though they knew quite well that deportation most likely meant death. These people did not answer the underground's call to join the rebellion, nor did they try to hide or to escape the ghetto.

The three ghettos differ substantially in their patterns of evasion. In my sample only one Białystok survivor escaped (and even that escape was not from the ghetto itself but from the city's jail where he was taken after the ghetto's liquidation). Five (out of 17) survivors chose evasion in Kraków, while almost everyone who managed to survive the Minsk ghetto did so by choosing evasion. For the Kraków and Białystok Jews, coping could eventually lead to survival, either thanks to Oscar Schindler or to their being selected for labor in various camps. For the vast majority of Minsk Jews, the choice was between evasion and death. Levels of integration into broader society are also associated with choosing the evasion strategy not only across, but also within ghettos. As almost every Minsk survivor escaped and virtually no Białystok survivor did, Kraków is the most useful case study. Among Kraków Jews who attended exclusively Jewish educational institutions, not one chose evasion.

A number of survivors engaged in organized resistance, but the coding results likely do not accurately reflect the actual frequency of this strategy. First, because Jewish resistance was (and for good reasons!) celebrated after the Holocaust, those who engaged in it were more likely to be interviewed and to leave their testimonies. Second, the OHD Kraków interviews were conducted for a project on Jewish resistance in the ghetto, thus affecting the choice of interviewees and the topics raised during the interview.

Everyone adopted the coping strategy at one point or another during their time in the ghetto, but the patterns of coping varied from one ghetto to another. Thus, 70 percent of Białystok survivors mention being in a hideout during a German Aktion. In Minsk the number is 58 percent. In Kraków hideouts were quite rare and only 18 percent of survivors mention them. In both Minsk and Białystok, 65 percent of the survivors smuggled food, money, and other items into the ghetto. In Kraków, only 41 percent did. The different material conditions in the three ghettos also can be deduced if we look at where the bartering of food was more prevalent. In Białystok, 47 percent of the survivors in my sample engaged in this high-risk activity. In Kraków, only 12 percent did. However, in Minsk, where hunger was prevalent and official rations were insufficient to ensure survival, 70 percent of the survivors were forced to barter their belongings for food, even though doing so was often punishable by death.

Pre–World War II levels of Jewish integration into non-Jewish society affected the amount of help extended by Jews and non-Jews. In Białystok, only 3 out of 17 survivors mention receiving help from non-Jews they knew prior to the German occupation. In Kraków, the number is twice that high, whereas 10 survivors were helped by their non-Jewish acquaintances in Minsk. If we look only at those survivors who were educated in exclusively Jewish schools, the numbers are striking. Taking all three cities together, there was only one survivor who reported being helped by a non-Jewish acquaintance. On the other hand, among Kraków survivors who did *not* attend Jewish schools, there was not one who recalled being helped by other Jews inside the ghetto—evidence of the fractured coping that prevailed in that city.

To summarize, the results of my coding show general trends that are consistent with the overall qualitative narrative that emerges from the totality of the testimonies. At the same time, while such coding is useful to observe general trends, the exact numbers and percentages presented here should be taken with a grain of salt, and not only because of the small N. Several systematic biases affect the overall universe of testimonies from which sampling is possible. Simply increasing the number of coded testimonies will not overcome the basic fact that the testimonies overrepresent the experiences of those who survived and were available and willing to be interviewed decades after World War II. For that reason, this appendix should be viewed mainly as supporting evidence for the qualitative narrative, and not as a substitute for it.

BEYOND THE THREE GHETTOS: ECONOMETRIC ANALYSIS OF UPRISINGS

Can the nature of a city's pre–World War II regime and the prewar activism of individuals in the city explain Jewish behavior in places other than Minsk, Kraków, and Białystok? Given the inevitable incompleteness and messiness of individual-level data, the only way to quantitatively test my arguments is by analyzing *collective* Jewish behavior in the ghettos, first and foremost anti-Nazi resistance.

The analysis of the Minsk, Kraków, and Białystok ghettos (chapter 7) suggests that *sustained* Jewish resistance should have been most common in Eastern Poland—the region where both Jewish communists (in 1919–39) and Zionists (in 1939–41) were subject to selective repression that spurred them to acquire operational security skills. Sustained Jewish resistance, conversely, should be less common in other parts of Poland and in the territory of the pre-1939 USSR. Coding underground organizations is not an easy task, however. Given the very nature of their work, resources, and environment, many Jewish resistance groups did their best to leave as minimal a paper trail as possible. If all the members of an underground group were deported and killed when the ghetto was liquidated, it is unlikely that we will even know that the organization existed. The second best, though certainly not ideal option, is to focus on resistance behavior that is more observable, namely ghetto uprisings—organized, open, armed resistance inside the ghetto.[1] Even if all the Jewish fighters engaged in such an action were killed, as happened in a number of uprisings, the instance of anti-German violence was noted, reported, and remembered by the German authorities, the local non-Jewish population, anti-Nazi guerillas in the forests, and the Allies' intelligence agents.

Ghetto uprisings could not be organized or carried out without a sustained underground effort, so they would be expected to concentrate in Eastern Poland, due to its prewar political regimes. The comparison of the

Minsk, Kraków, and Białystok ghettos, moreover, suggests that the likelihood of an uprising was greater when Zionists played a leading role in the underground (see chapter 7). Zionists, intent on defending Jewish honor, generally favored a symbolic albeit suicidal fight inside the ghetto; the communists, who placed no stress on Jewish identity, preferred smuggling people to the forests. Yet in Kraków the Zionist underground was weak, unskilled, and dependent upon a partnership with the communists, and it failed to rebel despite an explicit desire to do so. In Białystok, where the Zionists had gained underground experience prior to Nazi occupation, they not only rebelled inside the ghetto, but also managed to convince the communists to join the uprising.

I have collected data on more than one thousand ghettos established by the Nazis in Poland and the USSR—the main killing fields of the Holocaust. The number of uprisings in the ghettos is not high, yet the pattern is clear (Table A3.1). Eastern Poland was indeed the epicenter of ghetto uprisings, and given the gargantuan differences between the Jewish civilians and the German military in manpower and weapons, the fact that even 7 percent of the ghettos in that region openly rebelled is remarkable. No less astonishing is that the number of uprisings in Eastern Poland was almost seven times higher than in the rest of the country. The absolute number of ghettos in Eastern Poland and the rest of the country was similar, and in 1939 Polish territory was split almost equally between Germany and the USSR. The concentration of the Jewish population, however, was quite different in the two regions—there were just over one million Jews in Eastern Poland versus two million in the rest of the country. Thus, the concentration of an ethnic group—which, according to the literature, is an important driver of nationalist violence[2]—was substantially *higher* in the area that witnessed fewer uprisings. Even if we acknowledge that the much higher concentration of Jews in central and western Poland was driven to a substantial extent by the presence there of the two largest Jewish communities

Table A3.1. Ghetto uprisings during the Holocaust (1939 borders)

Region	Poland (East)	Poland (Rest)	USSR
Ghettos total	317	360	328
Uprisings	23	4	3
%	7.26	1.11	0.91

Pearson $X^2 = 29.1830(2)$, $p < 0.001$

in the country, Warsaw and Łódź, and we therefore remove them from the data, the concentration of Jews in Eastern Poland will still be lower than in the rest of the country.

The low number of uprisings in the USSR before 1939 is in line with my prediction, but the paucity of historical data does not allow me to completely rule out potential alternative explanations, such as Soviet evacuation policies.[3] This comparison cannot tell us either whether there is indeed a link between Zionism, location in the Soviet occupation zone in 1939, and the likelihood of an uprising. To better unpack this relationship, the most illuminating comparison would be between ghettos located in Eastern Poland and the rest of the country.

In the following pages I conduct a simple econometric analysis of patterns of uprisings in Jewish ghettos located in interwar Poland. First, I describe the data and then proceed to the analysis itself. The data consist of three main datasets: the Jewish Ghettos dataset, the 1928 Polish National Election Returns dataset, and the 1937 and 1939 Zionist Organization Elections Returns dataset.

THE JEWISH GHETTOS IN POLAND DATASET

The Jewish Ghettos in Poland dataset includes data on 677 ghettos established by the Nazis in the territory of pre-1939 Poland. It includes information on the ghetto population, the dates of its establishment and liquidation, whether the ghetto was enclosed by a physical barrier that prevented contact with the outside world, prewar census data on the Jewish community, and data on instances of rebellion. The bulk of the information comes from the most recent and comprehensive data collection effort on Jewish ghettos: namely, the second volume of the United States Holocaust Memorial Museum's (USHMM) *Encyclopedia of Camps and Ghettos*. Data that could not be found in the USHMM encyclopedia are from the *Yad Vashem Encyclopedia of the Ghettos during the Holocaust*; the *Encyclopedia of Jewish Life before and during the Holocaust*; the Hebrew-language *Encyclopedia of Jewish Communities (Pinkas Hakehilot)*; the 1921 Polish census; the Polish Jewish Historical Institute list of prewar Jewish communities in Poland; the *Blackbook of Localities Whose Jewish Population Was Exterminated by the Nazis*; and numerous Jewish communities' memorial (*Yizkor*) books.

I have compiled the largest existing dataset on Jewish ghettos in Poland. The data nonetheless have several shortcomings. First, there is an eighteen-year gap between the 1921 census data and the outbreak of World War II. Unfortunately, detailed community-level results of the 1931 Polish census seem not to have survived the war; the data that are available are mainly at the *powiat* (county) level. What mitigates this problem is the availability of data on ghetto populations, which can be substituted for census data (although the number of ghetto inhabitants fluctuated over time). This bias, however, is systematic and affects all of the ghettos in the dataset.

Second, the census data are not without problems. The number of Jews in the census is underreported due to the wording of census questions, which were explicitly designed to artificially increase the reported number of ethnic Poles in the country. While it is hard to determine which, if any, Jewish communities were more likely than others to be affected by this problem, the ghetto population data also mitigate the problem of biased census data.

THE 1928 POLISH NATIONAL ELECTIONS RETURNS DATASET

The data in this dataset are based on the results of the 1928 Polish election, published in Główny Urząd Statystyczny, *Statystyka Wyborów do Sejmu i Senatu Odbytych w Dniu 4 i 11 Marca 1928 Roku* (Warsaw, 1930). Election results were published at the locality level, hence, the electoral data correspond to the data on ghettos. Out of 677 Polish towns and villages in which ghettos were established, I have electoral returns from 569. The results were not published for localities with less than 500 voters, and several ghettos were created in places that before World War II were agricultural estates with no Jewish population. Figure A3.1 presents a typical excerpt from the 1928 election results data book.

The 1928 election was the last free (by the standards of the day) election held in prewar Poland and offered the Jewish electorate a wide range of voting choices. They could vote for the pro-government BBWR party, which was affiliated with the country's leader and founding father, Józef Piłsudski, a popular figure among Polish Jews; they could also vote for Jewish parties of various ideological stripes. While the Communist Party itself did not take part in the election, various pro-communist or proxy-communist parties did.[4] Following Kopstein and Wittenberg's coding, I aggregate all the pro-communist and communist proxy parties into one voting bloc.

Tabl. 1.

WYBORY DO SEJMU WEDŁUG OKRĘGÓW WYBORCZYCH (c. d.).
ÉLECTIONS À LA DIÈTE SUIVANT LES CIRCONSCRIPTIONS ÉLECTORALES (suite).

OKRĄG WYBORCZY NR. 4 (dok.) — *CIRCONSCRIPTION ÉLECTORALE N-o 4 (fin).*
POWIATY — *ARRONDISSEMENTS:* OSTRÓW, BIELSK, WYSOKIE MAZOWIECKIE.

Powiaty Miasta Gminy wiejskie / *Arrondissements Villes Communes rurales*	Liczba obwodów głosowania / *Nombre des sections de vote*	Liczba mieszkańców uprawn. do głosowania / *Nombre des habitants ayant le droit de vote*	Złożono głosów / *Nombre des votes déposés*	Unieważniono głosów w Komisjach / *Nombre des votes invalidés par les Commissions*		Oddano głosów ważnych ogółem / *Total des votes valables*	Głosy ważne oddane na listy Nr. Nr. / *Nombre des votes valables obtenus par les listes N-o N-o*										
				Obwodowej / *Primo-Locale*	Okręgowej / *Primo-pale*		1	2	3	4	5	10	11	18	20	24	33	36
Pow. — *Arr.* Bielsk . .	85	94 964	62 429	2 971	2 113	60 316	7 479	16 014	11 107	41	355	2 453	181	5 898	2 025	13 900	768	92
a) Miasta — *Villes* .	15	15 812	12 535	250	185	12 350	1 345	2 004	959	—	358	205	16	3 971	442	2 327	717	—
Bielsk	3	3 525	2 520	37	37	2 483	386	566	2	—	165	—	4	695	110	389	166	—
Boćki	1	1 117	945	64	—	945	116	79	117	—	—	112	—	327	17	186	1	—
Brańsk	2	2 217	1 864	49	49	1 815	113	250	2	—	114	—	1	614	26	649	46	—
Ciechanowice . .	2	2 086	1 789	12	11	1 778	182	227	5	—	79	72	11	539	4	473	247	—
Drohiczyn . . .	1	1 052	941	—	—	941	158	70	153	—	—	16	—	206	94	140	104	—
Kleszczele . . .	1	1 054	819	—	—	819	64	285	161	—	—	—	—	240	6	62	1	—
Mielnik	1	753	544	32	32	512	47	20	240	—	—	—	—	62	87	45	11	—
Narew	1	652	501	5	5	496	83	141	—	—	—	—	—	157	9	99	1	6
Siemiatycze . . .	3	3 422	2 612	51	51	2 561	197	366	279	—	—	5	—	1 141	89	344	140	—
b) Gminy wiejskie *Communes rurales*	70	79 152	49 894	2 721	1 928	47 966	6 134	14 010	10 148	41	—	2 248	165	1 927	1 583	11 573	51	86
Białowieża . . .	5	6 585	3 507	408	408	3 099	632	1 719	40	—	—	2	—	408	83	186	2	28
Domanowo . . .	3	1 533	1 507	5	4	1 503	330	30	236	—	—	47	2	—	558	—	—	—
Dubiażyn	2	2 650	1 894	26	26	1 858	123	1 106	520	—	—	7	3	—	—	100	—	3
Grodzisk	3	3 226	2 286	96	15	2 271	294	223	526	3	—	295	28	14	39	849	—	—
Kąty	2	2 159	1 557	12	12	1 545	252	60	747	—	—	3	—	3	38	442	—	—
Kleszczele . . .	2	2 208	1 397	—	—	1 397	124	1 031	124	—	—	20	—	63	7	28	—	—
Łosinka	3	4 582	1 949	94	84	1 865	205	1 431	103	—	—	—	—	58	42	20	—	6
Lubin	3	3 759	2 765	31	24	2 736	110	360	482	—	—	188	14	7	1	1 634	—	—
Masiewo	3	3 267	2 228	13	12	2 216	215	1 447	137	28	—	—	—	309	4	—	—	12
Milejcyce	4	3 744	2 337	181	181	2 156	172	1 023	414	4	—	—	—	216	214	98	11	4
Narew	3	4 504	1 595	450	450	1 145	214	654	19	—	—	1	—	34	31	170	—	22
Narojki	4	4 676	3 609	8	22	3 587	217	236	1 959	2	—	161	5	—	148	857	2	—
Orla	4	6 005	2 977	255	255	2 722	121	1 320	454	—	—	1	—	642	113	54	6	11
Pasynki	5	4 536	1 500	495	165	1 995	163	1 039	11	—	—	2	—	80	80	13	—	3
Radziwiłłówka .	5	4 438	1 580	32	31	1 558	92	362	958	—	—	7	—	30	61	27	21	—
Rudka	2	2 616	1 965	8	8	1 957	207	199	398	—	—	404	—	17	3	728	—	—
Siemiatycze . . .	3	4 628	2 676	34	34	2 642	258	298	1 298	—	—	28	—	4	118	636	2	—
Skórzec	5	5 385	4 605	19	19	4 586	985	265	630	—	—	926	33	6	—	1 736	5	—
Topczewo	4	3 179	2 366	23	23	2 343	570	311	7	—	—	58	93	16	37	1 321	—	—
Widźgowo	2	2 929	2 431	—	5	2 426	154	103	1 056	2	—	74	3	9	4	1 020	1	—
Wysokł	4	4 541	2 799	228	150	2 649	697	193	89	—	—	21	55	—	2	1 590	—	—
Pow. — *Arr.* Wysokie Mazowieckie . .	35	44 707	37 932	376	335	37 598	9 911	3 188	1 852	—	81	446	1 296	3 111	1	17 787	975	—
a) Miasta — *Villes*	4	7 835	6 739	97	97	6 642	1 628	1 175	26	—	23	—	125	2 053	1	1 296	415	—
Wysokie Mazowieckie .	2	2 015	1 816	39	39	1 777	350	161	26	—	—	1	—	762	—	332	145	—
Łapy	2	2 793	2 431	28	28	2 403	489	952	—	—	—	91	262	1	622	6	—	—
Sokoły	1	1 109	936	16	16	920	127	49	—	—	—	—	593	—	111	40	—	—
Tykocin	1	1 918	1 556	14	14	1 542	562	33	—	—	23	—	33	436	—	231	224	—
b) Gminy wiejskie *Communes rurales*	31	36 872	31 194	279	238	30 956	7 383	2 013	1 826	—	58	446	1 171	1 058	—	16 441	560	—
Dmochy-Gliski . .	3	3 650	2 904	18	18	2 886	664	340	37	—	1	45	14	312	—	1 080	393	—
Klukowo	3	5 402	4 542	55	61	4 481	522	516	18	—	57	307	232	405	—	2 296	68	—
Kowalewszczyzna . .	3	2 628	2 142	31	31	2 114	357	32	35	—	—	52	20	—	—	1 618	—	—
Piekuty	3	3 283	2 870	59	12	2 858	897	54	3	—	—	6	22	33	—	1 843	—	—
Piszczaty	3	2 733	2 087	7	3	2 084	328	8	266	—	—	—	291	33	—	1 145	13	—
Poświetne	3	3 895	2 919	18	18	2 901	1 128	433	67	—	19	163	21	33	—	1 079	—	—
Sokoły	3	3 011	2 599	37	40	2 559	932	98	42	—	—	—	26	43	—	1 429	1	—
Stelmachowo . . .	2	2 745	2 559	2	2	2 557	959	98	—	—	—	—	69	5	—	1 419	7	—
Szepietowo . . .	5	5 257	4 662	32	31	4 631	860	297	471	—	—	9	217	63	—	2 068	16	—
Wysokie Mazowieckie .	4	4 268	3 910	27	25	3 885	736	149	—	—	—	—	85	121	—	1 844	62	—

4. Nr. 36 — Lista Rolników i Robotników Kresowych — Liste des Agriculteurs et Ouvriers des Territoires del'Est.

Figure A3.1: A page from the *1928 Polish Elections Data Book*

There were four purely Jewish parties that competed in the elections: the socialist anti-Zionist *Bund*; the Zionist-Marxist *Poalei Tsion*; the Jewish National Union of Little Poland, dominated by moderate Zionists from former Austro-Hungarian Galicia; and the General Jewish National Bloc, representing the religious-orthodox *Agudas Yisroel* (also known as the *Aguda*). The Bloc of National Minorities (BNM), although striving to unite and represent all of Poland's ethnic minorities, was created and led by Yitzhak Greenboim, the leader of the Polish Zionists. It attracted numerous Jewish voters, mainly Zionists in the urban areas of central and Eastern Poland (with the exception of Galicia), where the vast majority of ghettos were located. Here I follow Kopstein and Wittenberg's "not perfect, but reasonable"[5] assumption that it was only ethnically non-Poles, and particularly the Jews, who supported the BNM. The BNM was a loose coalition established and led by Zionists. Some Zionists, however, were more committed and organized than others. The 1937 and 1939 Zionist Organization (ZO) Congresses' electoral returns allow for an analysis of the number and ideological preferences of these people.

THE 1937 AND 1939 ZIONIST ORGANIZATION ELECTIONS DATASET

The ZO was established in 1897 as an umbrella organization for the Zionist movement that sought the creation of a Jewish homeland in Palestine. ZO Congresses were held every two years, and the right to elect delegates was granted to every dues-paying member. Only Jews were allowed to join. For this study I use the local-level ZO Congress Electoral Commissions protocols from 1937 and 1939. These are the only existing local-level protocols from Poland, and they are located at the Central Zionist Archives (CZA) in Jerusalem.[6]

An advantage of the ZO returns is that the data cover the immediate prewar period—the 1939 ZO elections took place just a month before the Nazi invasion of Poland. The downside is that the data are incomplete—some protocols were most likely destroyed during the Holocaust and did not reach the CZA. Furthermore, the right-wing Revisionist Zionists split from the ZO in 1935 to establish the New Zionist Organization (NZO), and therefore not all Polish Zionists voted in the ZO Congress elections. Unfortunately, I was unable to find community-level data on the number of NZO members in Poland.

Ghettos were not established in all the localities that voted in the ZO elections, and there are places for which I have only the 1937 or 1939 elections results. However, in places for which I do have both 1937 and 1939 data, the local-level results are almost identical. In places for which both 1937 and 1939 data are available, I use averages. Several protocols remain unidentified—the names of the localities and the results are handwritten (almost exclusively in Hebrew, with a handful in Yiddish or Polish), and the name of the locality is most of the time given in its Yiddish form, which is often quite different from the Polish original. As a partial solution to this problem, when the handwritten locality name was impossible to decipher, I tried to identify the locality by looking for names of the local electoral commission members at the Yad Vashem Central Database of Shoah [Holocaust] Victims' Names. I was able to identify ZO elections results for 469 out of 667 ghetto localities. Of the 198 ghettos for which I do not have ZO elections data, about fifty are in Western Galicia, for which no protocols are available—most likely they were kept in Poland and were destroyed during the war. Outside Western Galicia, many localities for which I do not have protocols are very small towns, and hence it is likely that the elections were simply not held there. Otherwise, I do not see any additional, systematic pattern that might explain the missing data. Scholars have never previously analyzed the ZO's local election results.

Three main parties took part in the ZO Congresses' 1937 and 1939 elections: the moderate, centrist General Zionists A, the religious *Mizrahi*, and the left-wing Bloc for the Working Land of Israel (BWLI). There were also two minuscule parties, General Zionists B and the right-wing Jewish State Party, which received only a handful of votes and therefore were excluded from analysis. In 1939, two more parties took part in the elections (though they did not compete in Eastern Galicia) but received very few votes and they have been omitted as well.

ANALYSIS

In this analysis I match the data on ghettos with electoral returns from places in which ghettos were established. The dependent dichotomous variable is *Ghetto uprising*, and I include in the model a number of explanatory and control variables, described in table A3.2.

To interpret the results I estimate the percentage change in odds. In other words, I estimate by how many percentage points the likelihood of an uprising changes with a one unit or one standard deviation increase in a right-hand variable.[7] It should be noted that in my analysis I focus on why and where the uprisings took place and do not analyze their timing. The reason is that there is no variation in the timing of uprisings—they were virtually always a last resort measure and took place during the final liquidation of the ghetto, real or perceived. The Jews had little to no impact on the timing of a liquidation as the decision depended on German internal policies, goals, and holidays, such as Hitler's birthday. Therefore, after a decision to fight had been adopted, the exact date of the uprising

Table A3.2: Variables

Variable	Description
Percent Jews	Percent of Jews in the locality
Ghetto population	Ghetto population (logged)
Existence	Duration of ghetto's existence (months)
Enclosed	Closed or open ghetto (dummy)
Eastern Poland	Under Soviet occupation in 1939–41 (dummy)
Percent BBWR	Percent of votes received by BBWR in the locality
Percent communist	Percent of votes received by the communists and their allies in the locality
Percent Bund	Percent of votes received by Bund in the locality
Percent BNM	Percent of votes received by the Minorities Bloc in the locality
Percent Aguda	Percent of votes received by the General Jewish National Bloc in the locality
Percent Poalei Tsion	Percent of votes received by the Poalei Tsion in the locality
Percent Galicia Zionists	Percent of votes received by the Jewish National Union of Little Poland in the locality
ZO members	Number of ZO members in the locality (logged)
BWLI	Number of BWLI supporters in the locality (logged)
Gen Zionists	Number of General Zionists supporters in the locality (logged)
Mizrahi	Number of Mizrahi supporters in the locality (logged)

was a function of German, not Jewish, actions. The results are reported in table A3.3.

The results of the statistical test support my argument. A one-unit increase in the logged number of ZO members in a community is associated with a more than fivefold increase in the probability of an uprising; the estimated effect of location in Eastern Poland is associated with a 340% increase. The estimated effects of voting for the BNM and, interestingly, the communists, are small but statistically significant and positive. Although the data are scant, it is possible that, as in the case of Białystok, Jewish communists did join the Zionist-led underground in the uprising. It is also interesting to note that the estimated effects of the size of the ghetto population and the percentage of Jews in the local community prior to the

Table A3.3: Logit analysis of ghetto uprisings: Percentage change in odds

Variable	Increase of		Odds ratio (p value)	95% confidence interval	
	One unit	One SD			
ZO members**	540.3	872.2	6.403 (.011)	1.533	26.736
Eastern Poland*	344.2	—	4.442 (.059)	.947	20.842
Percent BNM*	4.6	73.3	1.046 (.054)	.999	1.094
Percent communist***	5.8	87.0	1.058 (.001)	1.022	1.095
BWLI members	−15.9	−24.6	.841 (.474)	.523	1.351
Gen Zionists	−34.8	−49.3	.652 (.108)	.387	1.099
Mizrahi	−13.7	−23.6	.863 (.465)	.581	1.282
Ghetto population	64.1	82.1	1.641 (.314)	.626	4.302
Percent Jews	2.1	49.4	1.021 (.243)	.986	1.057
Existence	−0.4	−3.7	.996 (.914)	.921	1.077
Enclosed	−6.1	—	.939 (.925)	.256	3.440
Percent BBWR	2.2	36.8	1.022 (.261)	.984	1.063
Percent Bund	0.9	3.4	1.009 (.910)	.863	1.181
Percent Aguda	−0.4	−2.5	.996 (.953)	.885	1.122
Percent Poalei Tsion	5.1	13.6	1.051 (.649)	.847	1.305
Percent Galicia Zionists	1.1	16.8	1.011 (.684)	.958	1.067

N = 339; Pseudo R2= 0.344; Log-likelihood = −53.430.
Notes: p values in parentheses (*p < 0.1; **p < 0.05; ***p < 0.01).

Holocaust are not statistically significant. As noted above, several studies of ethnically motivated violence put forward the concentration of groups and the "power in numbers" argument as an important explanatory variable. An opposite perspective that builds on the Olsonian logic of collective action argues that the organization of violence is easier in smaller groups. My analysis suggests that variables other than sheer numbers and demographic structures explain the ghetto revolts. The enclosure of a ghetto by a fence or a wall—a good measure of the level of German oppression during the ghetto's existence and an impediment to the acquisition of material resources and weapons—also has no statistically significant estimated effect.

It should be remembered, however, that the statistical analysis, while supporting the arguments derived from my argument and the comparison of the three ghettos, offers a plausibility test only. Because of the limitations of the data, I do not test the argument directly as there are no explicit measures of skills in the model. However, in ghettos where Jews were most likely to have operational security skills, uprisings were more likely.

Notes

Chapter 1: Introduction

1. The policies of the Yale University Fortunoff Video Archive for Holocaust Testimonies require listing the first letter of an interviewee's last name only.

2. Israel G. 1995.

3. Langer 1982.

4. Fujii 2009.

5. Andreas 2008.

6. Hilberg 1993; for a more nuanced classification, see Fujii 2009.

7. Browning 1993; Dean 2000; Fujii 2009; Goldhagen 1996; Straus 2006.

8. Darden forthcoming; Kalyvas 2006; R. Petersen 2001; J. Weinstein 2007; Wood 2003; Balcells 2016.

9. Browning 2010, 291.

10. Hilberg 2003.

11. See Paulsson 2002; Tec 1993.

12. Browning 2010.

13. Bauer 1989.

14. See Bettelheim 1980; Pawełczyńska 1979; Des Pres 1980. Bettelheim and Pawełczyńska were themselves prisoners of the Nazi camps.

15. See Aquino and Thau 2009; Carver and Connor-Smith 2010; Somer et al. 2007.

16. Hirschman 1970.

17. In Hirshman's framework, "loyalty" is an intervening factor, not a separate strategy, as loyalty "holds exit at bay and activates voice" (p. 78).

18. Baines and Paddon 2012; Jose and Medie 2015; Mégret 2009.

19. This argument builds on McAdam (1986), which I discuss in greater detail later in the book.

20. Botticini and Eckstein 2012; Darden and Grzymała-Busse 2006.

21. Kopstein and Wittenberg 2011; Varshney 2003; Wilkinson 2006.

22. Connelly et al. 2011, 340.

23. King 2012.

24. Dumitru and Johnson 2011; Goldhagen 1996; Hollander 2008; Kopstein and Wittenberg 2011; Braun 2016; Zeitlin 2010; Maher 2010; Einwohner 2003.

25. I discuss the concept of a "ghetto" in greater detail in chapter 2.

26. Fein 1979. Fein excludes the USSR from her analysis of Nazi controlled zones, but as I will demonstrate, Nazi policies in Minsk were no less (and in many respects substantially more) brutal than in the other two cities.

27. Appendix 2 further describes the variation in the distribution of strategies both within and across the three ghettos. Appendix 3 analyzes the differences in the patterns of Jewish armed resistance across ghettos.

28. Not all of the testimonies I read or viewed are referenced or cited in the book.

29. Friedländer 1997.

30. Jeffrey Kopstein and Jason Wittenberg use the same underlying data in their analysis of the Jews' voting patterns in interwar Poland and of the 1941 anti-Jewish pogroms. My dataset is more limited as it focuses only on communities in which ghettos were later established. Kopstein and Wittenberg kindly shared with me some of their data, but most of the dataset was coded independently.

31. Currently the World Zionist Organization.

32. King 2012.

33. On the paucity of comparative research in Jewish studies, see Endelman 1997.

34. Friedländer 1997, 2.

CHAPTER 2: SETTING THE STAGE: JEWISH GHETTOS DURING THE HOLOCAUST

1. Michman 2011, 1.

2. Browning 2012, xxvii.

3. Michman 2011, 3.

4. Dean n.d.

5. Kruglov and Dean 2012.

6. Hilberg 1981.

7. Corni 2002; Gringauz 1949; Michman 2011; Trunk 1972.

8. Manley 2012, 48.

9. Margarita F. 1995.

10. Arkadii P. 1995.

11. Okun' 1991, 3.

12. Bryson 2004.

13. Yoffe 2003, 51, 55, 62.

14. Girsh K. 1995.

15. Asja T. 1995.

16. Tatyana G. 1995.

17. Shalit-Galperin 1970, 19.

18. Yoffe 2003, 64.

19. Menke 1996; Parker 1995; Brauner 1996; Lane 1995.

20. Yoffe 2003, 78–79.

21. Blum 1995, 3–4.

22. Cichopek-Gajraj 2014, 66.

23. Crowe 2004, 140.

24. Crowe 2004, 148. The sole exception was the *Pod Orlem* (Under the Eagle) pharmacy, the only non-Jewish business in the ghetto.

25. Dora R. 1988.

26. Erna R. 1989.

27. Sinnreich, Phillips, and Dean 2012, 530.

28. Dobroszycki 1994, 22, 71, 78.

29. See Gotlib 1995, 5; Irene S. 1980.

30. J. T. Gross 2002; Bikont 2015; Kopstein and Wittenberg 2011.

31. Birk 1991, 10.

32. Lipa A. 1990.

33. Levkowitcz 1972, 4.

34. Bender 2008, chap. 6.

35. Bender 2008, 269–73.

36. Dobroszycki 1994, 69, 76.

37. Bemporad 2013, 16.

38. Zakai 1968, 7.

39. Bemporad 2013, 24, 27.

40. Bemporad 2013, chap. 5.

41. Bemporad 2013, chap. 2; Neria 1969; Rozin 1975.

42. Bemporad 2013.

43. Bemporad 2013, 3, 198. On Soviet nationalities policies in general, see Martin 2001. On the impact on these policies on the general population's attitude towards Jews, see Dumitru 2016.

44. Altshuler 1993, Table 4.

45. E.g., M. Epstein 1980.

46. Martin 2004, 31.

47. H. Petersen 2008.

48. Wróbel 1994, 103. Here I use "ghetto" in the medieval sense, as a separate Jewish quarter of the city, where Jews were forced to reside.

49. Wróbel 1994, 108, 117.

50. Wróbel 1994, 116.

51. Martin 2004, 15, 53, 169.

52. Martin 2004, 40–41.

53. Martin 2004, 84–89.

54. Galas and Polonsky 2011, 43.

55. In August 1945, the city also experienced an anti-Jewish pogrom. For details on the 1945 pogrom, see Cichopek-Gajraj 2014, chap. 4.

56. Galas and Polonsky 2011, 23.

57. Martin 2004, 16.

58. Melzer 2001, 214.

59. Martin 2004, 9.

60. Kobrin 2010, 19.

61. Kobrin 2010, 25–26.

62. Bender 2008, 3.

63. Kobrin 2010, 20.

64. Bender 2008, 21.

65. Kobrin 2010, 20.

66. Kobrin 2010, 52.

67. Kobrin 2010, 58–60.

68. Kobrin 2010, 63.

69. Kobrin 2010, 136–41.

70. Kobrin 2010, 140.

71. Bender 2008, 18–19.

72. Kobrin 2010.
73. Bender 2008, 22.
74. Zabuski and Brott 1996, 3.
75. Sztop-Rutkowska and Kobrin 2014.
76. Seder 1995.
77. Ari 1995, 4; Goldshmidt 1991, 6; Irene S. 1980.
78. Bikont 2015, 43.
79. Bender 2008, 43.
80. However, some Jewish organizations provided services to both Jewish and non-Jewish residents of the city.
81. Zvuluni n.d., 4–6.
82. A. Vered 1988, 18.
83. Lipa A. 1990.
84. Mielnicki and Munro 2000, 77.
85. Dorn 1991, 12.
86. Berkner 2001, 21; A. Vered 1988, 20.
87. On the consequences of ethnic hierarchy reversal in neighboring Lithuania, see R. Petersen 2001.
88. Dorn 1991, 28.
89. Bender 2008, 56.
90. Bender 2008, 55.
91. Levkowitcz 1972, 2.
92. Gofer 1996, 6.
93. Perlis 1987, 56.
94. Liak 1974, 1.
95. Bender 2008, 68–70.

Chapter 3: What Did the Jews Know?

1. Tversky and Kahneman 1974, 1124.
2. Slovic, Fischhoff, and Lichtenstein 1982, 464–65.
3. Gal'burt 2003, 7.
4. See Rubinshtein 2011, 6.
5. Margolina 2010, 11.
6. Leonid's image was certainly influenced by the Soviet 1938 classic movie "Alexander Nevskii," which depicted the victory, in 1242, of Russian prince Alexander over the German knights of the Teutonic Order, who wore horned helmets.
7. Okun' 2007.
8. Hecker 2007, 44.
9. Smolar 1989, 12.
10. Jackson 2000, 11, 14.
11. Shalit-Galperin 1970, 10.
12. Lapidus 1994, 16.
13. Tatyana G. 1995.
14. Goland 1980, 6.
15. Rubinshtein 2011, 22.

16. Rubin 1977, 16.

17. Lapidus 1994, 10.

18. YIVO is also the *Yidisher Visnshaftlekher Institut* (Yiddish Scientific Institute)—a famous Jewish history and culture research center, established in interwar Poland and currently located in New York.

19. Smolar 1989, 25.

20. See Movshenson 1993.

21. Cholawski 2001.

22. Davydova 2000, 214.

23. Movshenson 1993.

24. Karpilova 1993.

25. Perchonok-Kesler 1973, 5. According to the testimony this person was either an ethnic Czech or, more likely, an ethnic German from Czechoslovakia. In any case, the testimony explicitly mentions that the person wore a German military uniform.

26. Krasinskii 2011.

27. Pasherstnik 2008, 245–50.

28. Smilovitsky 1999, 67; see also Parker 1995.

29. Henry R. 1986.

30. Hecker 2007; Barkai 1989; Meinhart 1996.

31. Iaakov N. 1995.

32. Floss 1996.

33. See Menke 1996; Parker 1995; Lane 1995.

34. Leopold P. 1984; David W. 1988; Frederic B. 1991.

35. Rosalie S. 1985.

36. David R. 1987.

37. Solomon S. 1991.

38. Luna K. 1988.

39. Leon K. 1983.

40. Menachem S. 1979.

41. William S. 1991.

42. Reena F. 1987.

43. Ada A. 1989.

44. Rosalyn O. 1987.

45. Alexander A. 1994.

46. Peleg-Marianska and Peleg 1991, 7–8; Pemper 2008, 16.

47. Meir B. 1991.

48. Moshe B. 1990.

49. Peleg-Marianska and Peleg 1991, 124.

50. Henry S. 1996.

51. Pankiewicz 1987, 98.

52. Ludwig B. 1992.

53. N. Gross 1983, 5.

54. Henry T. 1990.

55. Solomon S. 1991.

56. Ida L. 1994.

57. Regina L. 1991.

58. Frederic B. 1991.
59. Shatyn 1985, 21; see also Bosak 1983, 2.
60. Avnon 2003, 25.
61. Ida L. 1994.
62. Edith W. 1994.
63. Leon F. 1994.
64. Mielnicki and Munro 2000, 35, 64, 73.
65. Kraczowska 1991a, 11.
66. Ralph B. 1986.
67. Zabuski and Brott 1996, 41.
68. Blumental 1962, 60.
69. Datner 1946, 21–22.
70. Goldshmidt 1991, 18.
71. Kraczowska 1991a, 26.
72. Bass 2006, 7.
73. Abraham O. 1980.
74. Tenenbaum-Tamaroff 1984, 74.
75. Birk 1991, 10.
76. Levkowitcz 1972; Levkowitcz 1980.
77. Pransky 1991, 36.
78. Jay M. 1983.
79. Olenski 2006, 43–44, 46.
80. Shtrauch 1991, 16, 19.
81. Levkowitcz 1980, 3.
82. Tenenbaum-Tamaroff 1984, 31.
83. Felicja N. 1991.
84. Avraham K. 1994. Semen Bekenshtein (1995), on the other hand, says he knew about Treblinka, but when he was deported to Auschwitz in February 1943 he had no idea where exactly he was going.
85. Mielnicki and Munro 2000, 125; italics in original.
86. Levkowitcz 1980, 13.
87. Yovin 1991, 9–10.
87. Yekutiel S. 1996.
89. Lahower 1980, 8.
90. Piletzki 2000, 13.
91. Levkowitcz 1980, 30.
92. Rabinovici 2011, 167.
93. Kozin 1996; Sokol'skaia 1988, 7.
94. Birman 1943.

Chapter 4: Cooperation and Collaboration

1. Miron 2009.
2. Arendt 2006, 125.
3. I thank Christopher Browning for stressing this crucial distinction.

4. Hilberg 1980, 110.
5. Trunk 1972.
6. Weiss 1973.
7. P. Friedman 1953; 1980 ch. 12–14.
8. Michman 2003, 159–76.
9. Compare p. 666 in the first edition with p. 1111 in the third edition.
10. Bauer 2001, 148. A very similar distinction between cooperation and collaboration is also proposed by the French historian Henry Michel in his work on World War II France.
11. Engelking and Leociak 2009, 218.
12. Weiss 1973.
13. Adler 1982; Friling 2009; Gombiński 2010; Perechodnik 1996.
14. Michman 2011; Weiss 1973.
15. Zhits 2000, 13–14.
16. B. Epstein 2008, 96.
17. Rubin 1965, 14.
18. Taubkin 2008, 262.
19. Smolar 1989, 20–21.
20. See Goland 1980, 5.
21. Gai 1991, 178.
22. Zhits 2000, 79–90.
23. Weiss 1973.
24. Lyall 2010; Milechina 1980, 5.
25. Gimel'shtein 1991, 15; Vera B. 1993.
26. Gal'burt 2003, 92.
27. Gai 1991, 254.
28. Treister 1992, 11.
29. See Gitlina 1993, 10–12. Mira Markman was also known for betraying to the Germans Jews who worked with the underground or tried to escape to the partisans (Alperovich 1997).
30. Lazar T. 1995.
31. Rubenchik 2006, 68.
32. Goland 1980, 9.
33. Vera S. 1995.
34. See, for instance, Dolts 1972, 14.
35. Hecker 2007, 50–51.
36. Menke 1996.
37. Zhits 2000, 79.
38. Peled 1993, 67–68.
39. Bosak 1983, 7–8.
40. Ganani 1997, 13.
41. According to other sources, he was originally from Silesia.
42. Pankiewicz 1987, 136.
43. Guter 2008, 24.
44. Meringer-Moskowicz 1996, 17; Henry T. 1990.
45. Jarkowska-Natkaniec 2013, 148.

46. Weiss 1973.
47. Jarkowska-Natkaniec 2013, 149.
48. See Avnon 2003, 19–20; Guter 2008.
49. Pankiewicz 1987, 136.
50. Frederic B. 1991.
51. Karter 1990, 30.
52. Staner 1999, 13.
53. Blonder 2002, 5; Peled 1993, 49; Bar-Meir 1982, 11.
54. One such Polish language song was recorded by Nathan Gross and is now available at the YVA (O.3/456).
55. J. Scott 1987.
56. Iaakov W. 1991.
57. Buchnik 1996, 5.
58. Blum 1995, 21.
59. Aneta W. 1993.
60. Edward S. 1991.
61. Meringer-Moskowicz 1996, 17.
62. Ganani 1997, 14–16.
63. Joseph B. 1995.
64. Katz 1996, 21.
65. See Wolf 1995a, 2.
66. Ida L. 1994.
67. Sonia W. 1989.
68. William S. 1991.
69. M. Gurewicz 1994, 12.
70. Teler 1995, 10–11.
71. For a (most probably incomplete) list of informers, see Pankiewicz (1987, 37).
72. Taubenschlag 1998, 57.
73. Wolf 1995a, 13.
74. See Hilfstein 1995, 17.
75. Y. Friedman 1984, 9.
76. Zaltsberg 1994, 10.
77. Pankiewicz 1987, 67.
78. Chwalba 2011, 353.
79. Blumental 1962.
80. Bender 2008, 97.
81. Shilhav 1961, 11, fn. 44.
82. Shilhav 1961, 17.
83. Levkowitcz 1972, 5.
84. Levkowitcz 1980; see also Bender 2008, 186.
85. Levkowitcz 1972, 5.
86. Bender 2008, 130.
87. Tenenbaum-Tamaroff 1984, 64.
88. Blumental 1962, 127–128, 166, מו.
89. Cukiert 1972, 4.
90. Levkowitcz 1980.

91. Sokol'skaia 1988, 23.
92. Bender 2008, 245.
93. Levkowitcz 1980, 7.
94. Trunk 1972; Weiss 1973.
95. Kozin 1996.
96. Zabuski and Brott 1996, 70.
97. Lipa A. 1990.
98. Bender 2008, 136.
99. Blumental 1962, 198–200.
100. Tenenbaum-Tamaroff 1984, 70.
101. Bender 2008, 201.
102. Jack R. 1990.
103. Avraham K. 1994.
104. Lipa A. 1990.
105. Piletzki 2000, 10.
106. Avraham K. 1994.
107. Piletzki 2000, 9.
108. See Gofer 1996, 15.
109. Levkowitcz 1980, 10.
110. Bender 2008, 203.
111. Sokol'skaia 1988, 23.
112. Kalyvas 2008.
113. Lyall 2010.

Chapter 5: Coping and Compliance

1. Quoted in Lower 2013, 94.
2. See Hilberg 2003.
3. A more generic definition of "coping," often used in psychology research is "constantly changing cognitive and behavioral efforts to manage specific external and/or internal demands that are appraised as taxing or exceeding the resources of the person" (Lazarus and Folkman 1984, 141).
4. Browning 2010, 297.
5. For instance, J. Scott 1987.
6. Bauer 2001, 134, 161, 165.
7. Rappoport 2008, 66.
8. Vera B. 1993.
9. Astashinskii 2008.
10. Arkadii T. 1995.
11. Movshenson 1993.
12. Treister 2008, 307.
13. Lazar T. 1995.
14. Arkadii T. 1995.
15. Vera B. 1993.
16. Vera S. 1995.

17. Bressler 1969, 15.
18. Matthäus 1996, 140.
19. Quoted in Smilovitsky 1999, 61–62.
20. Rubin 1977, 16.
21. Davydova 2000, 32–33.
22. Okun' 2007.
23. Lapidus 1994, 13.
24. Liond 1993, 60–64.
25. Malomed 2008, 71, 96–97.
26. Alexander 1996.
27. Iaakov N. 1995.
28. Margolina 2010, 19.
29. Rubenchik 2006, 81.
30. Gorelik 2010.
31. Gai 1991, 299–303.
32. Lazar T. 1995.
33. M. Epstein 1980, 14.
34. Movshenson 1993.
35. See, for instance, Virgili 2002.
36. But see Hedgepeth and Saidel 2010.
37. Margolina 2010, 34–35.
38. Samuil K. 1995.
39. Samuil K. 1995.
40. Hecker 2007, 116.
41. Treister 1992, 10.
42. Ruderman 1973, 4.
43. On stealing, see Parker 1995; Henry R. 1986.
44. Henry R. 1986.
45. Henry R. 1986; see also Lane 1995; Meinhart 1996.
46. Bar'am 1980, 38.
47. Pemper 2008, 100.
48. Else D. 1983.
49. In Minsk, unlike in Kraków, no ghetto existed prior to 1941.
50. Max H. 1994.
51. Irene F. 1987.
52. A Jew of German origin.
53. Cukier 1992, 10.
54. Wolf 1995a, 8.
55. Bar-Meir 1982, 4.
56. Treibicz 1984, 7.
57. Manheim 1984, 21.
58. Markowitcz 1998, 13.
59. Bosak 1983, 18.
60. Helen R. 1992.
61. Frederic B. 1991.
62. Maimon 1984, 1.
63. Browning, Hollander, and Tec 2007, 112.

64. N. Gross 1986; Pankiewicz 1987.
65. Rappoport 2008, 20.
66. Alexander A. 1994.
67. Tushia Z. 1995.
68. Henry E. 1988.
69. Victor L. 1994.
70. Victor L. 1994.
71. Aneta W. 1993.
72. Reena F. 1987.
73. Pankiewicz 1987, 29–30.
74. Max H. 1994.
75. Leopold P. 1984.
76. Victor L. 1994.
77. David W. 1988.
78. Bosak 1983, 21.
79. Anna N. 1984.
80. Ruter 1974, 6–9.
81. Edith W. 1994.
82. Alexander A. 1994.
83. David R. 1987.
84. Isaac W. 1994.
85. Leopold P. 1984.
86. Julian M. 1987.
87. Victor L. 1994.
88. Moshe B. 1990.
89. Raymond F. 1990.
90. Henry S. 1996.
91. Edith W. 1994.
92. Leon K. 1983.
93. Else D. 1983.
94. Rosalie S. 1985.
95. Iaakov W. 1991.
96. Levi 1996.
97. Joseph R. 1995.
98. Miriam H. 1990.
99. Bar-Meir 1982, 7.
100. Crowe 2004, 148.
101. Browning, Hollander, and Tec 2007.
102. Erna H. 1994.
103. Moshe B. 1990.
104. Sonia W. 1989.
105. Feiler-Felińska 1963.
106. Kobrin 2010.
107. Hadasah Levkowitcz (1980, 1–2) recalls how the Jundenrat leadership put very strong emphasis on using proper Yiddish in its public announcements, yet another indirect indicator of the city's proud, inward-looking, Yiddish-speaking identity.
108. Blumental 1962, 132.

109. Shedler 1992, 25.
110. Tzitron 1991, 13.
111. Levkowitcz 1980, 5.
112. Mielnicki and Munro 2000, 109.
113. Celina H. 1993.
114. Zabuski and Brott 1996, 71.
115. Bass 2006, 3, 5.
116. Yekutiel S. 1996.
117. Kizelstein 1985, 2–4.
118. Jack R. 1990.
119. Zabuski and Brott 1996, 62.
120. Avraham K. 1994.
121. Mielnicki and Munro 2000, 110, 119.
122. Blumental 1962, 80.
123. Blumental 1962.
124. Kraczowska 1991a, 19.
125. Zabuski and Brott 1996, 76.
126. Joe D. 1991.
127. Irene S. 1980.
128. Kraczowska 1991a, 17.
129. Zachary A. 1993.
130. J. Scott 1987.
131. Mielnicki and Munro 2000, 109.
132. Bernice S. 1989.
133. Yekutiel S. 1996.
134. Zachary A. 1993.
135. The song, in Polish, is available at the YVA O.3/6825.
136. Olenski 2006, 42.
137. Liak 1974, 3.
138. Abraham O. 1980.
139. Jay M. 1983.
140. Selene B. 1983.
141. Shtrauch 1991, 26.
142. Esther and Charles G. 1980.
143. Blumental 1962, 148.

CHAPTER 6: EVASION

1. Paulsson 2002, 2–3.
2. Grabowski 2013, 2.
3. Ringelblum 1974.
4. See chapter 2 for detailed description of various ghetto types.
5. See Gutman and Krakowski 1986.
6. Ringelblum 1974, 100–101.
7. Paulsson 2002, 3.

8. Grabowski 2013; J. T. Gross and Grudzinska Gross 2012.
9. Paulsson 2002, 3.
10. Monroe 2004; Monroe 2012; Monroe, Barton, and Klingemann 1990.
11. Fogelman 2011.
12. P. Friedman 1957.
13. Grabowski 2013; Paulsson 2002.
14. J. T. Gross 1979.
15. Tec 1986.
16. Ringelblum 1974, ch. 7.
17. Ringelblum 1974, 116.
18. Zuckerman 1993, 421.
19. Browning 2010, ch. 26.
20. Varese and Yaish 2000.
21. Tammes 2007.
22. E.g., Gutman and Krakowski 1986; Tec 1986.
23. E.g., Paulsson 2002.
24. Granovetter 1973, 1369.
25. Rubenchik 2006, 142.
26. Slepyan 2000.
27. Rubin 1965, 22.
28. Margolina 2010, 35–36.
29. Bruk and Bruk 2004, 56.
30. Shalit-Galperin 1970, 14.
31. Bemporad 2013.
32. Kukhta 1996, 9.
33. Lazar T. 1995.
34. The friend was a Soviet citizen of German ethnicity.
35. Rubin 1965, 31.
36. Asja T. 1995.
37. Fridland 1993.
38. Dadasheva 1999, 8–11.
39. Svoyatytskaia 1995.
40. Etinger 2001.
41. Ledvich 1995.
42. Vera B. 1993.
43. Lazar T. 1995.
44. B. Epstein 2008, 172–74.
45. Nikodimova 2010, ch. 2.
46. Tokarski 1993.
47. Greenstein 1968, 47.
48. Gorelik 2010.
49. Movshenson 1993.
50. Vera S. 1995.
51. Shalit-Galperin 1970, 26–27.
52. B. Epstein 2008, 29.
53. Vera B. 1993.

54. Bruk and Bruk 2004, 60–61.

55. Rappoport 2008, 59.

56. Okun' 1991, 14.

57. Alexander 1996.

58. Hecker 2007, 70. According to Curt Parker (1995), his cousin Günter escaped to the partisans together with a local Jewish girl. Their fate is unknown, but most likely they were caught and killed. As a punishment for the escape, the Germans murdered a group of Jews from the Hamburg ghetto.

59. Bar'am 1980, 42.

60. Gitlina 1993, 24.

61. Gutkovich 1993.

62. Gutkovich 1993.

63. Okun' 2007.

64. Krasinskii 2011.

65. See Gorelik 2010.

66. Kukhta 1996, 12.

67. Three Order of Glory decorations were equivalent to the "Hero of the Soviet Union"—the highest Soviet military honor.

68. M. Epstein 1980, 2.

69. Al B. 1995.

70. Celina R. 1995.

71. Aneta W. 1993.

72. Victor P. 1994.

73. Browning, Hollander, and Tec 2007, 130.

74. Immigration to the United States was guided by "country quotas," according to which only a certain number of immigrants from each country were allowed into the United States.

75. Browning, Hollander, and Tec 2007, 170, 203.

76. Ganani 1997, 7.

77. Buchbinder 1999, 6.

78. Zipporah S. 1992.

79. Celina S. 1979.

80. Leon K. 1983.

81. Louise J. 1988.

82. Barsuk 1996.

83. Peleg-Marianska and Peleg 1991, 62.

84. Irene F. 1987.

85. Peleg-Marianska and Peleg 1991, 6–7.

86. Victor P. 1994.

87. Celina S. 1979.

88. Marcel W. 1984.

89. David R. 1987.

90. Aneta W. 1993.

91. Joseph R. 1995.

92. Maria B. 1994.

 93. Sonia W. 1989.
 94. Ludwig B. 1992.
 95. Budik 1995, 18.
 96. Katz 1996, 12.
 97. Peleg-Marianska and Peleg 1991, 3.
 98. Chawka R. 1986.
 99. Marlow 2014.
100. Regina L. 1991.
101. Blum 1995, 34.
102. Pankiewicz 1987, 27.
103. Grabowski 2013.
104. Lieberman 1965.
105. Rotbard 2000.
106. Ruter 1974, 11.
107. Helen R. 1992.
108. Henry E. 1988.
109. Joseph B. 1995.
110. Rena R. 1985.
111. Victor P. 1994.
112. Regina L. 1991.
113. I. Gurewicz 1994, 13.
114. Barsuk 1996, 13–14.
115. Taubenschlag 1998, 29, 31–32, 36–37.
116. Quoted in Paulsson 2002, 110.
117. Shatyn 1985.
118. Victor P. 1994.
119. Anna N. 1984.
120. Alex G. 1990.
121. Irene F. 1987.
122. Ruter 1974, 18.
123. Sylvia F. 1981.
124. Mentioned in some sources as Bosko.
125. Pankiewicz 1987, 54–55.
126. Penski 1997.
127. Birk 1991, 4.
128. Yovin 1991, 2.
129. Tzitron 1991, 6.
130. Kraczowska 1991a, 2, 5–6.
131. Ari 1995, 4; Goldshmidt 1991, 6; Irene S. 1980.
132. Berkner 2001, 10; Mendelson 1998; Seder 1995.
133. Bass 2006, 5.
134. Blumental 1962, 262; Gofer 1996, 11.
135. Lipa A. 1990.
136. Lahower 1980, 8.
137. Irene S. 1980.

138. Bender 2008, 248.

139. M. Weinstein 1996.

140. Blumental 1962, טב.

141. Goldshmidt 1991, 19.

142. Shedler 1992, 34.

143. Bornstein-Bielicka 2003, 167.

144. Iwry 2004, 180–81.

145. Turlo 2011, 17.

146. Wender 2005, 22–23.

147. Cohen 2007, 21.

148. Kaminsky 1972, 18.

149. J. T. Gross 2002; Bikont 2015; Kopstein and Wittenberg 2011.

150. Grabowski 2013.

151. Jack R. 1990.

152. Schneider 1991, 9–10.

153. Felicja N. 1991.

154. Eventually she revealed the names of her saviors in the 1996 English translation of her Polish-language memoir.

155. Gotlib 1995, 12, 20.

156. Marlow 2014.

157. Celina H. 1993.

158. Dworzecka 1998.

159. Kraczowska 1991a.

160. Jay M. 1983.

161. Zachary A. 1993.

162. Sokol'skaia (1988, 22) does not discuss when this person was her colleague, but given the nature of the job, most likely this also happened during Soviet rule.

163. Bornstein-Bielicka 2003, 142, 148.

164. Bornstein-Bielicka 2003, 171.

165. Rud 1991, 6, 17.

166. Bornstein-Bielicka 2003, 204.

167. Dorn 1991, 55; Mendelson 1998.

168. At the same time, exclusively intraethnic social networks made for easier life and more opportunities *inside* the ghetto, thus making the coping strategy more attractive.

169. Granovetter 1973.

170. Mylonas 2013.

Chapter 7: Resistance

1. Bauer 2001, 120.

2. Maher 2010, 252.

3. Barnes 2005; Goldstone and Useem 1999; Rediker 2007; Rediker 2012.

4. Einwohner 2003; Varshney 2003; Wood 2003.

5. R. Petersen 2002.

6. Maher 2010.

7. McAdam 1986.

8. See Fearon and Laitin 2003.

9. Cederman, Wimmer, and Min 2010.

10. Kalyvas and Kocher 2007; Lichbach 1998.

11. Gould 1991; Parkinson 2013; R. Petersen 2001; Staniland 2014.

12. Kuran 1991.

13. Krakowski 1984.

14. Marrus 1995, 103.

15. Quoted in Marrus 1995, 103.

16. Parkinson 2013.

17. USA SOCOM 2013, 92.

18. McCormick and Owen 2000.

19. Bell 1989.

20. Maher 2010; see also Goldstone and Tilly 2001.

21. Goldman 2011, 311.

22. Here the term covers the communist parties of Poland, Western Ukraine, and Western Belorussia.

23. Bemporad 2013, 45–46.

24. B. Epstein 2008, 111.

25. Rubin 1965, 22–23.

26. Taits n.d.

27. Tec and Weiss 1997.

28. McAdam (1986, 70) defines biographical availability as "the absence of personal constraints that may increase the costs and risks of movement participation, such as full-time employment, marriage, and family responsibility."

29. Smolar 1989, 34, italics in original.

30. Smolar 1989, 36.

31. B. Epstein 2008, 16.

32. Lapidus 1994, 17–21.

33. Tatyana G. 1995.

34. Greenstein 1968, 47.

35. Astashinskii 2008.

36. Smolar 1989, 31.

37. B. Epstein 2008, 136.

38. Smolar 1989, 84.

39. Feigelman 1991, 9.

40. Karpilova 1993.

41. Taits n.d.

42. Gebeleva 2010, 30–31.

43. Reizman 2005, 160–61.

44. Khabai 1980, 7.

45. Perchonok-Kesler 1973, 3–4.

46. Nikodimova 2010, 23–24.

47. Greenstein 1968, 51.
48. Greenstein 1968, 62.
49. Porat 1997, 61.
50. Porat 1997, 60.
51. Tec 1993.
52. Krasinskii 2011.
53. Okun' 2007.
54. Feigelman 1991, 23–24.
55. Okun' 2007.
56. Boiko 1991, 32; Gorelik 2010.
57. Okun' 2007. It is also possible that Zorin simply had a softer character and therefore was amenable to pressure from above, but the available descriptions of his personality do not support this claim.
58. Liond 1993, 77; Press 1997.
59. Brauner 1996; Floss 1996.
60. Marcel W. 1984.
61. Pemper 2008, 16.
62. Katz 1996, 12–13.
63. Halutz is "pioneer" is Hebrew. The term refers to the early Zionist immigrants to Palestine.
64. Shlomo Sh. 1992.
65. Shlomo Sh. says that while he does not know whether Bauminger was a member of the communist party, he is certain that Bauminger did support the party and its cause. Kuper (1982, 33) defines him as "half-communist."
66. Shlomo Sh. 1992.
67. Peled 1993, appendix 11.
68. R. Kuper 1982.
69. Globerman 1982, 3–4.
70. Globerman 1982, 1.
71. Shlomo Sh. 1992.
72. McCormick and Owen 2000; Shapiro 2013.
73. Taube 1967, 5.
74. Davidson Draenger 1996, 37–38.
75. Bar-Meir 1982, 1.
76. Shifra Lustgarten 1981, Appendix 1, 5.
77. Peled 1993, Appendix 10.
78. Davidson Draenger 1996, 61.
79. Davidson Draenger 1996, 5, 62.
80. Shimon Lustgarten 1981; Maimon 1984; Nordlicht 1983, 7; Wolf 1995b; Sessler 1988, 10.
81. Globerman 1982; Shein 1988; Shenar 1983, 4.
82. Davidson Draenger 1996.
83. Shlomo Sh. 1992.
84. Maimon 1984, 9.
85. Davidson Draenger 1996, 83.

86. Mire was a cousin of Rivka Kuper, Dolek Liebeskind's spouse.
87. Zając 1965, 64.
88. Shlomo Sh. 1992.
89. R. Kuper 1982, 14.
90. Chawka R. 1986; Zuckerman 1993, 234.
91. Davidson Draenger 1996; Zaltsberg 1994, 9.
92. According to some sources—December 23.
93. See, for instance, Galas and Polonsky 2011, 46.
94. Wolf 1995a, 13.
95. See Y. Friedman 1984, 6; Hilfstein 1995, 17.
96. R. Kuper 1982, 15.
97. Shein 1988, 17.
98. Peled 1993, 283.
99. Crowe 2004, 192.
100. Rufeisen-Schüpper 1990, 89–90.
101. Ida L. 1994.
102. Frederic B. 1991; William S. 1991.
103. See Sessler 1988, 8.
104. Bender 2008, 155.
105. Baumetz 1980, 2.
106. Datner 1946, 18–19.
107. Reznik 1997, 2, 5.
108. Bender 2008; Porat 2000, 99.
109. Reznik 1997, 6–7.
110. Reznik 1997, 7.
111. Bender 2008, 167.
112. Liak 1974, 21–22; Bender 2008, ch. 5.
113. E. Vered 1973; E. Vered 1993.
114. See Cukiert 1972, 5; S. Goldberg 1972, 6; Kraczowska 1991b, 11.
115. Tenenbaum-Tamaroff 1984, 13–14, emphasis in original.
116. Kaminsky 1972, 16.
117. Cukiert 1972, 5.
118. Tenenbaum-Tamaroff 1984, 46.
119. Tenenbaum-Tamaroff 1984, 111–13.
120. Bornstein-Bielicka 2003, 190.
121. Bender 2008, 254.
122. Irene S. 1980.
123. Bornstein-Bielicka 2003; Grosman 1992; Klibanski 2002.
124. Cukiert 1972, 5.
125. Berkner 2001, 68.
126. Kraczowska 1991b, 30–31.
127. Pransky 1991, 23–24.
128. Fain 1990, 15.
129. Lahower 1980, 9.
130. S. Goldberg 1991, 38.

131. Klibanski 1993, 41.
132. Baumetz 1980, 4–5.
133. McAdam 1986, 71.

Chapter 8: Conclusions

1. King 2012.
2. Oscar Schindler did try to save his Jewish employees, but it was a private attempt by an individual entrepreneur.
3. McAdam 1986.
4. Varshney 2002.
5. Kopstein and Wittenberg 2011.
6. Bermeo 2003.
7. See Charny 1982; Fein 1979; L. Kuper 1981; Midlarsky 2005.
8. See, for instance, Levene 2005.
9. Kalyvas 2003.
10. Browning 1993.
11. Goldhagen 1996.
12. Straus 2006.
13. Fujii 2009.
14. Browning 2010.
15. Finkel and Straus 2012.
16. But see Straus 2015.
17. For additional work on historical legacies of regimes, see Darden forthcoming; Darden and Grzymała-Busse 2006; Putnam 1993.
18. On this point, see also Dumitru and Johnson 2011.
19. Mégret 2009; see also Jose and Medie 2015; Baines and Paddon 2012.

Appendix 1

1. For more information on the archive, see Shenker 2015, ch. 1.
2. Bartov 2011, 487; see also J. T. Gross 2002.
3. Shenker 2015.
4. Lustick 1996.
5. See Bazyler and Tuerkheimer 2015, ch. 7.
6. Lichtblau 2014, ch. 12.
7. Fujii 2010.
8. Schacter 2001, ch. 1. Schacter calls this well-known phenomenon "Transience."
9. Schacter 2001, 163.
10. Greenspan 2001.
11. Browning 2010; Grabowski 2013, 14.
12. Browning 2010, 9–10.
13. Browning 2010, 9.
14. On the same point, see Bartov 2011, 489.

15. The emergence of such a consistent, testimonies-based local narrative is also noted by a number of locality-centered studies of the Holocaust, such as Browning 2010; Bartov 2011. Elkins 2005 describes the emergence of a similarly consistent narrative in her testimonies based study of British camps in Kenya during the Mau-Mau rebellion.

16. Eric Grynaviski also makes this point in his interview for the APSA International History and Politics Newsletter (May 2016).

Appendix 2

1. The coding book and the data are available online at: https://sites.google.com/site/evgenyfinkel/resume.

Appendix 3

1. This definition excludes spontaneous, individual acts of resistance and resistance outside the ghettos.

2. See Toft 2003; Weidmann 2009.

3. Manley 2012.

4. Kopstein and Wittenberg 2003.

5. Kopstein and Wittenberg 2011, 9.

6. *Mahleket Irgun*, Folders S5\1703, S5\1773, S5\1774, S5\1801\1, S5\1801\2, and S5\1801\3.

7. I use the post-estimation commands developed by Long and Freese 2006.

Abbreviations of the Archives

CZA	Central Zionist Archives, Jerusalem
HVT	Yale University Fortunoff Video Archive for Holocaust Testimonies, New Haven, CT
JIA	Jabotinsky Institute in Israel Archive, Tel Aviv
Massuah	Massuah Institute for Holocaust Studies Archive, Tel Yitzhak
OHD	Oral History Division, Avraham Harman Institute of Contemporary Jewry, Hebrew University of Jerusalem
VHA	University of Southern California Shoah Foundation Visual History Archive, Los Angeles, CA
USF	University of South Florida Libraries Oral History Program, Tampa, FL
USHMM	United States Holocaust Memorial Museum Archive, Washington, DC
YVA	Yad Vashem Archive, Jerusalem
ŻIH	Jewish Historical Institute Archive, Warsaw

Bibliography

SURVIVORS' TESTIMONIES AND ARCHIVAL DOCUMENTS

Abraham O. 1980. "Abraham O. Holocaust Testimony." HVT-189.

Ada A. 1989. "Ada A. Holocaust Testimony." HVT-1546.

Al B. 1995. "Al B. Holocaust Testimony." HVT-2831.

Alex G. 1990. "Alex G. Holocaust Testimony." HVT-1327.

Alexander, Fred. 1996. "Fred Alexander Interview." VHA-48006.

Alexander A. 1994. "Alexander A. Holocaust Testimony." HVT-3642.

Alperovich, Dora. 1997. "Dora Alperovich Interview." VHA-35699.

Aneta W. 1993. "Aneta W. Holocaust Testimony." HVT-2696.

Anna N. 1984. "Anna N. Holocaust Testimony." HVT-588.

Ari, Avraham. 1995. "Avraham Ari Testimony." YVA O.3/9165.

Arkadii P. 1995. "Arkadii P. Holocaust Testimony." HVT-3619.

Arkadii T. 1995. "Arkadii T. Holocaust Testimony." HVT-3597.

Asja T. 1995. "Asja T. Holocaust Testimony." HVT-3595.

Avnon, Aliza. 2003. "Aliza Avnon Testimony." YVA O.3/12239.

Avraham K. 1994. "Avraham K. Holocaust Testimony." HVT-3639.

Bar-Meir, Yitzhak. 1982. "Interview with Yitzhak Bar-Meir." OHD-188(11).

Barsuk, Chana. 1996. "Chana Barsuk Testimony." YVA O.3/9828.

Bass, Harry. 2006. "Holocaust Testimony of Harry Bass : Transcript of Audiotaped Interview." Melrose Park, PA. D810.J4 G7 no. 172. Gratz College Holocaust Oral History Archive.

Baumetz, Eliasz. 1980. "Interview with Eliasz Baumetz." OHD-110(24).

Bernice S. 1989. "Bernice S. Holocaust Testimony." HVT-1336.

Birk, Hana. 1991. "Interview with Hana Birk." OHD-110(8).

Birman, Cipora. 1943. "List z Getta Białostockiego, z Prośbą o Odszukanie Siostry Szoszany Fink, Zamieszkalej w Jerozolimie." ŻIH 204.54.

Blonder, Menachem. 2002. "Menachem Blonder Testimony." YVA O.3/12098.

Blum, Avraham. 1995. "Avraham Blum Testimony." YVA O.3/8397.

Boiko, Tatyana. 1991. "Tatyana Boiko Testimony." YVA O.3/6593.

Bosak, Meir. 1983. "Interview with Meir Bosak." OHD-188(21).

Brauner, Walter. 1996. "Walter Brauner Interview." VHA-10982.

Bressler, Asia. 1969. "Interview with Asia Bressler." OHD-58(7).

Bryson, Tsilya. 2004. "My Life Story." USHMM 2004.606.

Buchbinder, Yisrael. 1999. "Yisrael Buchbinder Testimony." YVA O.3/11406.

Buchnik, Halina. 1996. "Halina Buchnik Testimony." YVA O.3/9862.

Budik, Shoshana. 1995. "Shoshana Budik Testimony." YVA O.3/8682.

Celina H. 1993. "Celina H. Holocaust Testimony." HVT-2521.

Celina R. 1995. "Celina R. Holocaust Testimony." HVT-3131.

Celina S. 1979. "Celina S. Holocaust Testimony." HVT-86.

Chawka R. 1986. "Chawka R. Holocaust Testimony." HVT-1821.

Cohen, Esther. 2007. "Esther Cohen Testimony." YVA O.3/13126.

Cukier, Eliezer. 1992. "Eliezer Cukier Testimony." YVA O.3/6572.

Cukiert, Fina. 1972. "Fina Cukiert Testimony." YVA O.3/3611.

Dadasheva, Daria. 1999. "Daria Dadasheva Testimony." YVA O.3/11442.

David R. 1987. "David R. Holocaust Testimony." HVT-1047.

David W. 1988. "David W. Holocaust Testimony." HVT-1246.

Dolts, Kolya. 1972. "Kolya Dolts Testimony." YVA O.3/5210.

Dora R. 1988. "Dora R. Holocaust Testimony." HVT-1230.

Dorn, Mina. 1991. "Mina Dorn Testimony." YVA O.3/6205.

Dworzecka, Maria. 1998. "Maria Dworzecka Interview." VHA-42475.

Edith W. 1994. "Edith W. Holocaust Testimony." HVT-2956.

Edward S. 1991. "Edward S. Holocaust Testimony." HVT-1876.

Else D. 1983. "Else D. Holocaust Testimony." HVT-3036.

Epstein, Maria. 1980. "Memoirs (1940–1980)." USHMM RG-02.132.

Erna H. 1994. "Erna H. Holocaust Testimony." HVT-2914.

Erna R. 1989. "Erna R. Holocaust Testimony." HVT-1381.

Esther and Charles G. 1980. "Esther and Charles G. Holocaust Testimony." HVT-186.

Fain, Zalman. 1990. "Zalman Fain Testimony." YVA O.3/5848.

Feigelman, Khaim. 1991. "Khaim Feigelman Testimony." YVA O.3/6679.

Feiler-Felińska, Maria. 1963. "Maria Feiler-Felińska Testimony." YVA O.3/2316.

Felicja N. 1991. "Felicja N. Holocaust Testimony." HVT-1874.

Floss, Eric. 1996. "Eric Floss Interview." VHA-16026.

Frederic B. 1991. "Frederic B. Holocaust Testimony." HVT-2016.

Fridland, Sophia. 1993. "Sophia Fridland Testimony." YVA O.3/4911.

Friedman, Yehuda. 1984. "Interview with Yehuda Friedman." OHD-188(23).

Ganani, Yitzhak. 1997. "Yitzhak Ganani Testimony." YVA O.3/10089.

Gimel'shtein, Grigorii. 1991. "Grigorii Gimel'shtein Testimony." YVA O.3/5162.

Girsh K. 1995. "Girsh K. Holocaust Testimony." HVT-3593.

Gitlina, Raisa. 1993. "Raisa Gitlina Testimony." YVA O.3/6809.

Globerman, Shalom. 1982. "Interview with Shalom Globerman." OHD-188(6).

Gofer, David. 1996. "David Gofer Testimony." YVA O.3/10477.

Goland, Sara. 1980. "Sara Goland Testimony." YVA O.3/4126.

Goldberg, Leo. 1969. "Interview with Leo Goldberg." OHD-58(2).

Goldberg, Shmuel. 1972. "Shmuel Goldberg Testimony." YVA O.3/3924.

———. 1991. "Interview with Shmuel Goldberg." OHD-110(13).

Goldshmidt, Moshe. 1991. "Zikhronot Migeto Bialystok Vemiblok 13 Birkenau." Massuah AR-T-042–12.

Gotlib, Shifra. 1995. "Shifra Gotlib Testimony." YVA O.3/8138.

Grosman, Chajka. 1992. "Chajka Grosman Testimony." YVA O.3/8650.

Gross, Natan. 1983. "Interview with Natan Gross." OHD-188(13).

Gurewicz, Irena. 1994. "Irena Gurewicz Testimony." YVA O.3/7861.

Gurewicz, Mieczysław. 1994. "Mieczysław Gurewicz Testimony." YVA O.3/7306.

Guter, Nurit. 2008. "Nurit Guter Testimony." YVA O.3/13294.

Gutkovich, Lea. 1993. "Interview with Lea Gutkovich." OHD-223(19).

Helen R. 1992. "Helen R. Holocaust Testimony." HVT-2236.

Henry E. 1988. "Henry E. Holocaust Testimony." HVT-1250.

Henry R. 1986. "Henry R. Holocaust Testimony." HVT-688.

Henry S. 1996. "Henry S. Holocaust Testimony." HVT-3380.

Henry T. 1990. "Henry T. Holocaust Testimony." HVT-1703.

Hilfstein, Josef. 1995. "Josef Hilfstein Testimony." YVA O.3/9486.

Iaakov N. 1995. "Iaakov N. Holocaust Testimony." HVT-3614.

Iaakov W. 1991. "Iaakov W. Holocaust Testimony." HVT-3249.

Ida L. 1994. "Ida L. Holocaust Testimony." HVT-2461.

Irene F. 1987. "Irene F. Holocaust Testimony." HVT-947.

Irene S. 1980. "Irene S. Holocaust Testimony." HVT-98.

Isaac W. 1994. "Isaac W. Holocaust Testimony." HVT-2958.

Israel G. 1995. "Israel G. Holocaust Testimony." HVT-3648.

Jack R. 1990. "Jack R. Holocaust Testimony." HVT-1516.

Jay M. 1983. "Jay M. Holocaust Testimony." HVT-430.

Joe D. 1991. "Joe D. Holocaust Testimony." HVT-1678.

Joseph B. 1995. "Joseph B. Holocaust Testimony." HVT-2832.

Joseph R. 1995. "Joseph R. Holocaust Testimony." HVT-3180.

Julian M. 1987. "Julian M. Holocaust Testimony." HVT-890.

Kaminsky, Aryeh. 1972. "Aryeh Kaminsky Testimony." YVA O.3/3718.

Karpilova, Anna. 1993. "Interview with Anna Karpilova." OHD-223(17).

Karter, Walter. 1990. "Walter Karter Testimony." YVA O.3/6706.

Katz, Edith. 1996. "Edith Katz Testimony." YVA O.3/10085.

Khabai, Sophia. 1980. "Khabai Sophia Testimony." YVA O.3/4212.

Kizelstein, Shamai. 1985. "Nativ Hagoral Shel Shamai Kizelstein Aushwitz-Birkenau Mispar B-1968." JIA K 7a-3/106.

Klibanski, Bronia. 1993. "Interview with Bronia Klibanski." OHD-110(17).

Kozin, Dora. 1996. "Dora Kozin Interview." VHA-11674.

Kraczowska, Eva. 1991a. "Interview with Eva Kraczowska." OHD-110(5).

———. 1991b. "Eva Kraczowska Testimony." YVA O.3/6239.

Kukhta, Boris. 1996. "Boris Kukhta Testimony." YVA O.3/10000.

Kuper, Rivka. 1982. "Interview with Rivka Kuper." OHD-188(4).

Lahower, Rachel. 1980. "Interview with Rachel Lahower." OHD-110(23).

Lane, Berny. 1995. "Berny Lane Interview." VHA-3066.

Lapidus, Albert. 1994. "Reminiscences of Albert Lapidus, from Baltimore, a Former Prisoner of the Minsk Ghetto." USHMM RG-02.174.

Lazar T. 1995. "Lazar T. Holocaust Testimony." HVT-3601.

Ledvich, Raisa. 1995. "A Memoir Relating to Experiences in the Minsk Ghetto and as a Hidden Child." USHMM 1995.A.0579.

Leon F. 1994. "Leon F. Holocaust Testimony." HVT-2903.

Leon K. 1983. "Leon K. Holocaust Testimony." HVT-3106.

Leopold P. 1984. "Leopold P. Holocaust Testimony." HVT-433.

Levkowitcz, Hadasah. 1972. "Hadasah Levkowitcz Testimony." YVA O.3/3809.

———. 1980. "Interview with Hadasah Levkowitcz." OHD-110(22).

Liak, Aharon. 1974. "Interview with Aharon Liak." OHD-110(4).

Lieberman, Jakob. 1965. "Jakob Lieberman Testimony." YVA O.3/2987.

Lipa A. 1990. "Lipa A. Holocaust Testimony." HVT-1842.

Louise J. 1988. "Louise J. Holocaust Testimony." HVT-1142.

Ludwig B. 1992. "Ludwig B. Holocaust Testimony." HVT-2303.

Luna K. 1988. "Luna K. Holocaust Testimony." HVT-1095.

Lustgarten, Shifra. 1981. "Interview with Shifra Lustgarten." OHD-188(3).

Lustgarten, Shimon. 1981. "Interview with Shimon Lustgarten." OHD-188(2).

Maimon, Yehuda. 1984. "Interview with Yehuda Maimon." OHD-188(1).

Manheim, Ester. 1984. "Interview with Ester Manheim." OHD-188(27).

Marcel W. 1984. "Marcel W. Holocaust Testimony." HVT-463.

Margarita F. 1995. "Margarita F. Holocaust Testimony." HVT-3621.

Maria B. 1994. "Maria B. Holocaust Testimony." HVT-2879.

Markowitcz, Gizela. 1998. "Gizela Markowitcz Testimony." YVA O.3/10850.

Max H. 1994. "Max H. Holocaust Testimony." HVT-2913.

Meinhart, Hans. 1996. "Hans Meinhart Interview." VHA-17039.

Meir B. 1991. "Meir B. Holocaust Testimony." HVT-3199.

Menachem S. 1979. "Menachem S. Holocaust Testimony." HVT-152.

Mendelson, Mery. 1998. "Mery Mendelson Interview." VHA-45421.

Menke, Arthur. 1996. "Arthur Menke Interview." VHA-16399.

Meringer-Moskowicz, Nachum. 1996. "Nachum Meringer-Moskowicz Testimony." YVA O.3/10082.

Milechina, Rachil. 1980. "Milechina Rachil Testimony." YVA O.3/4186.

Miriam H. 1990. "Miriam H. Holocaust Testimony." HVT-1737.

Moshe B. 1990. "Moshe B. Holocaust Testimony." HVT-1832.

Movshenson, Esfir. 1993. "Interview with Esfir Movshenson." OHD-223(16).

Neria, Zvi. 1969. "Interview with Rabbi Zvi Neria." OHD-(5).

Nordlicht, Tova. 1983. "Interview with Tova Nordlicht." OHD-188(12).

Okun, Leonid. 1991. "Leonid Okun' Testimony." YVA O.3/6278.

Parker, Curt. 1995. "Curt Parker Interview." VHA-6424.

Penski, Boris. 1997. "Boris Penski Interview." VHA-32711.

Perchonok-Kesler, Yekaterin. 1973. "Yekaterina Perchonok-Kesler Testimony." YVA O.3/3700.

Piletzki, Baruch. 2000. "Baruch Piletzki Testimony." YVA O.3/11804.

Pransky, Yisrael. 1991. "Yisrael Pransky Testimony." YVA O.3/6637.

Press, Boris. 1997. "Boris Press Interview." VHA-38746.

Ralph B. 1986. "Ralph B. Holocaust Testimony." HVT-801.

Raymond F. 1990. "Raymond F. Holocaust Testimony." HVT-1595.

Reena F. 1987. "Reena F. Holocaust Testimony." HVT-1118.

Regina L. 1991. "Regina L. Holocaust Testimony." HVT-1786.

Rena R. 1985. "Rena R. Holocaust Testimony." HVT-521.

Reznik, Nisan. 1997. "Hatsaadim harishonim behitargenut FPO." Massuah AR-T-042–16.

Rosalie S. 1985. "Rosalie S. Holocaust Testimony." HVT-737.

Rosalyn O. 1987. "Rosalyn O. Holocaust Testimony." HVT-945.

Rubin, Anatolii. 1965. "Interview with Anatolii Rubin." OHD-58(12).

Rud, Ania. 1991. "Interview with Ania Rud." OHD-110(10).

Ruderman, Motl. 1973. "Motl Ruderman Testimony." YVA O.3/3701.

Ruter, Eugenia. 1974. "Eugenia Ruter Testimony." YVA O.3/3720.

Samuil K. 1995. "Samuil K. Holocaust Testimony." HVT-3609.

Schneider, Anschel. 1991. "Interview with Anschel Schneider." OHD-110(9).

Seder, Allen. 1995. "Allen Seder Interview." VHA-8135.

Selene B. 1983. "Selene B. Holocaust Testimony." HVT-403.

Sessler, Leon. 1988. "Interview with Leon Sessler." OHD-188(32).

Shalit-Galperin, Nina. 1970. "Interview with Nina Shalit-Galperin." OHD-58(20).

Shedler, Yehiel. 1992. "Interview with Yehiel Shedler." OHD-110(15).

Shein, Selek. 1988. "Interview with Selek Shein." 188(9).

Shenar, Lea. 1983. "Interview with Lea Shenar." OHD-188(22).

Shlomo Sh. 1992. "Shlomo S. Holocaust Testimony." HVT-3496.

Shtrauch, Liza. 1991. "Interview with Liza Shtrauch." OHD-110(12).

Siegman, Frania. 1966. "Frania Siegman Testimony." YVA O.3/2979.

Sokol'skaia, Berta. 1988. "Berta Sokol'skaia Testimony." YVA O.3/4943.

Solomon S. 1991. "Solomon S. Holocaust Testimony." HVT-1696.

Sonia W. 1989. "Sonia W. Holocaust Testimony." HVT-1430.

Svoyatytskaia, Valentina. 1995. "A Memoir Relating to the Experiences at the Minsk Ghetto." USHMM 1995.A.0424.

Sylvia F. 1981. "Sylvia F. Holocaust Testimony." HVT-121.

Tatyana G. 1995. "Tatyana G. Holocaust Testimony." HVT-3594.

Taube, Anna. 1967. "Anna Taube Testimony." YVA O.3/3352.

Teler, Rivka. 1995. "Rivka Teler Testimony." YVA O.3/9087.

Tokarski, Katya. 1993. "Katya Tokarski Testimony." YVA O.3/7348.

Treibicz, Rina. 1984. "Rina Treibicz Testimony." YVA O.3/4295.

Treister, Mikhail. 1992. "Mikhail Treister Testimony." YVA O.3/4724.

Turlo, George. 2011. "Interview with George Turlo." USF-F60–00045.

Tushia Z. 1995. "Tushia Z. Holocaust Testimony." HVT-3175.

Tzitron, Tobia. 1991. "Interview with Tobia Tzitron." OHD-110(6).

Vera B. 1993. "Vera B. Holocaust Testimony." HVT-2744.

Vera S. 1995. "Vera S. Holocaust Testimony." HVT-3617.

Vered, Eliyahu. 1973. "Interview with Eliyahu Vered." OHD-110(3).

———. 1993. "Interview with Eliyahu Vered." OHD-110(19).

Victor L. 1994. "Victor L. Holocaust Testimony." HVT-2928.

Victor P. 1994. "Victor P. Holocaust Testimony." HVT-2887.

Weinstein, Masha. 1996. "Masha Weinstein Interview." VHA-16864.

Wender, Gedaliyah. 2005. "Gedaliyah Wender Testimony." YVA O.3/12746.

William S. 1991. "William S. Holocaust Testimony." HVT-2397.

Wolf, Yoel. 1995a. "Yoel Wolf Testimony." YVA O.3/9115.

———. 1995b. "Interview with Yoel Wolf." OHD-188(33).

Yekutiel S. 1996. "Yekutiel S. Holocaust Testimony." HVT-3823.

Yovin, Zvi. 1991. "Interview with Zvi Yovin." OHD-110(11).

Zachary A. 1993. "Zachary A. Holocaust Testimony." HVT-2575.

Zakai, David. 1968. "Interview with David Zakai." OHD- 58(1).

Zaltsberg, Esther. 1994. "Esther Zaltsberg Testimony." YVA O.3/8507.

Zipporah S. 1992. "Zipporah S. Holocaust Testimony." HVT-2043.

Zuperman, Solomon. 1993. "Interview with Solomon Zuperman." OHD-223(18).
Zvuluni, Shalom. n.d. "Ken Hanoar Hatsioni Bialystok." Massuah AR-T-028–26.

Published Sources

Adler, Stanislaw. 1982. *In the Warsaw Ghetto, 1940–1943: An Account of a Witness.* Jerusalem: Yad Vashem.
Altshuler, Mordechai. 1993. *Distribution of the Jewish Population of the USSR, 1939.* Jerusalem: Hebrew University of Jerusalem.
Andreas, Peter. 2008. *Blue Helmets and Black Markets: The Business of Survival in the Siege of Sarajevo.* Ithaca: Cornell University Press.
Aquino, Karl, and Stefan Thau. 2009. "Workplace Victimization: Aggression from the Target's Perspective." *Annual Review of Psychology* 60: 717–41.
Arendt, Hannah. 2006. *Eichmann in Jerusalem: A Report on the Banality of Evil.* New York: Penguin.
Astashinskii, Abram. 2008. "Interview with Abram Isakovich Astashinskii." At http://iremember.ru/memoirs/partizani/astashinskiy-abram-isaakovich/?sphrase_id=8939.
Baines, Erin, and Emily Paddon. 2012. "'This Is How We Survived': Civilian Agency and Humanitarian Protection." *Security Dialogue* 43, no. 3: 231–47.
Balcells, Laia. 2016. *Rivalry and Revenge: The Politics of Violence during Civil War.* New York: Cambridge University Press.
Bar'am, Hayim. 1980. *Hekhan Hayetah Ha-Shemesh? Divre Edut.* Tel Aviv: Beit lohamei ha-getaot.
Barkai, Avraham. 1989. "German-speaking Jews in Eastern European Ghettos." *Leo Baeck Institute Yearbook* 34, no. 1: 247–66.
Barnes, Steven A. 2005. "'In a Manner Befitting Soviet Citizens': An Uprising in the Post-Stalin Gulag." *Slavic Review* 64, no. 4: 823–50.
Bartov, Omer. 2011. "Wartime Lies and Other Testimonies: Jewish-Christian Relations in Buczacz, 1939–1944." *East European Politics & Societies* 25, no. 3: 486–511.
Bauer, Yehuda. 1989. *Jewish Reactions to the Holocaust.* Tel Aviv: MOD Books.
———. 2001. *Rethinking the Holocaust.* New Haven: Yale University Press.
Bazyler, Michael, and Frank Tuerkheimer. 2015. *Forgotten Trials of the Holocaust.* New York: NYU Press.
Bell, J. Bowyer. 1989. "Aspects of the Dragonworld." *International Journal of Intelligence and Counter Intelligence* 3, no. 1: 15–43.
Bemporad, Elissa. 2013. *Becoming Soviet Jews: The Bolshevik Experiment in Minsk.* Bloomington: Indiana University Press.
Bender, Sara. 2008. *The Jews of Bialystok during World War II and the Holocaust.* Waltham: Brandeis University Press.
Berkner, Sergei. 2001. *Zhizn' i bor'ba Belostokskogo getto: zapiski uchastnika Soprotivleniia.* Moskva: Fond "Kholokost."
Bermeo, Nancy Gina. 2003. *Ordinary People in Extraordinary Times: The Citizenry and the Breakdown of Democracy.* Princeton: Princeton University Press.
Bettelheim, Bruno. 1980. *Surviving and Other Essays.* New York: Vintage.

Bikont, Anna. 2015. *The Crime and the Silence*. New York: Farrar, Straus and Giroux.

Blumental, Nachman. 1962. *Darko Shel Yudenrat: Teudot Migeto Bialistok*. Jerusalem: Yad Vashem.

Bornstein-Bielicka, Chasia. 2003. *Ahat mimeatim: darkah shel lohemet umehanekhet, 1939–1947*. Tel Aviv: Moreshet.

Botticini, Maristella, and Zvi Eckstein. 2012. *The Chosen Few: How Education Shaped Jewish History, 70–1492*. Princeton: Princeton University Press.

Braun, Robert. 2016. "Religious Minorities and Resistance to Genocide." *American Political Science Review* 110, no. 1: 127–47.

Browning, Christopher. 1993. *Ordinary Men: Reserve Police Battalion 101 and the Final Solution in Poland*. New York: Harper Perennial.

———. 2010. *Remembering Survival*. New York: Norton.

———. 2012. "Introduction." *The United States Holocaust Memorial Museum Encyclopedia of Camps and Ghettos, 1933–1945*, Martin Dean, ed. Bloomington: Indiana University Press.

Browning, Christopher, Richard Hollander, and Nechama Tec. 2007. *Every Day Lasts a Year: A Jewish Family's Correspondence from Poland*. New York: Cambridge University Press.

Bruk, Lialia, and Berta Bruk. 2004. *Kogda Slova Krichat I Plachut*. Minsk: Asoby Dah.

Carver, Charles, and Jennifer Connor-Smith. 2010. "Personality and Coping." *Annual Review of Psychology* 61: 679–704.

Cederman, Lars-Erik, Andreas Wimmer, and Brian Min. 2010. "Why Do Ethnic Groups Rebel? New Data and Analysis." *World Politics* 62, no. 1: 87–119.

Charny, Israel. 1982. *How Can We Commit the Unthinkable? Genocide, the Human Cancer*. Boulder: Westview Press.

Cholawski, Shalom. 2001. *Meri ve Lohama Partizanit*. Jerusalem: Yad Vashem.

Chwalba, Andrzej. 2011. "The Ethnic Panorama of Nazi-occupied Krakow." Polin: Studies in Polish Jewry 23: 349–56.

Cichopek-Gajraj, Anna. 2014. *Beyond Violence: Jewish Survivors in Poland and Slovakia, 1944–48*. New York: Cambridge University Press.

Connelly, John, Mark Roseman, Andriy Portnov, Michael David-Fox, and Timothy Snyder. 2011. "Timothy Snyder, Bloodlands: Europe between Hitler and Stalin." *Journal of Genocide Research* 13, no. 3: 313–52.

Corni, Gustavo. 2002. *Hitler's Ghettos: Voices from a Beleaguered Society, 1939–1944*. London: Arnold.

Crowe, David. 2004. *Oskar Schindler*. Cambridge, Mass.: Westview Press.

Darden, Keith. Forthcoming. *Resisting Occupation: Mass Literacy and the Creation of Durable National Loyalties*. New York: Cambridge University Press.

Darden, Keith, and Anna Maria Grzymała-Busse. 2006. "The Great Divide: Literacy, Nationalism, and the Communist Collapse." *World Politics* 59, no. 1: 83–115.

Datner, Szymon. 1946. *Walka i zagłada białostockiego getta*. Łódź: Czytelnik.

Davidson Draenger, Gusta. 1996. *Justyna's Narrative*. Amherst: University of Massachusetts Press.

Davydova, Galina. 2000. *Ot Minska Do La-Mansha, Ili Dorogami Holokosta*. Minsk: Chetyre Chetverti.

Dean, Martin. n.d. "Ghettos in the Occupied Soviet Union."

———. 2000. *Collaboration in the Holocaust: Crimes of the Local Police in Belorussia and Ukraine, 1941–44*. New York: St. Martin's Press.

Des Pres, Terrence. 1980. *The Survivor: An Anatomy of Life in the Death Camps*. New York: Oxford University Press.

Dobroszycki, Lucjan. 1994. *Survivors of the Holocaust in Poland: A Portrait Based on Jewish Community Records, 1944–1947*. Armonk: M.E. Sharpe.

Dumitru, Diana. 2016. *The State, Antisemitism, and Collaboration in the Holocaust*. New York: Cambridge University Press.

Dumitru, Diana, and Carter Johnson. 2011. "Constructing Interethnic Conflict and Cooperation: Why Some People Harmed Jews and Others Helped Them during the Holocaust in Romania." *World Politics* 63, no. 1: 1–42.

Einwohner, Rachel. 2003. "Opportunity, Honor, and Action in the Warsaw Ghetto Uprising of 1943." *American Journal of Sociology* 109, no. 3: 650–75.

Elkins, Caroline. 2005. *Imperial Reckoning: The Untold Story of Britain's Gulag in Kenya*. New York: Henry Holt.

Endelman, Todd. 1997. *Comparing Jewish Societies*. Ann Arbor: University of Michigan Press.

Engelking, Barbara, and Jacek Leociak. 2009. *The Warsaw Ghetto: A Guide to the Perished City*. New Haven: Yale University Press.

Epstein, Barbara. 2008. *The Minsk Ghetto, 1941–1943: Jewish Resistance and Soviet Internationalism*. Berkeley: University of California Press.

Etinger, Iakov. 2001. *Eto Nevozmozhno Zabyt'*. Moskva: Ves' Mir.

Fearon, James, and David Laitin. 2003. "Ethnicity, Insurgency, and Civil War." *American Political Science Review* 97, no. 1: 75–90.

Fein, Helen. 1979. *Accounting for Genocide*. New York: Free Press.

Finkel, Evgeny, and Scott Straus. 2012. "Macro, Meso, and Micro Research on Genocide." *Genocide Studies and Prevention* 7, no. 1: 56–67.

Fogelman, Eva. 2011. *Conscience and Courage: Rescuers of Jews during the Holocaust*. New York: Anchor.

Friedländer, Saul. 1997. *Nazi Germany and the Jews: The Years of Persecution 1933–1939*, vol. 1. New York: Harper Collins.

Friedman, Philip. 1953. "The Messianic Complex of a Nazi Collaborator in a Ghetto." *Bitzaron* 28, no. 5: 29-40.

———. 1957. *Their Brothers' Keepers*. New York: Crown Publishers.

———. 1980. *Roads To Extinction: Essays on the Holocaust*. New York: The Jewish Publication Society of America and the Conference on Jewish Social Studies.

Friling, Tuvia. 2009. *Mi Ata, Leon Berzhe*. Tel Aviv: Resling.

Fujii, Lee Ann. 2009. *Killing Neighbors: Webs of Violence in Rwanda*. Ithaca: Cornell University Press.

———. 2010. "Shades of Truth and Lies: Interpreting Testimonies of War and Violence." *Journal of Peace Research* 47, no. 2: 231–41.

Gai, David. 1991. *Desiatyi Krug*. Moskva: Sovetskii pisatel'.

Galas, Michal, and Antony Polonsky. 2011. "Introduction." *Polin: Studies in Polish Jewry* 23: 3–48.

Gal'burt, Aleksandr. 2003. *Vyzhivshii v Adu*. Minsk: Entsiklopediks.

Gebeleva, Svetlana. 2010. *Dolgii Put' K Zavetnoi Ulitse*. Minsk: Logvinov.

Goldhagen, Daniel. 1996. *Hitler's Willing Executioners: Ordinary Germans and the Holocaust.* New York: Knopf.

Goldman, Wendy. 2011. *Inventing the Enemy.* New York: Cambridge University Press.

Goldstone, Jack, and Charles Tilly. 2001. "Threat (and Opportunity): Popular Action and State Response in the Dynamics of Contentious Action," in Silence and Voice in the Study of Contentious Politics, Ronald Aminzade et al., eds. Cambridge: Cambridge University Press, 179–94.

Goldstone, Jack, and Bert Useem. 1999. "Prison Riots as Microrevolutions." *American Journal of Sociology* 104, no. 4: 985–1029.

Gombiński, Stanisław. 2010. *Wspomnienia policjanta z warszawskiego getta.* Warsaw: ZIH.

Gorelik, Moisei. 2010. "Interview with Moisei Gorelik." iremember.ru. At http://iremember.ru/memoirs/partizani/gorelik-moisey-khaimovich/, accessed April 20, 2015.

Gould, Roger. 1991. "Multiple Networks and Mobilization in the Paris Commune, 1871." *American Sociological Review* 56, no. 6: 716–29.

Grabowski, Jan. 2013. *Hunt for the Jews: Betrayal and Murder in German-Occupied Poland.* Bloomington: Indiana University Press.

Granovetter, Mark. 1973. "The Strength of Weak Ties." *American Journal of Sociology* 78, no. 6: 1360–80.

Greenspan, Henry. 2001. The Awakening of Memory: Survivor Testimony in the First Years after the Holocaust, and Today. Washington, DC: USHMM. At http://www.ushmm.org/research/center/publications/occasional/2001–02/paper.pdf.

Greenstein, Jakob. 1968. *Ud Mikikar Hayovel.* Tel Aviv: Beit Lohamei Hagetaot.

Gringauz, Samuel. 1949. "The Ghetto as an Experiment of Jewish Social Organization (Three Years of Kovno Ghetto)." *Jewish Social Studies* 11, no. 1: 3–20.

Gross, Jan Tomasz. 1979. *Polish Society Under German Occupation: The General-gouvernement, 1939–1944.* Princeton: Princeton University Press.

———. 2002. *Neighbors: The Destruction of the Jewish Community in Jedwabne, Poland.* New York: Penguin Books.

Gross, Jan Tomasz, and Irena Grudzinska Gross. 2012. *Golden Harvest: Events at the Periphery of the Holocaust.* New York: Oxford University Press.

Gross, Natan. 1986. *Mi Ata, Adon Grymek.* Tel Aviv: Moreshet.

Gutman, Yisrael, and Shmuel Krakowski. 1986. *Unequal Victims: Poles and Jews during World War Two.* New York: Holocaust Library.

Hecker, Clara. 2007. *Nemetskie Evrei v Minskom Getto.* Minsk: Istoricheskaia Masterskaia.

Hedgepeth, Sonja Maria, and Rochelle Saidel. 2010. *Sexual Violence against Jewish Women during the Holocaust.* Waltham: Brandeis University Press.

Hilberg, Raul. 1980. "The Ghetto as a Form of Government." *The Annals of the American Academy of Political and Social Science* 450, no. 1: 98–112.

———. 1981. "The Ghetto as a Form of Government: An Analysis of Isaiah Trunk's Judenrat," in Yehuda Bauer and Nathan Rotenstreich, eds., *The Holocaust as Historical Experience.* New York: Holmes and Meier.

———. 1993. *Perpetrators Victims Bystanders: Jewish Catastrophe, 1933–1945.* New York: Harper Collins.

———. 2003. *The Destruction of the European Jews*, 3rd ed. New Haven: Yale University Press.

Hirschman, Albert. 1970. *Exit, Voice, and Loyalty*. Cambridge: Harvard University Press.

Hollander, Ethan J. 2008. "The Final Solution in Bulgaria and Romania: A Comparative Perspective." *East European Politics & Societies* 22, no. 2: 203–48.

Iwry, Shmuel. 2004. *To Wear the Dust of War: From Bialystok to Shanghai to the Promised Land : An Oral History*. New York: Palgrave Macmillan.

Jackson, Carlton. 2000. *Joseph Gavi: Young Hero of the Minsk Ghetto*. Paducah, Ky.: Turner Publishing Company.

Jarkowska-Natkaniec, Alicja. 2013. "Jüdischer Ordnungsdienst in Occupied Kraków during the Years 1940–1945." *Scripta Judaica Cracoviensia* no. 11: 147–60.

Jose, Betcy, and Peace A. Medie. 2015. "Understanding Why and How Civilians Resort to Self-Protection in Armed Conflict." *International Studies Review* 17, no. 4: 515–35.

Kalyvas, Stathis. 2003. "The Ontology of 'Political Violence:' Action and Identity in Civil Wars." *Perspectives on Politics* 1, no. 3: 475–94.

———. 2006. *The Logic of Violence in Civil War*. New York: Cambridge University Press.

———. 2008. "Ethnic Defection in Civil War." *Comparative Political Studies* 41, no. 8: 1043–68.

Kalyvas, Stathis, and Matthew Kocher. 2007. "How Free Is 'Free Riding' in Civil Wars? Violence, Insurgency, and the Collective Action Problem." *World Politics* 59, no. 2: 177–216.

King, Charles. 2012. "Can There Be a Political Science of the Holocaust?" *Perspectives on Politics* 10, no. 2: 323–41.

Klibanski, Bronia. 2002. *Ariadneh*. Tel Aviv: Gevanim.

Kobrin, Rebecca. 2010. *Jewish Bialystok and Its Diaspora*. Bloomington: Indiana University Press.

Kopstein, Jeffrey, and Jason Wittenberg. 2003. "Who Voted Communist? Reconsidering the Social Bases of Radicalism in Interwar Poland." *Slavic Review* 62, no. 1: 87–109.

———. 2011. "Deadly Communities." *Comparative Political Studies* 44, no. 3: 259–83.

Krakowski, Shmuel. 1984. *The War of the Doomed : Jewish Armed Resistance in Poland, 1942–1944*. New York: Holmes and Meier.

Krasinskii, Arkadii. 2011. "Interview with Krasinskii Arkadii Borisovich." At http://iremember.ru/memoirs/partizani/krasinskiy-arkadiy-borisovich/?sphrase_id=10126.

Kruglov, Alexander, and Martin Dean. 2012. "Trembowla." *The United States Holocaust Memorial Museum Encyclopedia of Camps and Ghettos, 1933–1945*. Bloomington: Indiana University Press.

Kuper, Leo. 1981. *Genocide: Its Political Use in the Twentieth Century*. New Haven: Yale University Press.

Kuran, Timur. 1991. "Now Out of Never." *World Politics* 44, no. 1: 7–48.

Langer, Lawrence. 1982. *Versions of Survival: The Holocaust and the Human Spirit*. Albany: SUNY Press.

Lazarus, Richard, and Susan Folkman. 1984. *Stress, Appraisal, and Coping*. New York: Springer.

Levene, Mark. 2005. *Genocide in the Age of the Nation State*. Vol. 1. London: I.B.Tauris.

Levi, Primo. 1996. *Survival in Auschwitz*. New York: Touchstone.

Lichbach, Mark. 1998. *The Rebel's Dilemma. Economics, Cognition, and Society*. Ann Arbor: University of Michigan Press.

Lichtblau, Eric. 2014. *The Nazis Next Door*. New York: Houghton Mifflin Harcourt.

Liond, Reuven. 1993. *Partizan Yehudi Beyaar*. Tel Aviv: Sifriyat Poalim.

Long, J. Scott and Jeremy Freese. 2006. *Regression Models for Categorical Dependent Variables Using Stata*. College Station, Md.: Stata Press.

Lower, Wendy. 2013. *Hitler's Furies: German Women in the Nazi Killing Fields*. New York: Houghton Mifflin Harcourt.

Lustick, Ian S. 1996. "History, Historiography, and Political Science: Multiple Historical Records and the Problem of Selection Bias." *American Political Science Review* 90, no. 3: 605–18.

Lyall, Jason. 2010. "Are Coethnics More Effective Counterinsurgents? Evidence from the Second Chechen War." *American Political Science Review* 104, no. 1: 1–20.

Maher, Thomas. 2010. "Threat, Resistance, and Collective Action." *American Sociological Review* 75, no. 2: 252–72.

Malomed, Berta. 2008. "Menia Rasstreliali 2-Go Marta 1942-Go Goda," in Inna Gerasimova and Vyacheslav Selemenev, eds., *Vyzhit'—Podvig*. Minsk: NARB.

Manley, Rebecca. 2012. *To the Tashkent Station*. Ithaca: Cornell University Press.

Margolina, Sima. 2010. *Ostat'sia Zhit'*. Minsk: Logvinov.

Martin, Terry. 2001. *The Affirmative Action Empire: Nations and Nationalism in the Soviet Union, 1923-1939*. Ithaca, N.Y.: Cornell University Press.

Marlow, Jennifer. 2014. "Polish Catholic Maids and Nannies: Female Aid and the Domestic Realm in Nazi-Occupied Poland." PhD diss., Michigan State University, East Lansing.

Marrus, Michael. 1995. "Jewish Resistance to the Holocaust." *Journal of Contemporary History* 30, no. 1: 83–110.

Martin, Sean. 2004. *Jewish Life in Cracow, 1918–1939*. London: Vallentine Mitchell.

Matthäus, Jurgen. 1996. "What about the 'Ordinary Men'?: The German Order Police and the Holocaust in the Occupied Soviet Union." *Holocaust and Genocide Studies* 10, no. 2: 134–50.

McAdam, Doug. 1986. "Recruitment to High-Risk Activism: The Case of Freedom Summer." *American Journal of Sociology* 92, no. 1: 64–90.

McCormick, G. H., and G. Owen. 2000. "Security and Coordination in a Clandestine Organization." *Mathematical and Computer Modeling* 31, no. 6–7: 175–92.

Mégret, Frédéric. 2009. "Beyond the 'Salvation' Paradigm: Responsibility to Protect (Others) vs the Power of Protecting Oneself." *Security Dialogue* 40, no. 6: 575–95.

Melzer, Emanuel. 2001. "Hamaarakh hapoliti shel yehude Krakov bein shtei milhamot olam," in Elchanan Reiner, ed., *Kroke-Kazimierz-Cracow: mehkarim betoldot Yehude Krakov*. Tel Aviv: ha-Merkaz le-heker toldot ha-Yehudim be-Polin u-morashtam, ha-Makhon le-heker ha-tefutsot, Universitat Tel-Aviv.

Michman, Dan. 2003. *Holocaust Historiography—A Jewish Perspective : Conceptualizations, Terminology, Approaches, and Fundamental Issues*. London: Vallentine Mitchell.

———. 2011. *The Emergence of Jewish Ghettos During the Holocaust*. New York: Cambridge University Press.

Midlarsky, Manus. 2005. *The Killing Trap: Genocide in the Twentieth Century*. Cambridge: Cambridge University Press.

Mielnicki, Michel, and John A. Munro. 2000. *Bialystok to Birkenau : The Holocaust Journey of Michel Mielnicki*. Vancouver: Ronsdale Press.

Miron, Guy. 2009. "Zhmerinka." *Yad Vashem Encyclopedia of the Ghettos during the Holocaust*. Jerusalem: Yad Vashem.

Monroe, Kristen R. 2004. *The Hand of Compassion: Portraits of Moral Choice during the Holocaust*. Princeton: Princeton University Press.

———. 2012. *Ethics in an Age of Terror and Genocide: Identity and Moral Choice*. Princeton: Princeton University Press.

Monroe, Kristen R., Michael C. Barton, and Ute Klingemann. 1990. "Altruism and the Theory of Rational Action: Rescuers of Jews in Nazi Europe." *Ethics* 101, no. 1: 103–22.

Mylonas, Harris. 2013. *The Politics of Nation-Building: Making Co-Nationals, Refugees, and Minorities*. New York: Cambridge University Press.

Nikodimova, Zoia. 2010. *Arkhiv Khasi Pruslinoi: Minskoe Getto, Antifashistskoe Podpol'e, Repatriatsiia Detei Iz Germanii*. Minsk: Logvinov.

Okun', Leonid. 2007. "Interview with Leonid Isakovich Okun'." At http://iremember .ru/partizani/okun-leonid-isaakovich.html.

Olenski, Luba. 2006. *A Life Reclaimed: A Child among the Partisans*. Caulfield South (Victoria, Australia): Makor Jewish Community Library.

Pankiewicz, Tadeusz. 1987. *The Cracow Ghetto Pharmacy*. New York: Holocaust Library.

Parkinson, Sarah. 2013. "Organizing Rebellion: Rethinking High-Risk Mobilization and Social Networks in War." *American Political Science Review* 107, no. 3: 418–32.

Pasherstnik, Lev. 2008. "Pobeg Iz Getto," in Z. Tsukerman, ed., *Katastrofa—Poslednie Svidetei.* Moskva: Dom evreiskoi knigi.

Paulsson, Gunnar. 2002. *Secret City: The Hidden Jews of Warsaw, 1940–1945*. London: Yale University Press.

Pawełczyńska, Anna. 1979. *Values and Violence in Auschwitz: A Sociological Analysis*. Berkeley: University of California Press.

Peled, Yael. 1993. *Krakov haYehudit, 1939–1943*. Tel Aviv: Beit Lohamei Hagetaot.

Peleg-Marianska, Miriam, and Mordecai Peleg. 1991. *Witnesses: Life in Occupied Krakow*. New York: Routledge.

Pemper, Mietek. 2008. *The Road to Rescue: The Untold Story of Schindler's List*. New York: Other Press.

Perechodnik, Calel. 1996. *Am I a Murderer? Testament of a Jewish Ghetto Policeman*. Boulder, Co.: Westview Press.

Perlis, Rivka. 1987. *Tenuot hanoar hahalutsiyot bePolin hakevushah*. Tel Aviv: Hakibuts hameuhad.

Petersen, Heidemarie. 2008. "Kraków before 1975," in *YIVO Encyclopedia of Jews in Eastern Europe*, Gershon David Hundert, ed. New Haven, Ct.: Yale University Press.

Petersen, Roger. 2001. *Resistance and Rebellion: Lessons from Eastern Europe*. New York: Cambridge University Press.

———. 2002. *Understanding Ethnic Violence: Fear, Hatred, and Resentment in Twentieth-Century Eastern Europe*. New York: Cambridge University Press.

Porat, Dina. 1997. "Zionists and Communists in the Underground during the Holocaust: Three examples—Cracow, Kovno and Minsk." *Journal of Israeli History* 18, no. 1: 57.

———. 2000. *Meever legishmi: parashat hayav shel Aba Kovner*. Tel Aviv: Am Oved.

Putnam, Robert D. 1993. *Making Democracy Work: Civic Traditions in Modern Italy*. Princeton: Princeton University Press.

Rabinovici, Doron. 2011. *Eichmann's Jews*. Cambridge: Polity.

Rappoport, Rakhil. 2008. "Ostat'sia Soboi," in Inna Gerasimova and Vyacheslav Selemenev, eds., *Vyzhit'—Podvig*. Minsk: NARB.

Rediker, Marcus. 2007. *The Slave Ship: A Human History*. New York: Penguin.

———. 2012. *The Amistad Rebellion: An Atlantic Odyssey of Slavery and Freedom*. New York: Viking.

Reizman, Frida. 2005. *Zhiva . . . Da, Ia Zhiva: Minskoe Getto Vvospominaniiakh Maii Krapinoi i Fridy Reizman*. Minsk: Istoricheskaia Masterskaia.

Ringelblum, Emanuel. 1974. *Polish-Jewish Relations during the Second World War*. Jerusalem: Yad Vashem.

Rotbard, Shemuel. 2000. *Parashim Yerukim: Temunot Yaldut Be-Krakov*. Tel Aviv: Moreshet.

Rozin, Aharon. 1975. "Hayishuv Hayehudi Beminsk Beshanim 1917–1941," in Shlomo Even-Shoshan, ed., *Minsk: Ir Va-Em*. Tel Aviv: Hakibuts hameuhad.

Rubenchik, Abram. 2006. *V Minskom Getto i Partizanakh*. Tel Aviv: Abram Rubenchik.

Rubin, Anatolii. 1977. *Magafaim Humim, Magafaim Adumim: Mi Geto Minsk Ad Mahanot Sibir*. Tel Aviv: Dvir.

Rubinshtein, Leonid. 2011. *Nel'zia Zabyt'*. Minsk: Medisont.

Rufeisen-Schüpper, Hella. 1990. *Peridah Mi-Mila 18: Sipurah Shel Kasharit*. Tel Aviv: Hakibuts hameuhad.

Schacter, Daniel. 2001. *The Seven Sins of Memory*. New York: Houghton Mifflin.

Scott, James. 1987. Weapons of the Weak: Everyday Forms of Peasant Resistance. New Haven: Yale University Press.

Shapiro, Jacob. 2013. *The Terrorist's Dilemma*. Princeton: Princeton University Press.

Shatyn, Bruno. 1985. *A Private War: Surviving in Poland on False Papers, 1941–1945*. Detroit: Wayne State University Press.

Shenker, Noah. 2015. *Reframing Holocaust Testimony*. Bloomington: Indiana University Press.

Shilhav, Yaakov Moshe. 1961. "Haminhal Hayehudi Haatsmi (Hayudenrat) Begeto Biyalistok." MA thesis, Hebrew University of Jerusalem.

Sinnreich, Helene, Shannon Phillips, and Martin Dean. 2012. "Krakow," in *USHMM Encyclopedia of Camps and Ghettos*, Martin Dean, ed. Bloomington: Indiana University Press.

Slepyan, Kenneth. 2000. "The Soviet Partisan Movement and the Holocaust." *Holocaust and Genocide Studies* 14, no. 1: 1–27.

Slovic, Paul, Baruch Fischhoff, and Sarah Lichtenstein. 1982. "Facts Versus Fears: Understanding Perceived Risk," in Daniel Kahneman, Paul Slovic, and Amos Tversky, eds. *Judgement under Uncertainty: Heuristics and Biases*. New York: Cambridge University Press.

Smilovitsky, Leonid. 1999. "Llya Ehrenburg and the Holocaust in Byelorussia." *East European Jewish Affairs* 29, no. 1–2: 61.

Smolar, Hersh. 1989. *The Minsk Ghetto: Soviet-Jewish Partisans against the Nazis*. New York: Holocaust Library.

Somer, Eli, Ayalla Ruvio, Ilana Sever, and Erez Soref. 2007. "Reactions to Repeated Unpredictable Terror Attacks." *Journal of Applied Social Psychology* 37, no. 4: 862–86.

Staner, Mieczyslaw. 1999. *The Eyewitness*. Kraków: Hagoda.

Staniland, Paul. 2014. *Networks of Rebellion*. Ithaca: Cornell University Press.

Straus, Scott. 2006. *The Order of Genocide: Race, Power, and War in Rwanda*. Ithaca: Cornell University Press.

———. 2015. *Making and Unmaking Nations: War, Leadership, and Genocide in Modern Africa*. Ithaca: Cornell University Press.

Sztop-Rutkowska, Katarzyna, and Rebecca Kobrin. 2014. "Żydzi W Międzywojennym Białymstoku. Między Lokalnością a Diasporą," in Daniel Boćkowski, ed., *Białystok—Mayn Heym*. Białystok: Muzeum Wojska w Białymstoku.

Taits, Mark. n.d. "Interview with Mark Taits." At http://netzulim.org/R/OrgR/Articles/Stories/Zubarev07.html#z01.

Tammes, Peter. 2007. "Survival of Jews during the Holocaust: The Importance of Different Types of Social Resources." *International Journal of Epidemiology* 36, no. 2: 330–35.

Taubenschlag, Stanislaw. 1998. *To Be a Jew in Occupied Poland: Cracow, Auschwitz, Buchenwald*. Oswiecim: Frap-Books.

Taubkin, David. 2008. "Moi Gorod, Znakomyi Do Slioz," in Z. Tsukerman, ed., *Katastrofa—Poslednie Svidetili*. Moscow: Dom evreiskoi knigi.

Tec, Nechama. 1986. *When Light Pierced the Darkness: Christian Rescue of Jews in Nazi-Occupied Poland*. New York: Oxford University Press.

———. 1993. *Defiance: The Bielski Partisans*. New York: Oxford University Press.

Tec, Nechama, and Daniel Weiss. 1997. "Historical Injustice: The Case of Masha Bruskina." *Holocaust & Genocide Studies* 11, no. 3: 366.

Tenenbaum-Tamaroff, Mordehai. 1984. *Dapim min hadlekah*. Jerusalem: Yad Vashem.

Toft, Monica Duffy. 2003. *The Geography of Ethnic Violence: Identity, Interests, and the Indivisibility of Territory*. Princeton: Princeton University Press.

Treister, Mikhail. 2008. "Probleski Pamiati," in Z. Tsukerman, ed., *Katastrofa—Poslednie Svidetili*. Moscow: Dom evreiskoi knigi.

Trunk, Isaiah. 1972. *Judenrat: The Jewish Councils in Eastern Europe under Nazi Occupation*. New York: The Macmillan Company.

Tversky, Amos, and Daniel Kahneman. 1974. "Judgment under Uncertainty: Heuristics and Biases." *Science* 185, no. 4157: 1124–31.

USASOC. 2013. Human Factor Considerations of Undergrounds in Insurgencies, 2nd ed. Fort Bragg: USASOC. At http://www.soc.mil/ARIS/HumanFactorsS.pdf.

Varese, Federico, and Meir Yaish. 2000. "The Importance of Being Asked. The Rescue of Jews in Nazi Europe." *Rationality and Society* 12, no. 3: 307–34.

Varshney, Ashutosh. 2002. *Ethnic Conflict and Civic Life: Hindus and Muslims in India*. New Haven: Yale University Press.

———. 2003. "Nationalism, Ethnic Conflict, and Rationality." *Perspectives on Politics* 1, no. 1: 85–99.

Vered, Abraham. 1988. *Liheyot betsel hashoah*. Ramot Menasheh: Author.

Virgili, Fabrice. 2002. *Shorn Women: Gender and Punishment in Liberation France*. Oxford: Berg.

Weidmann, Nils. 2009. "Geography as Motivation and Opportunity : Group Concentration and Ethnic Conflict." *Journal of Conflict Resolution* 53, no. 4: 526–43.

Weinstein, Jeremy. 2007. *Inside Rebellion: The Politics of Insurgent Violence*. New York: Cambridge University Press.

Weiss, Aharon. 1973. "Jewish Police in the 'General Gouvernement' and Upper Silesia during the Holocaust." PhD diss., The Hebrew University of Jerusalem.

Wilkinson, Steven. 2006. *Votes and Violence: Electoral Competition and Ethnic Riots in India*. New York: Cambridge University Press.

Wood, Elisabeth. 2003. *Insurgent Collective Action and Civil War in El Salvador*. New York: Cambridge University Press.

Wróbel, Piotr. 1994. "The Jews of Galicia under Austrian-Polish Rule, 1869–1918." *Austrian History Yearbook* 25: 97–138.

Yoffe, Emmanuil. 2003. *Belorusskie Evrei: Tragediia i Geroizm, 1941–1945*. Minsk: s.n.

Zabuski, Charles, and June Sutz Brott. 1996. *Needle and Thread: A Tale of Survival from Białystok to Paris*. Oakland: Popincourt Press.

Zając, Józef. 1965. *Toczyły się boje*. Warsaw: Czytelnik.

Zeitlin, Maurice. 2010. "The Last Stand of Jews in Small Town Ghettos of German Occupied Poland, 1941–43," in Zaheer Baber and Joseph Bryant, eds. *Society, History, and the Global Human Condition*. Lanham: Lexington.

Zhits, Dan. 2000. *Geto Minsk ve-Toldotav Le-or Ha-Teud He-Hadash*. Ramat Gan: Bar Ilan University.

Zuckerman, Yitzhak. 1993. *A Surplus of Memory*. Berkeley: University of California Press.

Glossary

Aktion   A large-scale operation, usually involving the killing of Jews by German forces and their collaborators or a deportation from the ghetto to death or labor camps.

Aryan Side   A part of the city outside the ghetto boundaries, or the outside world more generally.

Betar (Hebrew acronym for Brit Yosef Trumpeldor)   A Zionist youth movement affiliated with right-wing Revisionist Zionism.

Bund (officially the General Jewish Labor Bund of Lithuania, Poland and Russia)   A socialist, anti-Zionist Jewish party.

Dror (Hebrew for "Freedom")   A socialist Zionist youth movement.

Gestapo (German abbreviation of Geheime Staatspolizei, "Secret State Police")   Nazi Germany's secret/political police. It operated both in Germany proper and throughout the Nazi-occupied territories.

Ghetto   A part of a city designated exclusively for Jewish settlement and concentration, which the Jews generally were not allowed to leave and the non-Jews were not allowed to enter. In German official sources ghettos are usually referred to as Jewish Residential Districts/Areas.

Hashomer Hatzair (Hebrew for "Young Guard," also referred to as "Hashomer")   A socialist, Zionist youth movement; Marxist and to the left of Dror.

Judenrat (German for "Jewish Council")   An institution, headed and staffed by Jews, that was tasked by the German authorities with administering Jewish communities under Nazi rule and implementing German orders and instructions.

Partisans   Anti-German organized armed guerilla units, which operated in the forests and the countryside.

SS (German abbreviation of Schutzstaffel, "Protection Squadron")   A Nazi elite organization, a "state within a state." The SS controlled the German police forces, was in charge of the concentration camps, and led the implementation of the Final Solution. It also had its own military units, called the *Waffen SS*.

Wehrmacht   Nazi Germany's regular armed forces.

Acknowledgments

This book is the culmination of a long process that started as a vague, but intriguing idea in 2009, progressed to become a doctoral dissertation, and eventually matured into a manuscript. During these years I benefited from the help, generosity, wisdom, and support of very many people.

Throughout the entire period of my graduate studies at the University of Wisconsin-Madison, Yoi Herrera was the best advisor ever—sharp, committed, enthusiastic, critical when needed, and always, always supportive and caring. My other mentors, Scott Gehlbach, Andrew Kydd, Nadav Shelef, and Scott Straus, were and remain professional role models. Scott Straus showed me how to study mass violence by using the tools of the social sciences. Nadav Shelef taught me to take ideas and identities seriously and provided meticulous comments on each and every chapter draft just a couple of hours after I sent it to him. Andy Kydd helped me to think clearly about complex ideas and messy processes. Scott Gehlbach, with whom I am now writing a book on another large-scale political upheaval, was always (and still is) there to give advice on striking the right balance between qualitative and quantitative work, methods, analysis, and research in general.

Jeffrey Kopstein is the intellectual godfather of this book. It was a conversation with him, during a 2009 car ride in Jerusalem, that led me to think seriously about studying the impact of pre–World War II politics on Jewish behavior during the Holocaust. Jeff's own work, coauthored with Jason Wittenberg, showed me that it is possible to study the Holocaust and be a political scientist. I am very grateful to Jeff and Jason for their constant support, advice, guidance, and encouragement.

A year spent at the Order, Conflict, and Violence Program at Yale University was crucial for turning general ideas and intuitions into scholarship, and I thank Stathis Kalyvas for choosing me as one of the 2011–2012 OCV fellows. OCV was also where I met Sarah Parkinson and Janet Lewis, amazing scholars and friends who influenced my thinking about sub-state violence more than anyone else.

The George Washington University Department of Political Science and the Institute for European, Russian and Eurasian Studies (IERES) provided intellectual and financial support while I was turning the dissertation into a book. My colleagues Celeste Arrington, Michael Barnett, Brandon Bartels, Nathan Brown, Bruce Dickson, Alex Downes, Harvey Feigenbaum, Martha Finnemore, Eric Grynaviski, Henry Hale, Eric Kramon, Eric Lawrence, James Lebovic, Yon Lupu, Marc Lynch, Mike Miller, Kimberly Morgan, Harris Mylonas, Robert Orttung, John Sides, Rachel Stein, Manny Teitelbaum, Paul Wahlbeck, Cory Welt, and Adam Ziegfeld read and commented on portions of the manuscript, provided professional advice, and helped me to navigate the unfamiliar terrain of book writing.

I am especially grateful to Peter Rollberg, the IERES director, for providing financial support for a book workshop in May 2015. Evan Alterman expertly dealt with the workshop's logistics. Christopher Browning, Jeffrey Kopstein, Janet Lewis, Irfan Nooruddin, Abdulkader Sinno, Cathy Schneider, Aviel Roshwald, Jocelyn Viterna, Bruce Dickson, and James Lebovic read the entire manuscript and did an incredible job helping me to turn a messy text into a real book.

The final version of the book was completed during a short-term fellowship at New York University's Jordan Center for the Advanced Study of Russia. I thank the Center for providing me with such an opportunity.

Taras Demczuk, Daniel Nerenberg, Annelle Sheline, Dot Ohl, Daniil Romanovsky, Lee Rotbart, Julian Waller, and Marko Zilovic provided research assistance in Israel, Poland, and the United States. Leonid Rein helped me access documents from the Yad Vashem Archive, Vadim Altskan advised on materials available at the U.S. Holocaust Memorial Museum Archive, and Joanne Rudoff and Stephen Naron made my work at the Fortunoff Video Archive for Holocaust Testimonies as smooth as possible. Mitia Frumin expertly produced the maps.

I am also grateful to numerous people in the United States, Canada, Israel, and Poland for their support, advice, and suggestions. Ana Arjona, Dominique Arel, Sanja Badanjak, Omer Bartov, Galina Belokurova, Elissa Bemporad, Max Bergholz, Michael Bernhard, Yitzhak Brudny (who got me interested in Eastern European politics in the first place), Hannah Chapman, Keith Darden, Georgi Derluguian, Jan Grabowski, Marko Grdesic, Kathryn Hendley, Liesbet Hooghe, Charles King, Matthew Kocher, Aliza Luft, Jason Lyall, Kyle Marquardt, Lauren McCarthy, Dan Miodownik, Lilach Nir, Tricia Olsen, Raz Segal, Emily Sellars, Dan Slater, Timothy Snyder, Yang Su, Erik Wibbels, and Elisabeth Wood helped me with this book in various ways. I am sure there are others to whom I am grateful and whose names I have forgotten to mention here. I apologize for the omission.

At Princeton University Press, Eric Crahan was a dream editor—supportive, enthusiastic, thoughtful, and forgiving when I constantly failed to meet deadlines. Leslie Grundfest, Ben Pokross, and Hannah Zuckerman guided me through the production process. Eva Jaunzems expertly copy-edited the text. I also thank the anonymous reviewers for their comments and suggestions, which substantially strengthened the book. Parts of chapter 7 were previously published as "The Phoenix Effect of State Repression: Jewish Resistance during the Holocaust" in the *American Political Science Review* (109[2]: 339–353). I thank Cambridge University Press for permission to reproduce parts of the article in this book.

Finally, but most importantly, I want to thank my family, and especially Julie. Without their love, understanding, and forgiveness, this book would have never been written. Thank you, thank you, thank you!

Index